LEVEL 1
AWARD IN
BOOKKEEPING

STUDY TEXT

Qualifications and Credit Framework

AAT Level 1

Q2022

KAPLAN PUBLISHING'S STATEMENT OF PRINCIPLES

LINGUISTIC DIVERSITY, EQUALITY AND INCLUSION

We are committed to diversity, equality and inclusion and strive to deliver content that all users can relate to.

We are here to make a difference to the success of every learner.

Clarity, accessibility and ease of use for our learners are key to our approach.

We will use contemporary examples that are rich, engaging and representative of a diverse workplace.

We will include a representative mix of race and gender at the various levels of seniority within the businesses in our examples to support all our learners in aspiring to achieve their potential within their chosen careers.

Roles played by characters in our examples will demonstrate richness and diversity by the use of different names, backgrounds, ethnicity and gender, with a mix of sexuality, relationships and beliefs where these are relevant to the syllabus.

It must always be obvious who is being referred to in each stage of any example so that we do not detract from clarity and ease of use for each of our learners.

We will actively seek feedback from our learners on our approach and keep our policy under continuous review. If you would like to provide any feedback on our linguistic approach, please use this form (you will need to enter the link below into your browser).

https://forms.gle/U8oR3abiPpGRDY158

We will seek to devise simple measures that can be used by independent assessors to randomly check our success in the implementation of our Linguistic Equality, Diversity and Inclusion Policy.

British Library Cataloguing-in-Publication Data

A catalogue record for this book is available from the British Library.

Published by
Kaplan Publishing UK
Unit 2, The Business Centre
Molly Millars Lane
Wokingham
Berkshire
RG41 2QZ

ISBN 978 1 83996 294 3

The text in this material and any others made available by any Kaplan Group company does not amount to advice on a particular matter and should not be taken as such. No reliance should be placed on the content as the basis for any investment or other decision or in connection with any advice given to third parties. Please consult your appropriate professional adviser as necessary. Kaplan Publishing Limited and all other Kaplan group companies expressly disclaim all liability to any person in respect of any losses or other claims, whether direct, indirect, incidental, consequential or otherwise arising in relation to the use of such materials.

© Kaplan Financial Limited, 2023

Printed and bound in Great Britain.

VAT Value-Added Tax

CREDIT MEMO = CREDIT NOTE

CONTENTS

INTRODUCTION

HOW TO USE THESE MATERIALS

These Kaplan Publishing learning materials have been carefully designed to make your learning experience as easy as possible and to give you the best chance of success in your AAT assessments.

They contain a number of features to help you in the study process.

The sections on the Unit Guide, the Assessment and Study Skills should be read before you commence your studies.

They are designed to familiarise you with the nature and content of the assessment and to give you tips on how best to approach your studies.

STUDY TEXT

This Study Text has been specially prepared for the revised AAT Level 1 qualification introduced in 2022, based on the specification published in June 2022.

It is written in a practical and interactive style by expert classroom tutors.

In this Study Text:

- key terms and concepts are clearly defined

- all topics are illustrated with practical examples with clearly worked solutions based on sample tasks provided by the AAT in the new assessment style

- frequent activities throughout and at the end of the chapters ensure that what you have learnt is regularly reinforced

- 'Test your understanding' activities are included within each chapter to apply your learning and develop your understanding

- a 'Case Study' brings the subject to life and puts the content covered into a real life context

- Mock Assessments and end of chapter activities reinforce understanding to prepare you for the assessment.

ICONS

The chapters include the following icons throughout.

They are designed to assist you in your studies by identifying key definitions and the points at which you can test yourself on the knowledge gained.

 Definition

These sections explain important areas of Knowledge which must be understood and reproduced in an assessment

 Example

The illustrative examples can be used to help develop an understanding of topics before attempting the activity exercises

Test your understanding

These are exercises which give the opportunity to assess your understanding of all the assessment areas.

 Case study

These examples put the chapter content into a real life context, using the case study of Jessica and her role at How Two Ltd.

Case study activities

Following the chapter summary, these questions enable further practice using the real life context of the above case study.

throughout
preposition - in every part of
adverb = in every part of place or object.

UNIT GUIDE

Introduction

The Level 1 Award in Bookkeeping offers students the opportunity to develop practical bookkeeping skills. This qualification may help students to move on to further study in either accountancy or bookkeeping with AAT, offer a route into employment or be of interest to those already in employment.

This qualification will particularly suit those students who have had minimal work experience or those who need some additional support to progress. This may include younger students seeking tangible and finance-specific skills, adults seeking to validate their existing skills to enter into or progress in their career, or students who would like to test their abilities before progressing further with AAT. This qualification may also interest those who are self-employed or working in small businesses who wish to do their own bookkeeping.

Students should choose to study the Level 1 Award in Bookkeeping if they wish to develop an understanding of the basics of manual bookkeeping. Students completing this qualification may wish to pursue careers in finance or business in either the private or public sectors. This qualification may be combined with the Level 1 Award in Business Skills to lay a strong foundation for further study with AAT in either accountancy or bookkeeping.

The skills developed by studying this qualification will give students a solid base from which to seek employment with greater confidence or enable them to progress to the next level of learning.

The skills developed in this qualification can lead to employment in junior or supporting administrative roles in companies across a wide range of sectors, for example, as a:

- trainee bookkeeper
- accounts administrator
- billing/payments administrator/coordinator
- accounts junior
- accounts receivable/payable assistant
- procurement and finance assistant
- assistant cashier.

The skills developed in this qualification may also underpin those developed further in the following Level 2 qualifications:

- Level 2 Certificate in Bookkeeping
- Level 2 Certificate in Accounting

Overview and learning outcomes

Overview

This qualification covers a range of skills and the relevant supporting knowledge in one mandatory unit - Bookkeeping Fundamentals. The qualification is assessed in one end-of-qualification assessment.

Students completing this qualification will develop an understanding of the role of the bookkeeper, including the need to produce timely and accurate work and to follow ethical principles. Students will learn underpinning theory including how to identify assets, liabilities, income, expenses, capital profit or loss, and the differences between trading for cash and trading on credit.

Students will also develop the skills to process customer and supplier transactions, to enter receipts and payments into the cash book and check amounts against the bank statement in preparation for bank reconciliation. Students will be introduced to the dual effect of transactions. This is a fundamental underpinning concept for double-entry bookkeeping and will support students who go on to study bookkeeping at Level 2.

Students will also learn the role that software can have in bookkeeping and the benefits and risks that different types of software may bring. They will explore the differences between cloud accounting software and traditional accounting software and learn about the importance of software security and the steps that can be taken to keep data secure.

Learning outcomes

The Level 1 Award in Bookkeeping comprises of five learning outcomes:

1. Understand the role of the bookkeeper
2. Understand financial transactions
3. Process customer and supplier transactions
4. Process receipts and payments
5. Understand the benefits and risks of using accounting software to complete bookkeeping tasks

Scope of content and assessment criteria

Understand the role of the bookkeeper (Chapters 1, 4 & 8)

1.1 Duties and responsibilities of a bookkeeper

Learners need to know:

1.1.1 the duties and responsibilities of a bookkeeper:

- record and check financial transactions
- prepare and check financial documentation
- prepare information that is timely and accurate
- prepare information that may be used by managers/business owners in making decisions
- required to follow ethical principles
- must refer to a supervisor or seek authorisation where appropriate
- have money laundering obligations.

1.2 The importance of timely and accurate information

Learners need to know:

1.2.1 the potential effect of inaccurate information:

- incorrect accounting records: overstatement, understatement
- incorrect profit or loss
- incorrect tax payments to authorities
- delayed receipts from customers
- incorrect chasing of customers
- incorrect payments to suppliers: overpayment, underpayment
- duplicated payment to suppliers
- delayed receipt of goods from suppliers
- loss of customer/supplier goodwill
- incorrect information on external/internal reports: incorrect management/client decision making
- time spent tracing and correcting errors

1.3 Ethical principles

Learners need to know:

1.3.1 the five fundamental principles of ethics:

- confidentiality
- professional behaviour
- professional competence and due care
- integrity
- objectivity.

1.3.2 the potential effect of not keeping information confidential:

- unauthorised sharing of information
- breach of data protection/General Data Protection Regulations
- breach of AAT Code of Professional Ethics
- breach of employment contract
- loss of business / personal reputation.

1.3.3 ways to keep information confidential/secure:

- use of strong passwords / not sharing passwords
- screensavers
- encryption
- firewalls
- use of secure network: remote / hybrid working
- storage of hard-copy records, physical access restrictions
- storage of soft-copy records: cloud-storage, archives, secure back-ups, restricted access, cybersecurity
- authentication required to access cloud-based information
- not sharing laptops/computers with others
- not leaving confidential information where non-authorised personnel may see/not working in a public space
- not discussing confidential information where non-authorised personnel may hear
- anti-virus software
- cookies and privacy settings
- the importance of only sharing information with authorised personnel
- checking correct recipient before sending required information.

1.4 Money laundering obligations

Learners need to know:

1.4.1 key money laundering obligations:

- bookkeeping is an accountancy service
- bookkeepers must register for anti-money laundering supervision if they provide external bookkeeping services
- money laundering is a criminal offence
- reports of suspicious activity should be made
- failure to report a suspicion of money laundering is a criminal offence.

Understand financial transactions (Chapter 2)

2.1 The dual effect of transactions

Learners need to know:

2.1.1 that items that can be classified as:

- assets
- liabilities
- income
- expenses
- capital
- profit / loss.

2.1.2 that items can be recorded in the bookkeeping system

2.1.3 that each transaction changes the records of at least two items in the bookkeeping system: item amounts may increase and/or decrease.

2.2 The accounting equation

Learners need to know:

2.2.1 the accounting equation

2.2.2 that profits result in increases in capital and losses result in decreases in capital

2.2.3 that the accounting equation will always balance.

Process customer and supplier transactions (Chapters 3, 4 & 5)

3.1   The buying and selling process

Learners need to know:

3.1.1   the difference between trading for cash and trading on credit:

- cash sales
- cash purchases
- credit sales
- credit purchases
- customers
- suppliers
- receivables
- payables.

3.1.2   relevant documents and how they are used:

- sales and purchase invoice
- sales and purchase credit note
- quotation
- sales and purchase orders
- delivery note
- goods received note
- goods returned note
- cash receipt
- remittance advice.

3.2   Preparing sales invoices and credit notes

Learners need to know:

3.2.1 the documents used to prepare sales invoices and credit notes:

- quotation
- delivery note
- price list
- sales order.

Learners need to be able to:

3.2.2 complete sales invoice and credit note details with:

- customer name
- customer address

- invoice number
- invoice date
- credit note number
- credit note date
- product description
- product code

3.2.3 complete sales invoice and credit note amounts:
- unit price and price for multiple units
- discounts for buying in large quantities
- amounts (net, VAT and total)

3.3 Check purchase invoices and credit notes

Learners need to know:

3.3.1 the documents used to check purchase invoices and credit notes:
- quotation
- purchase order
- goods received note
- goods returned note.

Learners need to be able to:

3.3.2 recognise errors:
- customer reference
- product description
- product code
- unit price and price for multiple units
- discounts for buying large quantities
- amounts: net, VAT at standard rate, total.

3.4 Record sales and purchase invoices and credit notes in the books of prime entry

Learners need to know:

3.4.1 the books of prime entry:
- sales day book
- purchases day book
- sales returns day book
- purchases returns day book.

3.4.2 the columns within the books of prime entry:

- date
- customer/supplier name
- customer/supplier invoice number/credit note number
- amounts (net, VAT and total).

Learners need to be able to:

3.4.3 make entries in the books of prime entry

3.4.4 total columns in the books of prime entry

3.4.5 cross cast columns in the books of prime entry.

Process receipts and payments (Chapters 6 & 7)

4.1 Enter receipts and payments into a cash book

Learners need to know:

4.1.1 the format of the cash book:

- receipts side
- payments side.

4.1.2 the columns within the cash book:

- date
- customer/supplier
- cash and/or bank
- analysis columns (including VAT analysis).

4.1.3 the resources and documents used:

- cash receipts
- cheque stubs
- remittance advices
- lists of receipts and/or payments
- lists of Direct Debits and/or standing orders
- lists of Faster Payments and/or BACS
- bank statements
- automatic bank feeds.

Learners need to be able to:

4.1.4 make entries in the cash book:

- receipts

- payments
- total columns in the cash book
- cross cast columns in the cash book.

4.2 Use the cash book to calculate closing amounts of cash in hand and cash in the bank

Learners need to be able to:

4.2.1 calculate the closing amount of cash in hand from the opening amount, amounts received and amounts paid

4.2.2 calculate the closing amount of cash in the bank from the opening amount, amounts received and amounts paid.

4.3 Check the closing amount of cash in the bank against the closing balance on the bank statement

Learners need to be able to:

4.3.1 recognise receipts and payments on the bank statement

- counter credits
- cash withdrawals
- standing orders
- Direct Debits
- cheques
- BACS
- Faster Payments
- bank charges
- bank interest received.

4.3.2 recognise balances on the bank statement

4.3.3 recognise items in the cash book that are not on the bank statement

4.3.4 recognise items on the bank statement that are not in the cash book.

4.4 Identify outstanding amounts for individual customers and suppliers

Learners need to know:

4.4.1 the documents used:

- sales and purchase invoices
- sales and purchase credit notes
- lists of invoices and/or credit notes
- cheque stubs / paying-in book
- remittance advices

- lists of receipts and/or payments
- bank statements / bank feeds
- software reports: individual customer reports, individual supplier reports, receivables report, aged receivables analysis, aged payables analysis.

4.4.2 the records used:

- sales day book
- purchases day book
- sales returns day book
- purchases returns day book.

Learners need to be able to:

4.4.3 calculate amounts owed by customers

4.4.4 calculate amounts owed to suppliers

4.4.5 use an opening amount owed.

Understand the benefits and risks of using accounting software to complete bookkeeping tasks (Chapters 1 & 8)

5.1 Features of accounting software compared to manual bookkeeping

Learners need to know:

5.1.1 that digital systems can import transactions from a number of sources:

- bank records
- CSV files
- third party software / Apps.

5.1.2 The benefits of being able to integrate, import and export data to and from other programs:

- to work with data more flexibly
- save time
- reduce risk of human error
- communicate information in various formats
- receive information in reali-time: live bank feeds, wider accessibility
- easy access to information from a single system.

5.1.3 that digital systems can produce real-time reports.

5.1.4 that reports may be produced in accounting software:

- real-time financial position
- analysis of income and expenses
- individual customer reports
- individual supplier reports
- receivables reports
- payables reports
- aged receivables analysis
- aged payables analysis
- bank payments analysis for a specified time period
- bank receipts analysis for a specified time period.

5.1.5   that accounting software can provide benefits to processing customer and supplier transactions:

- pro forma invoices
- automated calculations
- automated emailing of invoice
- automated updates of changes to invoices
- pro forma purchase orders
- automatic conversion of quotes to sales invoices
- recurring invoicing schedules
- duplicate previously raised invoices
- automatic checks for accuracy.

5.1.6 that accounting software can provide benefits to processing receipts and payments:

- match bank receipts to sales invoices
- match bank payments to purchase invoices
- Software learning to suggest automated matching based on previous transactions
- automatic identification of differences in amounts paid/received to expectation
- automated allocation of amount received to cash book and customer account
- automated remittance advice
- automated reminders of when payments are due

- automated payment set up for due dates
- automatic checks for accuracy
- customer statements in real time to show amounts outstanding
- supplier statements in real time to show amounts outstanding.

5.1.7 that accounting software can have disadvantages:

- can create errors when the amount or frequency of a recurring entry changes
- manual errors at initial point of entry may still occur.

5.2 Advantages and disadvantages to users of different types of accounting software

Learners need to know:

5.2.1 the differences between 'off the shelf' versus bespoke software:

- cost
- levels of support for users
- timeframe for development
- range of functions used by business
- frequency and ease of updates
- level of training required to use software
- type of subscription.

5.2.2 the differences between traditional accounting software versus cloud software:

- cost
- levels of support for users
- range of functions used by business
- frequency and ease of updates
- upgrade capacity
- level of training required to use software
- access from multiple devices
- access/useability from mobile devices
- ability to integrate with third party software / Apps
- type of subscription
- access to internet.

5.3 Accounting software security

Learners need to know:

- potential threats to data security:
  - viruses
  - hacking
  - phishing
  - system crashes
  - employee fraud
  - corrupt files
  - natural disasters (flood, fire)
  - accidental deletion.

The assessment

Students must successfully pass one mandatory unit assessment, Bookkeeping Fundamentals, to achieve this qualification.

The proportion of this qualification assessed by externally marked assessment is 100%.

The assessment in this qualification:

- is set and marked by AAT
- is computer based
- is time-limited
- is scheduled by training providers or assessment venues
- takes place at approved training providers and assessment venues under controlled conditions.

This qualification is not graded.

Assessment for this award will be by Computer based assessment (CBA), under timed conditions. The time allowed for the assessment is 90 minutes.

The weighting of the learning outcomes is as follows:

1. Understand the role of the bookkeeper	17%
2. Understand financial transactions	10%
3. Process customer and supplier transactions	29%
4. Process receipts and payments	34%
5. Understand the benefits and risks of accounting software to complete bookkeeping tasks	10%
Total	100%

STUDY SKILLS

Preparing to study

Devise a study plan

Determine which times of the week you will study.

Split these times into sessions of at least one hour for study of new material. Any shorter periods could be used for revision or practice.

Put the times you plan to study onto a study plan for the weeks from now until the assessment and set yourself targets for each period of study – in your sessions make sure you cover the whole course, activities and the associated questions with answers at the back of the Study Text.

When working through your course, compare your progress with your plan and, if necessary, re-plan your work (perhaps including extra sessions) or, if you are ahead, do some extra revision/practice questions.

Effective studying

Active reading

You are not expected to learn the text by rote, rather, you must understand what you are reading and be able to use it to pass the assessment and develop good practice.

A good technique is to use SQ3Rs – Survey, Question, Read, Recall, Review:

1   **Survey the chapter**

    Look at the headings and read the introduction, knowledge, skills and content, so as to get an overview of what the chapter deals with.

2   **Question**

    Whilst undertaking the survey ask yourself the questions you hope the chapter will answer for you.

3   **Read**

    Read through the chapter thoroughly working through the activities and, at the end, making sure that you can meet the learning objectives shown within the summary.

4   **Recall**

    At the end of each chapter, try to recall the main ideas of the section/chapter without referring to the text. This is best done after short break of a couple of minutes after the reading stage.

5   **Review**

    Check that your recall notes are correct.

You may also find it helpful to re-read the chapter to try and see the topic(s) it deals with as a whole.

Note taking

Taking notes is a useful way of learning, but do not simply copy out the text. The notes must:

- be in your own words
- be concise
- cover the key points
- be well organised
- be modified as you study further chapters in this text or in related ones.

Trying to summarise a chapter without referring to the text can be a useful way of determining which areas you know and which you don't.

Three ways of taking notes

1 **Summarise the key points of a chapter**

2 **Make linear notes**

A list of headings, subdivided with sub-headings listing the key points.

If you use linear notes, you can use different colours to highlight key points and keep topic areas together.

Use plenty of space to make your notes easy to use.

3 **Try a diagrammatic form**

The most common of which is a mind map.

To make a mind map, put the main heading in the centre of the paper and put a circle around it.

Draw lines radiating from this to the main sub-headings which again have circles around them.

Continue the process from the sub-headings to sub-sub-headings.

Highlighting and underlining

You may find it useful to underline or highlight key points in your study text – but do be selective.

You may also wish to make notes in the margins.

Further reading

In addition to this text, you should also read the 'Student section' of the 'Accounting Technician' magazine every month to keep abreast of any guidance from the examiners.

The role of a bookkeeper

1

Introduction

In this chapter we will look at the role of a bookkeeper and what it entails. Having established the different tasks carried out by a bookkeeper, it will become clear why they play such a vital role in an accounting function.

As information provided by accounting professionals may be commercially sensitive, it is also important to understand why a bookkeeper needs to know how to handle this data confidentially and behave in an ethical manner, including a bookkeeper's money laundering obligations.

We will also look at the importance of bookkeepers keeping their knowledge up to date and what their professional responsibilities are.

KNOWLEDGE	CONTENTS
Understand the role of a bookkeeper	1 Duties and responsibilities of a bookkeeper
1.1 Duties and responsibilities of a bookkeeper	2 Ethical principles and obligations
1.2 The importance of timely and accurate information	3 Confidentiality and data security
1.3 Ethical principles	4 Summary and further questions
1.4 Money laundering	
Understand the benefits and risks of using accounting software to complete bookkeeping tasks	
5.3 Accounting software security	

1 Duties and responsibilities of a bookkeeper

1.1 Case study: an introduction

 Case study

Jessica has completed full-time education and, having gained some work experience in her uncle's shop, she is keen to pursue a career in accountancy. She has always enjoyed mathematics and has a good eye for detail.

Jessica has started an apprenticeship with the finance department at How Two Ltd, a supplier of computer components. As a result of the knowledge and skills she has acquired during her apprenticeship, Jessica has been given the task, as a junior bookkeeper, of getting all the financial records at How Two up to date. Jessica's manager stresses the need to ensure that the records balance accurately and to complete the task in a timely manner.

Jessica considers the importance of her role as a bookkeeper and the factors she needs to think about when completing this task.

Her progress will be monitored and checked by her mentor as Jessica completes a series of activities to ensure that she fully understands.

1.2 Why do we need bookkeepers?

 Case study

One of the reasons that Jessica entered the accounting profession, and one of the first things she learnt when she started working in the finance department at How Two Ltd, was that *no matter where you live or work in the world, an organisation will always need a bookkeeper.*

The main reasons bookkeepers will always be needed are:

- So that the owner/manager knows the income and expenditure of the business.

- So that the owner/manager can make decisions that will improve/expand the business.

- So that the organisation pays the correct amount of taxes due.

All governments need money to finance their activities, and they obtain that money from businesses and individuals in the form of taxes.

1.3 The role of the bookkeeper

The role of the bookkeeper is to keep an accurate record of all financial transactions carried out by an organisation. In most organisations, a bookkeeper will be required to prepare and check financial documentation before recording the financial transactions.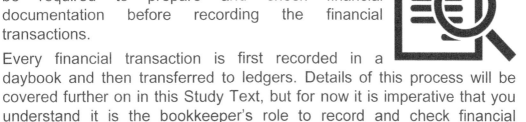

Every financial transaction is first recorded in a daybook and then transferred to ledgers. Details of this process will be covered further on in this Study Text, but for now it is imperative that you understand it is the bookkeeper's role to record and check financial transactions. Ultimately, they are responsible for keeping the accounting records up to date and accurate.

 Example

A bookkeeper checks the details of purchase orders against delivery notes which state what goods have been delivered to the customer. If the delivery note has been signed by the customer and everything agrees, the bookkeeper is then required to prepare a sales invoice to be sent to the customer, checking that it is accurate before sending it out.

In larger organisations, the bookkeeping work is often separated into different business activities carried out by clerks.

 Example

A sales ledger clerk will produce customer invoices and statements and chase up outstanding debts.

A purchases ledger clerk will keep a record of all invoices received from suppliers and process payments.

Cashiers are responsible for recording all monies received and paid by the business.

In smaller organisations, a bookkeeper will perform all of these activities.

Once the data has been entered, the information will be analysed by an accountant who will produce financial reports for the owner/manager of the business to enable them to make business decisions.

Accountants are also given the power to authorise certain transactions within a business whereas a bookkeeper simply processes them. Accountants help this decision-making process by interpreting and offering alternative strategies.

1.4 Information from the accounting function

The accounting function provides help and support to all other functions within the organisation. The managers of these other functions will rely on the information provided by accounting staff in order to run their departments effectively and contribute to the overall smooth running of the organisation.

The table below gives examples of the key information provided by the accounts department to other functions in the organisation.

Information	Function
Management will need information about the profit or loss of the organisation. For example, they may want to know whether a particular product is making a profit or a loss, or which department is making the most profit.	Management
The manager of the production department may want to know if the department has spent more or less than budgeted. They may need to know the cost of raw materials, discounts, the cost of any machinery and the budget for any replacements.	Production
The sales function may want to know about the income received from a particular product or the level of sales each sales person has been responsible for.	Sales
Human Resources may want the total salary cost of the staff, if there is a recruitment budget and whether there are any bonuses, overtime or commission due.	Human Resources

Therefore, it is essential that the information provided by bookkeepers or accounts clerks is accurate (free from errors), up to date and complete (nothing is missing). If there is something that a bookkeeper is unsure of, or that they feel is outside of the scope of their role, it is vital that they refer to their supervisor/manager for advice or seek approval from the accountant before acting upon it.

1.5 The importance of timely and accurate information

Due to the above, the bookkeeper plays a pivotal role in the successful operation of a business. Failure to carry out bookkeeping duties in an accurate and timely manner can have a detrimental impact on the organisation in a variety of ways.

It is therefore important for bookkeepers to consistently check and review their own work to make sure the information produced is accurate and free from error. Where possible, it is good practice to ask someone else to also review their work before submission.

Tracing and correcting errors further down the line could prove to be costly in terms of time, and could impact on other tasks unnecessarily. There are many features with accounting software which allow checks to be performed within the system. These will identify errors which can then be investigated in the most appropriate manner. Alternatively, finance department processes may include internal checks, again to reduce the risk of errors within the financial records.

In Chapter 4, we will look at some specific examples of the importance of checking documents, and how a bookkeeper's failure to do so can have a negative impact on a business.

1.6 Time management and deadlines

As a bookkeeper, it is important to take your time when processing financial transactions and entering information into the accounting records. For example, if totals are checked and do not agree, it is essential that time is spent identifying any errors and correcting them.

Time management is key to providing information both accurately and in a suitable amount of time. Therefore it is important that bookkeepers identify how long it will take to complete a task (e.g. processing the sales invoices) and plan their time accordingly. They should avoid taking on more work than is possible in the time available and discuss any worries about their workload with their supervisors, who can help to prioritise these tasks appropriately.

Failure to complete tasks in a timely manner can also have a negative impact on the organisation in a number of ways, as shown by the following examples.

 Example

A failure to process customer invoices in a timely manner could result in delayed receipts from customers which will have a negative impact on cash flow.

Note: If there are queries with customer invoices, accounts staff should not be afraid of contacting the customer/client for clarification. This helps promote positive working relationships and will instil confidence in their ability from the customer's perspective, thus increasing goodwill.

 Example

If accounting records are not kept up to date, supplier payments could be duplicated. These overpayments could go undetected, which would prove costly to the organisation.

When completing tasks such as supplier payments, a bookkeeper needs to be conscious of deadlines. Payment terms will be agreed when entering into a business relationship with a supplier of goods/services (e.g. 10 days, 14 days or 30 days after the date of invoice).

To maintain supplier goodwill, it is important that these timescales are met, and a positive working relationship is maintained. Failure to meet these timescales could result in late payments which could delay the receipt of goods from suppliers.

Timekeeping is crucial both when working alone or as part of a team. Knowing how long a particular task will take helps with both individual and team planning. The use of planning aids such as diaries, calendars or planning software enables you to keep track of the tasks for which you are responsible and to identify and be conscious of timescales and deadlines.

Managers can delegate tasks to individual team members, each working towards a common goal. It is important that managers can trust individuals to complete their work to the required standard. Mistakes can be costly to an organisation and can damage the relationship between managers and their staff.

If team members do not work efficiently and keep to the expected timescales, others within the team may be impacted, as they may be relying on the completion of that work before they can start theirs. If struggling to meet a deadline, a team member should highlight this to their manager so that arrangements can be made for other members of the team to help complete the work, or deadlines can be amended to prevent issues further down the line. Failure to highlight issues with meeting deadlines could result in work being rushed and mistakes being made.

 Example

Kim's manager asks her to complete some bookkeeping duties, but the deadline set is unrealistic. Kim wants to create a good impression so rushes the work to make sure it is completed on time, but she does not have time to review her own work before submitting it to her manager.

The figures inputted contain mistakes which leads to the month end reports being incorrect. The sales figures have been understated considerably which means the profit figure showing within the accounts is lower than it should be.

This has resulted in Kim's manager making incorrect business decisions and incorrect taxes being paid to the authorities.

Deadlines are exceptionally important in accounting and finance. All businesses must comply with external regulations such as the submission of year-end accounts, payroll information and tax information.

These regulations set out strict deadlines to ensure taxes are paid on time. They also provide a set of rules that must be followed to ensure financial information is processed accurately, to show a true reflection of the financial position of the organisation. If these rules and regulations are not adhered to, it could result in penalties being imposed on the business which could have a negative impact on its reputation.

Internal deadlines (those required within the organisation) are another important aspect of working in accounting and finance. As workload will often be distributed throughout the organisation, each department will be relying on timely and accurate information. If internal deadlines are missed, this could result in out of date information being communicated to all departments. This will lead to incorrect business decisions being made which could have a detrimental impact on the organisation as a whole.

If your manager delegates a task to you which you have not done before, it is important to assess your ability to take on the task. If you are unsure, discuss it in more detail with them and do not take on any work that is beyond your ability. Accepting work beyond your capabilities could lead to mistakes, again leading to negative consequences for both you and the organisation. Therefore, despite deadlines, it is important that if unsure of how to process something, you seek advice to clarify the correct course of action, rather than rushing to complete the task simply as you think it should be done without the relevant knowledge.

As detailed below, learning new skills and seeking advice on how to perform such tasks is a crucial part of any bookkeeper's development.

1.7 Continuing Professional Development (CPD)

Bookkeepers and accounts clerks are entry level job roles, but there are a lot of opportunities for career progression by work experience and gaining bookkeeping and accounting qualifications.

A bookkeeper is responsible for their own continuing professional development. Continuing professional development is where an individual enhances or maintains their professional skills and experience to keep their knowledge of their chosen profession up to date.

When considering their professional development, bookkeepers will need to assess and look to develop their skills. Some of their career skills are professional, whereas some are their personal attributes. Professional skills include:

Professionalism   Accounting professionals should be able to demonstrate a high level of competence in their work and be able to meet the required standards of the profession.

Integrity	Accounting professionals should adopt an approach to work guided by strong moral principles. They are expected to be straightforward, honest and trustworthy.
Numeracy	Accounting professionals are expected to have good numeracy skills. They should be able to process numerical information quickly and accurately and be able to understand and explain calculations.
Literacy	Accounting professionals need to be skilled at dealing with written content.
Communication Skills	Accounting professionals need to be able to speak and deal with a wide range of people using a range of communication skills: e.g. writing, speaking, presenting, and listening.

As well as the key skills mentioned above, accounting professionals are expected to display certain personal attributes. These include:

Reliability	Employers and your team workers will need to rely on you to do the work that you promised to do.
Punctuality	Being punctual means being on time, both in terms of arriving at your place of work on time and completing a required task at an agreed time.
Willingness to learn	Showing a willingness to learn demonstrates that you are interested in your job role and the organisation. It also suggests you are not afraid of learning new skills which will help you and the organisation to develop.
Organisation	Employers will expect you to be able to complete work within an agreed time frame. If you are well-organised you are more likely to be able to complete your work effectively and efficiently.

New skills and knowledge can be acquired in a variety of ways.

Accounting professionals will undertake **formal training** to learn technical skills, for example by enrolling on a college course to take AAT qualifications. Knowledge and experience can also be acquired through **informal training** such as self-study or on the job training. Examples of informal training are given below.

Example

Job Rotation	Job rotation involves switching employees round through a range of jobs. Job rotation can mean that employees are given a wider knowledge of the organisation. It can also help the organisation if cover is needed for absent staff.
Job Shadowing	Job shadowing means working with an experienced employee who can pass on the skills and knowledge required to perform the task
Professional Journals	Professional journals are magazines written by professionals in a particular field of interest. For example, the AAT Accounting Technician magazine.
Internet/ newspapers	These sources provide up to date financial news and information relevant to accounting professionals.

The AAT's Continuing Professional Development (CPD) policy follows a four-stage cycle: Assess, Plan, Action, Evaluate. The AAT recommend that the cycle is followed at least twice each year in order for its members to develop their skills and further their career.

When considering their personal development, the AAT CPD cycle can help bookkeepers and their line managers to evaluate your performance and set appropriate development goals and targets. It also will enable them to continually assess their learning needs to keep up to date with professional developments.

Assess learning and development needs and goals.

What skills do I need to be able to perform my duties effectively?

Plan appropriate activities to meet learning and development needs and goals.

Research how skills can be developed and discuss training opportunities with your manager. It might be by enrolling on a college course, or having informal training from a colleague.

Evaluate whether the activities did meet the developmental goals.

Can I now perform the tasks the organisation needs me to?

Action the plan

Enrol on a college course/ schedule training with a mentor.

Test your understanding 1

Fill in the gaps from the pick list below to complete the paragraph about bookkeepers.

The bookkeeper is responsible for _inputting_ the financial _transactions_ of an organisation. An accountant is responsible for _interpreting_ the financial _information_ of an organisation. The _Accountant_ suggests alternative strategies, based on the interpretation of the financial information. The _manager_ will make the decisions.

A bookkeeper may start as a _bookkeeper_, but, with hard work and study, can progress to _senior_ accountant.

Pick list

Accountant	bookkeeper	information	interpreting
manager	senior	inputting	transactions

 Test your understanding 2

Below is a list of duties that are performed in the accounting department. Tick the column to suggest who would typically perform each task.

Role	Bookkeeper	Accountant
Authorising the purchase of a new printer		✓
Coding the printer invoice	✓	
Entering the printer invoice into the system	✓	
Authorising payment of the printer invoice		✓

 Test your understanding 3

Lucy has been asked to complete some work for her colleague while she is on annual leave. Her colleague showed her quickly what to do but Lucy has forgotten. What should she do?

Options	✓
Ask one of her other colleagues to do it instead	
Attempt the task anyway, when she sees it, she should remember what she is supposed to do	
Speak to her manager and explain the situation	✓

Test your understanding 4

Identify whether the following statements are true or false.

Statement	True	False
Spending time tracing and correcting errors does not cost the business any money		✓
Delayed receipts from customers due to inaccurate information do not impact on the organisation		✓
Planning work using an online calendar helps ensure deadlines can be met	✓	

Test your understanding 5

It is lunchtime and you have completed all of your work for the day. Your colleague is struggling to meet their deadline of the end of the day.

What do you do?

Options	✓
Keep quiet and look busy	
Book a half day holiday	
Offer to help them complete their work to ensure the deadline is met	✓

2 Ethical principles and obligations

2.1 Ethical principles

Behaving ethically means doing the right thing at the right time. Accounting professionals are trusted by their employers to handle confidential and sensitive information in an appropriate manner.

The AAT has published a set of ethical guidelines to follow - www.aat.org.uk/membership/standards-requirements/professional-ethics.

These fundamental principles form part of the guidelines:

- **Confidentiality** – as described later in this chapter, it is important that information is not disclosed to third parties, used for personal gain or shared unless there is a legal or professional duty to do so.
- **Objectivity** – accountants should remain independent and show sound judgement rather than allowing bias, personal interests or pressure from others to influence them.
- **Integrity** - being straightforward and honest when you perform your duties.
- **Professional behaviour and competence** – being able to perform your job to an acceptable level and provide a good service. All accounting professionals should undergo regular training to keep their technical knowledge up-to-date.

Test your understanding 6

Which of the following are principles that a professional accountant should follow in order to demonstrate ethical behaviour?

Tick ALL that apply.

Options	✔
Confidentiality	✓
Flexibility	
Integrity	✓
Confidence	
Numeracy	

[handwritten note at top: lavagem de dinheiro = usar dinheiro ilícito para comprar objetos e revendê-los. Colocar dinheiro ilegal em meios formais]

Test your understanding 7

In each of the following situations decide whether this is an example of ethical behaviour or not. For each, state which ethical principle is being considered.	Is this ethical behaviour?		Which ethical principle is being considered?
	Yes	No	
Discussing the issues one of your clients is facing when with your friends over dinner.		✓	*Confiden-tiality*
Providing advice on an area of tax accounting you are not familiar with to a customer.		✓	*Integrity*
Completing the accounts on time and bearing in mind all recent changes in legislation.	✓		*Professional Behaviour and competence*
Changing the contents of a report because your manager offered you a financial bonus to do so.		✓	*Objectivity*

2.2 Money laundering obligations

Definition

Money laundering is a way of making large amounts of money through criminal activities such as terrorist activities and drug trafficking, and in particular, hiding the true origin of this money behind a seemingly legitimate venture.

In other words, the income generated through these types of activities is considered 'dirty' and needs to be 'laundered' in order to make it look 'clean'.

The process of money laundering costs the UK billions of pounds each year, and often includes the passing of financial proceeds through UK businesses and banks to make it look legitimate.

The UK National Risk Assessment of money laundering and terrorist financing 2020 (NRA) concluded that there is a particularly high risk of criminals (exploiting) accountancy services for the purposes of money laundering. Bookkeeping is an accountancy service and is therefore at risk of (exploitation.) Bookkeepers have a number of obligations to follow with regards to money laundering to prevent their role being used to further criminal activities.

[handwritten note in right margin: exploit = explorar no sentido de ...]

It is essential that bookkeepers who provide external bookkeeping services, register for anti-money laundering supervision. Anti-money laundering supervision helps bookkeepers take the necessary steps to protect themselves from money laundering.

Bookkeepers who provide internal bookkeeping services do not need to register as their services are overseen by external accountants who are registered for anti-money laundering supervision.

Failure to follow the rules and regulations around anti-money laundering could result in the bookkeeper being held personally liable. As money laundering is a criminal activity, penalties can include up to 14 years in prison, a large fine or both.

Any suspicious activity should be reported, following the correct procedures. Failure to report any suspicion of money laundering is a criminal offence and can result in penalties.

Test your understanding 8

Identify whether the following statements are true or false.

Statement	True	False
Money laundering is not a criminal offence		✓
Bookkeepers who provide internal bookkeeping services must register for anti-money laundering supervision		✓
Suspicious activity should be reported following the correct procedures	✓	

KAPLAN PUBLISHING

3 Confidentiality and data security

3.1 Confidentiality

Information that is being processed by a bookkeeper will be both sensitive and/or private. Whether the information is held on paper or held electronically on a computer, a bookkeeper must make sure that confidential information is kept in a safe and secure way. This will help to prevent loss and the unauthorised sharing of information.

The potential impact of not keeping this information confidential should be serious for both the individual and the organisation. It could be considered a breach of the individual's employment contract (most users will need to complete some form of IT security/ 'Acceptable use of IT' training when joining a company), a breach of the AAT Code of Professional Ethics, or a data protection violation or breach (see section 3.3), which could result in a fine for the business.

3.2 Commercial information

Information held by the accounts department or being processed by a bookkeeper may be commercially sensitive. For example, the price paid for a particular product, or discounts given to customers. If a competitor of the business knew this information they might be able to use it as a competitive advantage. It is therefore imperative to protect customer information and to only share information with authorised personnel, otherwise this could be damaging to the business.

3.3 Personal information

Personal information held about individuals such as employees, customers, supplier etc. is protected by law. The Data Protection Act 2018 is the UK's implementation of the General Data Protection Regulation (GDPR). This sets out rules about how personal data can be used.

The act sets out the following principles that must be followed when processing and using personal data.

The information must be:

1. collected and used fairly, transparently, and lawfully

2. used for limited, specifically stated purposes

3. used in a way that is adequate, relevant, and limited to what is necessary in relation to the purposes for it is intended

4. accurate and kept up to date

5. kept for no longer than is absolutely necessary

6. kept safe and secure - the principle of integrity and confidentiality requires businesses to handle personal data in a manner that will protect against accidental loss or damage

7. handled responsibly in compliance with the other principles – organisations should have written policies and processes to ensure all staff are accountable for the way in which data is handled.

Any organisations who process personal data must register with the Information Commissioner's Office in order to be permitted to process data. The information Commissioner's Office (ICO) is the UK's independent body set up to uphold information rights. You can find out how personal information is protected by visiting their website: https://ico.org.uk/

Whether personal and sensitive information is held on a computer or in paper based format, it is vitally important that it is kept safe and secure. This means necessary steps must be taken to reduce the risk of unauthorised access or sharing of information.

When sending information to others, it is important to make sure they are authorised to receive the details and if sending this information via email, the sender should double check they have the correct recipient to prevent information getting into the wrong hands.

Without the correct safety precautions in place, information could be lost or corrupted due to computer failure or viruses. Information should only be shared with people who are authorised to view it. It is a legal requirement of all businesses to keep sensitive information such as customer details confidential, any breach could result in penalties being imposed on the individual who has caused the issue, the company or both.

Not only would this be a breach of the individual's contract of employment and GDPR regulations, but it would also be a breach of the AAT Code of Professional Ethics. This could have a detrimental impact on the individual's reputation, the reputation of the organisation and ultimately could result in loss of business.

General
Data
Protection
Regulation

3.4 The security of confidential information

Advances in technology have enabled organisations to process more and more personal data, and to share information more easily. This has obvious benefits, but it also gives rise to equally obvious security risks.

If a bookkeeper is given sensitive information to work with, it is their responsibility to keep it safe and secure. There are some basic steps that can be taken such as:

- not sharing laptops/computers
- not working in public spaces where others may be able to see what you are doing
- conducting meetings in private
- the agenda for meetings not covering anything that is confidential and cannot be shared with all attendees
- discussing confidential matters with others in a place where unauthorised personnel are unable to hear what is being discussed
- using a secure network or VPN (Virtual Private Network) for remote or hybrid working
- restricting staff access to systems to the level required for their role. For example, an employee responsible for inputting invoices on the accounting system, does not necessarily need access to the bank account.

Although it is important to not keep unnecessary information, organisations do need to consider legal requirements. Financial information must be kept for 6 years from the end of the last company financial year they relate to. It is best practice to archive old records whether that be physically archiving and storing paperwork or archiving electronic files so they are hidden and only retrieved if and when required.

Below are some examples of how to keep confidential information secure in the role of a bookkeeper.

retrieved = recuperar, restaurar.

💡 Example

Situation	Paper based filing system	Information held on a computer
Confidential information you are currently working with.	Any confidential information you are responsible for should be kept close by you at all times so that you are aware if anyone tries to read it. To avoid the information being seen by anyone passing by your desk, all confidential paperwork should be kept face down or in a folder until you need to work with it.	You may need to change the position of your computer screen to make sure that unauthorised people cannot see information on your computer screen as you are working. If this is not possible, you may need to move desks or offices to ensure that you can carry out the work. Sensitive information held on computers should be protected by multi-level passwords so that employees only see what is relevant to them. Never share your password with unauthorised people.
If you have to leave your workstation	If you have to leave your desk always put any confidential papers in a locked drawer or filing cabinet.	You should use the screen lock on your computer so that confidential information cannot be read by people passing your desk when you are away.
Storage of confidential information	Sensitive information should be kept in a locked filing cabinet, until it is needed.	Regular back-ups of computer data should be taken and stored in fireproof cabinets.
Out of date information	When confidential information is no longer needed it should be shredded before being recycled.	Data should be removed or deleted from computers by authorised staff from the Information Technology (IT) department.

🔍 Definition

Authorised person – Someone who has been given permission to do something on somebody else's behalf. For example, an employee who has been authorised to input confidential information onto a computer.

KAPLAN PUBLISHING

Test your understanding 9

Tick the appropriate box for the statements provided:

Commercial information is information that can be sold to anyone, so it does not have to be kept confidential.

True ☐ or False ☒

You have finished working on a document, you have made notes on paper that you do not need anymore. Are you going to:

Discard the paper in the bin ☐   Shred the paper ☒

You have sent an e-mail containing personal information to the wrong client. Is this:

A breach of data protection regulations (GDPR) ☒

Nothing to worry about, as the data is not commercial ☐

3.5 Cybersecurity

Definition

Cybersecurity is how individuals and organisations protect hardware, software and data cyberattacks.

Businesses need to consider the best way of protecting themselves such as using a secure network, installing firewalls or asking for authentication before allowing access to cloud-based information.

Remote working/hybrid working is becoming more common, but it does increase the risk to the security of confidential information. Many companies use Microsoft Office for their day to day operations and this now operates in the cloud via Office 365. It is best practice to enable two factor authentication so that if a person is logging onto their Office Sharepoint, a code will be sent to another device such as their mobile phone to verify it is them before access is granted.

Firewalls provide protection against outside cyber attackers by shielding your computer or network from malicious or unnecessary network traffic. Firewalls can also prevent malicious software from accessing your computer or network via the internet.

escudo
shield =
protect
from a
danger,
risk, or
unpleasant
experience.

Businesses Businesses Businesses
businesses businesses businesses

3.6 Passwords

As a bookkeeper, you will have many passwords for different systems and processes. For example, you will have a password to be able to gain access to the computer system itself, you will then need another password to gain access to the accounting software and the chances are that other documents will be password protected for you to be able to view them.

It is important that you keep your password safe and secure and change it regularly in line with the company procedures or immediately if you suspect that someone has found out what your password is. You should avoid the use of names or dates that are personal to you as quite often these can be easy to guess. Ideally you should create a password that contains both upper and lower case letters, numbers and symbols. The harder it is for someone to guess your password, the harder it is for them to access sensitive information.

📝 Test your understanding 10

You have recently set up online banking for your current account.

You need to set a password for access to the online banking facilities. Which of the following would make a good password? Tick the TWO best answers from the options given.

Options	✔
Something you cannot remember	
Something other people are not likely to know	✓
Something obvious	
The word 'password'	
Your name and year of birth	
A combination of letters, numbers and symbols	✓
Something you saved on your PC in a file called Passwords	

Test your understanding 11

Below is a list of statements. State which are true and which are false.

Statement	True/False
Passwords can be shared with colleagues who are doing the same type work.	*FALSE*
All cabinet drawers with personal or commercial information in should be kept locked.	*TRUE*
If leaving your work station, you must ensure that the screen is blank and computer access blocked.	*TRUE*

3.7 Viruses

The best way to understand the concept of a computer virus is to think about a human being having the flu virus; let's call them the 'host.' When they come into contact with another human they infect them with the virus.

The virus can just keep on replicating itself and spreading from human to human until there is an epidemic. In the same way a computer virus needs a 'host' cell such as a program, file or document. When that is sent to another computer that too becomes infected.

unwittingly = not aware of the full facts! / not done on purpose / unintentional / involuntariamente / unwitting / involuntario

These viruses are cleverly hidden and can be unwittingly sent from user to user. People often do not realise that they have an infected computer until they experience problems with their programs. The more severe viruses have been known to spread to millions of users and have damaged their systems, or in some cases have destroyed them completely.

Unfortunately, viruses are created by people who write bad codes intended to change the way in which a computer operates. There have been instances where people experimenting have accidently sent out bad codes, however it is usually an intentional action by someone who is commonly known as a **cybercriminal**. They send the bad code out and it will attach itself to a program or file on the recipient user's computer. The virus may not do any damage immediately, it will only become active when you run the file that it has attached itself to (until then it is effectively sleeping). Once you run that program the bad code becomes active, you now have an infected computer that can infect other computers on the same network.

A virus attack can completely destroy accounting data/files resulting in the loss of client and business information. A severe attack can destroy an accounting system completely making it unusable. An attack can also create openings for unauthorised users known as hackers to view and steal sensitive information and data. The nature of accounting often means sending customers information electronically and therefore if you have a virus on your computer, it could be inadvertently sent to the client.

3.8   Backups

The first line of defence against a virus is to backup data and save it in a safe place such as a locked fire proof cabinet. It is good practice to have a further backed up copy stored in outside premises in case something happens to the file that is kept in the office. If storing data in the cloud, backups should be regularly updated to capture new data, the computer is set to automatically do a backup and as the information stored is real-time information, the most up to date data is always available to access.

3.9   Anti-virus software

Anti-virus software is another key way in which an organisation can keep confidential information safe and secure. This is a piece of software that is installed onto the computer system which will then scan information such as emails for viruses and will block any content that appears suspect. Viruses can be extremely dangerous as they can shut down a whole system in a very short space of time. If data becomes corrupt, you will not be able to see or use it therefore it is very important that an organisation protects itself with anti-virus software.

Test your understanding 12

You have been working on a confidential document on your computer and have to leave the office for ten minutes to deal with a customer. How can you keep the information on your screen confidential?

Options	✓
Switch the computer off	
Use the screen lock facility to lock the computer screen	✓
Stay at your desk	
Put some papers over the screen to hide the information	

Test your understanding 13

Complete the following sentences:

a) I need to go to the bathroom, I should use my computer _____*screen*_____ lock.

b) I have finished with this confidential paper so I am going to _____*shred*_____ it.

c) I don't want anyone to read this paperwork so I am going to put it _____*face down*_____ on my desk.

d) _____*Anti - virus*_____ software is another way of keeping information safe and secure.

e) Backed up computer data should be stored in _____*fireproof*_____ cabinets.

3.10 Hacking

Just like a burglar enters premises without permission, hackers gain access to people's computers without permission. Once they have done so, the hackers can do anything from stealing information to having control of the computer. Sophisticated hackers can see everything that the user is doing.

Hackers can gain access to computers in several ways such as through viruses, insecure wireless connections, e-mails, fake internet sites and social media. Hackers are constantly looking for weaknesses in computer programs and, just like a burglar will take advantage of an open window and sneak in, a hacker will do the same with a vulnerable computer.

If a hacker manages to access accounting data they can cause irreparable damage to the business. They can access all the clients' information and use it to commit identity theft, steal passwords and change or delete data.

These kind of attacks can cause huge financial losses to an organisation. The firm would have to inform all its clients that this had happened, resulting in damage to the reputation of the company and potentially the loss of clients.

To protect accounting data from hackers, effective use of passwords by employees is key. It is important to keep passwords safe and secure and change them regularly in line with the company procedures or immediately suspecting that someone has found out what the password is.

An organisation with a number of employees will usually have a system that prompts the user to change their password when it is time to do so. In addition, you should not use the same password for different programs, this way if a hacker guesses one password they do not have access to everything.

Encrypting data is effective against hackers. This is where your information is scrambled up so that it looks like nonsense. Only people who have access to the key stored on your hardware can unscramble it. So, a hacker may still manage to break in to the computer but they would not be able to understand the information.

Another way of protecting an organisation from hackers is to only keep the data that is of use. Client/customer information such as credit card numbers, dates of birth or other personal or sensitive data may be of no use, but is tempting for hackers. Therefore employees must be vigilant and remove the information yourself or get your client to remove it. Again, ensuring that you have a good security software package and keeping it updated is another way in which data can be kept secure. Individuals should NEVER share your password with anyone and should always close your computer screen when you leave your workstation and lock the screen to avoid unauthorised people from viewing information or using your computer.

3.11 Phishing (financial theft)

Phishing is an attempt to trick people into revealing sensitive information such as passwords, bank details or any other kind of sensitive financial information. The ultimate goal is financial theft. There are also phishing attacks where they not only try to steal information but also attach a virus to your system.

Phishing usually occurs in the form of an e-mail that looks like it came from a genuine organisation, for example a bank. A common trick is to tell the recipient that there has been some unusual activity on their account. They must sign into the account using the link provided (fake web address that looks like the banks) and verify their details in order to be able to continue using their account. It will say that an immediate response is required or your account will be suspended or closed.

Anyone clicking the link and providing the information has just given a thief all they need to steal from their bank account. People often receive these kinds of e-mails from organisations that they don't even have an account with. Companies may receive an e-mail that appears to be from one of their genuine clients. They are designed to trick the user into giving out financial information about the company or may activate a virus once opened.

Example

A recent phishing scheme e-mail reported in the USA targeted accounting firm employees. It looked like it was from a genuine client and asked the employee to open an attachment.

When opened, key-logging malware was launched that could see every keystroke the employee made.

It even got past encrypted data because the keystrokes were recorded by the malware before they were encrypted.

Phishing can cause a major threat to accounting data because sensitive data about clients and their customers can be used to gain access to their bank accounts or be used for other fraudulent financial transactions. Information about a company can be divulged to competitors or in some cases sold for the purpose of causing financial ruin.

If users wish to protect your data from phishing, they need to remember that no reputable organisation will EVER contact them and ask for a password. If the sender of an e-mail is not known, e-mails should not be opened and a virus scan should be performed.

If you are unsure of an e-mail because you know the sender, contact them to ask if they have sent you the e-mail. Hover over any strange looking links with your cursor to see if it is spelled correctly or is an unusual address. You should delete any obvious suspicious e-mail unopened and if you are unsure, you should report any strange activity to the I.T department.

3.12 System crashes

If a system crashes, it means that the system stops working properly and shuts itself down. This happens because data or other files can suddenly develop errors that the system cannot handle or recognise. These corrupt files are commonly known as computer bugs.

Power failures and problems with other programs or networks can also cause a system to crash. If this happens, there is a chance that all data files could be lost and therefore it is essential to protect data by taking regular backups. If a system has to be restored using a backup from before the crash happened, any transactions completed since would need to be re-entered. However, if data is stored in the cloud, it is automatically backed up on a regular basis. This means that when the system is backup and running, the number of transactions that need to be re-entered is minimal.

3.13 Employee fraud in accounting

Employee fraud is where an employee steals money from a business by altering or creating accounting records, in order to make missing money that they have stolen, look like legitimate transactions.

There are many ways in which this can happen, as shown here:

 Example

Accounts payable fraud – an employee sets up a fake supplier and charges the company for goods or services that have not actually been provided.

Personal purchases – an employee uses company funds to pay for personal purchases and records the payments as legitimate business expenses in the accounting system.

Payroll fraud – an employee processing payroll transactions sets up ghost employees on the system and pays them, intercepting the money for themselves.

Not only do these instances of fraud cause financial losses for the business, but often the employee is altering data either by deleting, adding or changing figures. This affects the integrity of the accounting data which is used to produce the year-end financial statements and to calculate their taxes. Incorrect information can lead to penalties and fines. There is also a risk of the system crashing or the employee causing a bad code to be generated and introduce a virus.

To protect accounting data from employee fraud, the company should introduce segregation of duties across the department/accounting process. Segregation of duties is where more than one employee is responsible for every stage of an accounting process. By having work checked more than once, this reduces the risk of employee fraud occurring and the temptation to attempt it.

 Examples

The cashier taking cash to the bank on behalf of a business should not be the same person who writes out the paying in slip to the bank. This reduces the danger of cash disappearing into the cashier's pocket.

There should also be a supervisor/line manager overseeing accounting activities on a regular basis. This involves checking things such as data entries onto computers, payments etc. with specified limits on payments over a certain amount e.g. payments over £2,500 need to be authorised by a senior member of staff.

Employees should also be encouraged to report suspicious activity.

3.14 Corrupt files

Corrupt files are files that suddenly stop working. There are several reasons for this happening.

A common reason is that the file has developed a bad sector - this is something that can happen randomly and unfortunately little can prevent it. Sometimes there is a fault or bug that may cause a file not to work properly, but it starts working again. The problem may never recur but the system needs checking by the IT department to ensure nothing more serious is happening behind the scenes.

The more serious way of files becoming corrupt is if a bug occurs due to the system having a virus. This poses a threat to accounting data as it can result in the loss of some or all accounting data. To protect against this, regular backups of data should be taken. Storing data in a cloud will ensure that the most up to date information is always available. Frequent virus checks will also help protect files from becoming corrupt.

3.15 Natural disasters and accidental deletion

Unexpected events occur in all over the world and are classed as natural disasters. These include fires, floods and earthquakes. Data is always vulnerable in the case of one of these events.

Accidental deletion is when someone removes a file or other data that should not have been removed from the system. This is usually by mistake or because of human error. Accidental deletion can happen by clicking on the wrong key or sequence of keys on the computer or by trying to correct an entry by deleting it incorrectly. Sometimes people try to speed up some of their working practices by copying and pasting information but sometimes this can lead to accidental data loss.

Accidental deletion or natural disasters could result in the loss of all accounting data files which causes major setbacks for a business. If client information is lost, this could lead to financial loss as well as having a negative effect on their reputation.

In order to protect accounting data, backup data should be stored in a fireproof cabinet high off the floor. Backups should be taken on a regular basis, and at least once a day in most businesses. In addition, individual files should regularly be backed up whilst working on them. There is little more frustrating than spending an hour producing a document or a spreadsheet only to lose it and not to have a backup.

Copies of backups should be kept securely to prevent unauthorised access or accidental damage. It is good practice to keep a backup at a secure location off the premises. This way, if there is a fire or a burglary the backup data will not be destroyed or stolen. Storing data in cloud is also another secure method as it is always accessible from anywhere with an internet connection.

equal chances for each item

r° statistic = in the way that involves item

aleatoriamente — randomly = without method or conscious decision; indiscriminately

---

📝 Test your understanding 14

Viruses can…..

Tick all of the options below that complete the sentence correctly.

Options	✔
Cause loss of information	✓
Can be easily fixed	
Cause the system to crash	✓
Infect all computers on the same network	✓
Only be harmful for s short period of time	
Cause a loss in productivity	✓

📝 Test your understanding 15

You receive an email from a client asking you to click on a link. It is unusual for them to contact you via email, what do you do?

There are TWO correct answers. Put a tick in the relevant boxes.

Options	✔
Ignore the email	
Hover over the address and if it looks genuine, click on the link	✓
Forward it to your supervisor	
Click on the link	
Contact the client to ask if they have sent the email	✓

KAPLAN PUBLISHING

Test your understanding 16

Match the relevant threat from the picklist below to its statement.

Statement	Threat
Enters your computer from infected files or programs	*viruses*
Enters your computer through emails	*phishing*
Can trace every stroke of a key you make on your computer	*hacking*

Picklist

Hacking

Phishing

Viruses

4 Summary and further questions

In this chapter we have described the role of a bookkeeper. You should now know that bookkeepers prepare and check financial documents and transactions to be authorised by an accountant, as well as the importance that this information is provided in a timely and accurate manner.

You should also understand the importance of keeping information confidential and secure in this role. We have considered a number of the key data threats and established a number of different methods for keeping data secure and confidential as required.

Whilst looking at the wider role of the bookkeeper, we have recognised the importance of working in an ethical manner and how this helps to protect the bookkeeping data.

Let us return to our case study to see how Jessica applies this knowledge.

 Case study activity 1

Jessica is asked to attend a staff meeting at How Two Ltd. Otto, the Sales Manager, asks Jessica what her role as a bookkeeper for the company entails.

Which TWO of the following answers would be the most appropriate?

Options	✓
Analysing the financial performance of the business	
Advising the Managing Director	
Recording and checking financial transactions	✓
Processing documents such as sales invoices as required	✓
Deciding pay increases	
Saving costs for the business	

Case study activity 2

Jessica is aware that there are many departments for which the accounting team at How Two Ltd provide information.

Match the department with the correct definition.

Department	Definition
PRODUCTION	This department sells the company's goods and services to customers.
SALES	This department is responsible for typing, collecting and distributing mail, keeping & filing records, organising meetings and maintaining resources.
ADMINISTRATION	This department deals with the recruitment of new staff, the training of new and existing staff, pay negotiations and regular staff appraisals.
ACCOUNTING	This department is responsible for producing the goods or services that a business provides by making best use of the various inputs.
HUMAN RESOURCES	This department is responsible for keeping records and accounts, for giving advice on budgets to other departments, and for paying wages and salaries.

 ## Case study activity 3

Jessica is discussing her future professional plans with a colleague who seems reluctant to take part in further training courses given their experience.

Why is it important for Jessica and other accounting professionals to continually develop their skills?

 ## Case study activity 4

Jessica has been asked to create her own unique password for the accounting system.

Which of the following passwords should she use?

a) Password123

b) JHoward011200

c) JessHowTw0

d) 4yXkj2fR!*

Case study activity 5

During a conversation in the staff canteen, several members of staff were discussing their rates of pay and the company bonus.

One of them, Neelam is upset that other people are being paid more than her. She asks Jessica to find out for her if one of her colleagues, Jason, is indeed being paid more than her.

What reply should Jessica give?

Statement	Correct?
Jessica confirms the amount that Jason does indeed receive more money than Neelam.	
Jessica tells Neelam that she will speak to her manager to see if she can tell her the information.	
Jessica explains to Neelam that this information is confidential and cannot be disclosed.	✓
Jessica ensures that all pay rates are accessible to all employees to avoid any future debate.	

 Case study activity 6

Jessica has a colleague who is also a good friend. They have forgotten their password to the system and need to quickly amend some figures before their meeting.

They have asked to use your password temporarily, what do you do?

Put a tick in the correct box.

Options	✓
Give them her password but tell them not to tell anyone else what it is	
Give them her password for now and then change it when they have gone into their meeting	
Refuse to give them her password	✓
Log in for them so they don't know what her password is	

Answers to chapter activities

Test your understanding 1

Fill in the gaps from the pick list below to complete the paragraph about bookkeepers.

The bookkeeper is responsible for **inputting** the financial **transactions** of an organisation. An accountant is responsible for **interpreting** the financial **information** of an organisation.

The **Accountant** suggests alternative strategies, based on the interpretation of the financial information. The **manager** will make the decisions.

A bookkeeper may start as a **bookkeeper**, but, with hard work and study, can progress to **senior** accountant.

Test your understanding 2

Role	Bookkeeper	Accountant
Authorising the purchase of a new printer		✓
Coding the printer invoice	✓	
Entering the printer invoice into the computer	✓	
Authorising payment of the printer invoice		✓

Test your understanding 3

Options	✓
Ask one of her other colleagues to do it instead	
Attempt the task anyway, when she sees it, she should remember what she is supposed to do	
Speak to her manager and explain the situation	✓

Test your understanding 4

Statement	True	False
Spending time tracing and correcting errors does not cost the business any money		✓
Delayed receipts from customers due to inaccurate information do not impact on the organisation		✓
Planning work using an online calendar helps ensure deadlines can be met	✓	

Test your understanding 5

Options	✓
Keep quiet and look busy	
Book a half day holiday	
Offer to help them complete their work to ensure the deadline is met	✓

Test your understanding 6

Options	✓
Confidentiality	✓
Flexibility	
Integrity	✓
Confidence	
Numeracy	

Test your understanding 7

	Ethical?		Ethical principle
	Yes	No	
Discussing the issues one of your clients is facing when with your friends over dinner.		✓	Confidentiality
Providing advice on an area of tax accounting you are not familiar with to a customer.		✓	Integrity
Completing the accounts on time and bearing in mind all recent changes in legislation.	✓		Professional behaviour & competence
Changing the contents of a report because your manager offered you a financial bonus to do so.		✓	Objectivity

Test your understanding 8

Statement	True	False
Money laundering is not a criminal offence		✓
Bookkeepers who provide internal bookkeeping services must register for anti-money laundering supervision		✓
Suspicious activity should be reported following the correct procedures	✓	

Test your understanding 9

Commercial information is information that can be sold to anyone, so it does not have to be kept confidential.

False ☑

You have finished working on a document, you have made notes on paper that you do not need anymore. Are you going to:

Shred the paper ☑

You have sent an e-mail containing personal information to the wrong client. Is this:

A breach of data protection regulations (GDPR) ☑

Test your understanding 10

Options	✓
Something you cannot remember	
Something other people are not likely to know	✓
Something obvious	
The word 'password'	
Your name and year of birth	
A combination of letters, numbers and symbols	✓
Something you saved on your PC in a file called Passwords	

Test your understanding 11

Statement	True/False
Passwords can be shared with colleagues who are doing the same type work.	False
All cabinet drawers with personal or commercial information in should be kept locked.	True
If leaving your work station, you must ensure that the screen is blank and computer access blocked.	True

KAPLAN PUBLISHING

Test your understanding 12

Options	✓
Switch the computer off	
Use the screen lock facility to lock the computer screen	✓
Stay at your desk	
Put some papers over the screen to hide the information	

Test your understanding 13

a) I need to go to the bathroom, I should use my computer **screen** lock.

b) I have finished with this confidential paper so I am going to **shred** it.

c) I don't want anyone to read this paperwork so I am going to put it **face down** on my desk.

d) **Anti-virus** software is another way of keeping information safe and secure.

e) Backed up computer data should be stored in **fireproof** cabinets.

Test your understanding 14

Options	✓
Cause loss of information	✓
Can be easily fixed	
Cause the system to crash	✓
Infect all computers on the same network	✓
Only be harmful for s short period of time	
Cause a loss in productivity	✓

Test your understanding 15

Options	✓
Ignore the email	
Hover over the address and if it looks genuine, click on the link	✓
Forward it to your supervisor	
Click on the link	
Contact the client to ask if they have sent the email	✓

Test your understanding 16

Statement	Threat
Enters your computer from infected files or programs	**Viruses**
Enters your computer through emails	**Phishing**
Can trace every stroke of a key you make on your computer	**Hacking**

📖 Case study activity 1

Options	✓
Analysing the financial performance of the business	
Advising the Managing Director	
Recording and checking financial transactions	✓
Processing documents such as sales invoices as required	✓
Deciding pay increases	
Saving costs for the business	

📖 Case study activity 2

Department	Definition
PRODUCTION	This department is responsible for producing the goods or services that a business provides by making best use of the various inputs.
SALES	This department sells the company's goods and services to customers.
ADMINISTRATION	This department is responsible for typing, collecting and distributing mail, keeping & filing records, organising meetings and maintaining resources.
ACCOUNTING	This department is responsible for keeping records and accounts, for giving advice on budgets to other departments, and for paying wages and salaries.
HUMAN RESOURCES	This department deals with the recruitment of new staff, the training of new and existing staff, pay negotiations and regular staff appraisals.

📖 Case study activity 3

Jessica and all bookkeepers and accounting professionals need to ensure that they remain competent for the work they do.

To do so, they will need to keep up to date with changing regulations that affect their work.

They will also need to keep up to date with technologies that help them do their work efficiently and effectively.

Case study activity 4

She should use:

d)   4yXkj2fR!*

Case study activity 5

Statement	Correct?
Jessica confirms the amount that Jason does indeed receive more money than Neelam.	
Jessica tells Neelam that she will speak to her manager to see if she can tell her the information.	
Jessica explains to Neelam that this information is confidential and cannot be disclosed.	✓
Jessica ensures that all pay rates are accessible to all employees to avoid any future debate.	

Case study activity 6

Options	✓
Give them her password but tell them not to tell anyone else what it is	
Give them her password for now and then change it when they have gone into their meeting	
Refuse to give them her password	✓
Log in for them so they don't know what her password is	

KAPLAN PUBLISHING

Bookkeeping terminology

2

Introduction

The purpose of accounting is to be able to provide financial information about an organisation. For example, managers will want to keep track of the profit made by the organisation in a certain period, and they will also want to see how much the organisation is worth at a specific point in time.

This chapter will introduce you to the accounting terminology used to complete the accounting equation in relation to this.

It also covers the basics of bookkeeping within an organisation, providing an overview of both single entry and double entry bookkeeping, and explaining the dual effect of transactions.

KNOWLEDGE	CONTENTS
Understand financial transactions	1 Assets and liabilities
2.1 The dual effect of transactions	2 Income and expenditure
2.2 The accounting equation	3 Basic sales terminology
	4 Profit and loss
	5 The dual effect principle
	6 The accounting equation
	7 Summary and further questions

1 Assets and liabilities

1.1 Case study: an introduction

Case study

Having established the importance of accuracy and confidentiality, Jessica is now more aware of what a career in bookkeeping entails.

She now needs to understand some of the key words and concepts she will encounter during her apprenticeship at How Two Ltd. To be effective, Jessica will need to use the correct terminology for each task so it will help her when it comes to completing her work, as well as when she takes her accountancy exams moving forward.

Jessica also wants to gain a greater understanding of the effect expenditure and income has on profit/loss. She is aware of the terms single entry and double entry bookkeeping, but needs to learn what they mean in practice and applied within an organisation's record keeping system.

She finds that practising activities helps to understand these concepts.

1.2 What is an asset?

Assets are items of value which an organisation owns in order to generate profit by selling goods or providing a service.

Assets can be physical such as cash, land, buildings etc. or non-physical such as copyrights, trademarks and patents. Either way, an asset is something that a company acquires to help increase its value or to improve its overall operations.

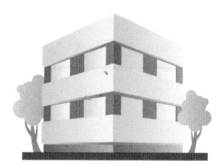

Definition

An asset is an item of value owned by an organisation.

1.3 Different types of asset

 Examples

Assets include:

Premises – organisations usually need a building from which to carry out their business. These premises could be an office building, a shop, or a factory.

Fixtures and fittings – these are items in the premises which are used to provide goods or services. For example, the computers in an office, the shelving in a shop, or machinery in a factory.

Vehicles – vehicles may be needed to deliver goods or provide a service to customers.

Inventory – goods which are ready to sell to customers are kept in stock

Bank – the funds available in the organisation's bank account may be used to purchase more stock to sell.

Cash – some organisations keep money on the premises so that they can buy small items. *or debtor*

Trade Receivables – amounts owed to the organisation by customers as a result of sales made on credit.

Copyrights – a legal right which protects any work created by an organisation. It prevents others from using it or distributing it without their permission

Trademarks – the brand, logo or slogan of an organisation which helps to distinguish it from another organisation. For example, Tesco is a 'brand'. Nobody would be allowed to set up a shop of their own and call it Tesco, as the name belongs to them.

Patents – if an organisation invents a new product, they may apply for a patent from the government which stops others for a limited period of time from creating, using or selling it without their permission.

1.4 What is a liability?

A liability is an amount of money that an organisation owes to a supplier, bank or other lender. An organisation will have a legal obligation to pay back the money that they owe. The money will usually have been used to buy assets for the organisation to use.

Total liabilities are deducted from total assets to calculate an organisation's worth at a specific period in time.

Definition

A liability is a debt owed by an organisation to other organisations, businesses and individuals.

1.5 Different types of liability

 Examples

Liabilities include:

Payables – amounts owed by the organisation to suppliers of goods and services.

Bank Overdraft – an arrangement that allows an organisation to take more money out of its bank than it has put in. The money is owed to the bank on a short-term basis.

Bank Loan – a fixed amount of money an organisation borrows from the bank usually over a longer period of time.

 Test your understanding 1

Jessica had to classify the following as an asset or a liability to be able to identify them accurately within the system.

Classify them accurately by putting a tick in the correct box.

	Asset	Liability
Machinery	✓	
A bank loan		✓
A bank overdraft		✓
Inventory	✓	
Receivables	✓	
Payables		✓
A patent	✓	

KAPLAN PUBLISHING

2 Income and expenditure

2.1 Introduction

The purpose of most organisations is to make a profit or to raise funds so that they can continue supplying goods and services to customers. To calculate profit, **expenditure** is deducted from **income**.

2.2 What is income?

Any money received from the supply of goods and services to customers is known as income.

2.3 What is expenditure?

Any money paid for purchasing the goods and services and day to day expenses is known as expenditure.

🔍 Definitions

Income is the money received by an organisation from selling its goods and services.

Expenditure is the money paid by an organisation to purchase goods and services.

📝 Test your understanding 2

Jessica needs to classify the following as income or expenditure to be able to identify them accurately within the system. Classify them accurately by putting a tick in the correct box.

	Income	Expenditure
Payments to suppliers		✓
Electricity bill		✓
The cost of goods and services		✓
Cash sales	✓	
Sales of services	✓	
Telephone bill		✓
Water bill		✓

---

3 Basic sales terminology

3.1 Cash and credit sales

As we have now established, income is the amount of money received by an organisation from its sales.

> **Definitions**
>
> **Sales** is the exchange of goods or services to an individual or organisation in exchange for money.

- Sometimes the money is received immediately, this is called a **cash sale.**
- Sometimes the money is received later, this is called a **credit sale**.

More detail about the differences between cash and credit customers and the sales and purchasing processes will follow in Chapter 3.

However, it is important to make the distinction between cash and credit transactions before looking at how items are entered in the bookkeeping system. Cash and credit transactions need to be recorded separately so that the organisation knows how much money it is owed by customers, and how much it owes to suppliers.

3.2 Customers and suppliers

> **Definitions**
>
> A **customer is** an individual or organisation to whom the goods or services have been sold. The organisation supplying the goods or services will then receive money in exchange.
>
> A **trade receivable (also known as a debtor)** is a customer who has been sold goods on credit and who owes the business the money in respect of the sale.
>
> A **supplier is** an individual or organisation providing goods or services to another in exchange for money.
>
> A **trade payable is** a supplier who is owed money for goods purchased on credit.

We will look at both customers and suppliers, and the business documentation which relates to them, in Chapter 3.

4 Profit and loss

4.1 What is a profit or loss?

A business needs to make money in order to operate. By selling goods or services they generate income, from this they need to deduct their expenses for buying in those goods and services. This is called the 'profit' or 'loss'.

In order for a business to generate a 'profit', their income needs to be more than their expenses. If their expenses are more than their income, they would make a loss which could make the business fail.

 Definitions

Profit is the amount of money an organisation earns after expenditure has been deducted from income.

Loss is when an organisation has spent more money than it has earned from income.

4.2 What happens when a business makes a profit?

An organisation's main goal should be to make a profit. No business can survive long-term if they don't make a profit.

Profit is paid to the owners of a company or its shareholders. Alternatively, it can be used as a saving opportunity to enable the organisation to re-invest and therefore grow the business. Growing a business means expanding it, making it bigger. This may be through investing in research or new technology, opening new offices, operating in new markets or obtaining other businesses. A bigger company means a bigger part of the market share and therefore increased profitability.

4.3 What happens when a business makes a loss?

If a business is spending more on expenses than they are making from the sales of goods or services, they will be making a loss.

If an organisation is making a loss then the chances are that their bank account may become overdrawn. Ultimately, they will be charged high amounts of interest for this which only increases their expenditure even more. If this were to happen, the business may not have enough money to pay their suppliers which could result in the suppliers putting their account on hold, or even withdrawing their credit agreement.

As a result, the business would find it difficult to purchase goods or services for resale, meaning that they would struggle to meet their customer's demands. If this is the case, it can cause problems and the business could fail.

Test your understanding 3

Jessica has been asked to identify which of the following are indicators of a business making a profit or a loss.

Put a tick in the correct box.

	Profit	Loss
The business could fail		✓
The bank account is overdrawn		✓
A saving opportunity	✓	
There is an opportunity for growth	✓	
There is a high volume of sales	✓	
Money has been invested in new ventures	✓	
Not enough money to pay for purchases		✓
Suppliers withdraw their credit agreement		✓

Example

JBU Wines has recorded all sales income and expenditure for the previous month.

Alan, the Accounts Assistant, has been asked to calculate the profit for the month.

	£
Sales income	125,000
Cost of sales	75,000
Wages	15,000
Premises expenses	3,000
Vehicle expenses	2,500

Solution:

To calculate **profit (or loss)** the cost of sales are deducted from the sales income.

	Sales income:	£125,000
−	Cost of sales	- £75,000
−	Wages	- £15,000
−	Premises expenses	- £3,000
−	Vehicle expenses	- £2,500
=	**Total Profit**	**£29,500**

Therefore, Alan can report a profit of £29,500 for the month.

Note: If Alan had ended up with a minus figure at the end of her calculation, she would know that the company had made a loss i.e. JBU Wines' expenses were more than the company's income.

 Case study

In September, How Two Ltd's Liverpool office had recorded income from sales of £82,000. The cost of those sales was £66,000 and the other expenses were £25,000. Jessica is asked whether the Liverpool office made a profit or a loss.

Solution:

	Sales income:	£82,000
−	Cost of sales	- £66,000
−	Other expenses	- £25,000
	=	**-£9,000**

Their expenses are more than their income so the Liverpool office of How Two Ltd made a loss of £9,000 in September.

 Test your understanding 4

To assess the performance of How Two Ltd's Liverpool office in September, Jessica looks at the figures from the previous month. In August, the Liverpool office recorded income of £85,000. The cost of those sales was £69,000 and the other expenses were £18,000.

Did they make a profit or a loss? How do the two months compare?

LOSS

AUGUST: INCOME £85,000
COST OF SALES -£69,000
OTHER EXP. -£18,000
-£2,000

SEPTEMBER -£9,000

AUGUST IS £7,000 LESS LOSS THAN SEP.

Test your understanding 5

Jessica has been asked to see if the performance of the Liverpool office is similar to the nearest office, in Manchester. The Manchester office of How Two Ltd has recorded all sales income and expenditure for the previous month.

Jessica needs to calculate the profit or loss for the month given the following information:

	£
Sales income from cash and credit sales	78,000
Cost of sales	– 50,700
Wages	– 7,500
Premises expenses	– 1,750
Vehicle expenses	– 2,000

PROFIT   16,050

 Test your understanding 6

Jessica concludes that in some cases, How Two Ltd offices have total income lower than costs of sales plus expenses.

Jessica must look at this statement and then determine – have these offices made a profit or a loss? She must provide a brief explanation for her answer for one of the departmental managers.

As their sales income is lower than cost of sales plus expenses, the business has made a loss.

5 The dual effect principle

5.1 Introduction

Having now looked at the basic bookkeeping terminology and established how to classify accounting items under the headings of assets, liabilities, income or expenditure, we will now discover how these items are recorded in the bookkeeping system.

5.2 Single entry bookkeeping

Many small businesses, particularly sole traders, are cash based, or do not have many transactions to record.

For this reason the owner will often only use a cash book or spreadsheet to record the income and expenditure of the business.

	A	B
1	Cstd	Sstd
2	0.000	0.00
3	0.100	12.36
4	0.200	24.83
5	0.300	35.91
6	0.400	48.79
7	0.500	60.42

The spreadsheet will often have columns analysed by type. The cash book may not.

It is quicker and easier for the owner to record the transactions this way, but the records are incomplete, and will have to be reconstructed in order to work out the taxable profit.

5.3 Double entry bookkeeping

Each of these items are recorded into the bookkeeping system via double entry.

Most organisations use the **double entry bookkeeping system** to record the financial transactions of the business. As double entry is based upon the principle of the dual effect, it is important that you understand what it is and how this impacts the assets, liabilities, income or expenses of the business.

For the purpose of your assessment you don't need to be able to perform double-entry bookkeeping as this will be covered comprehensively in the AAT Level 2, but you do need to understand the principle of it.

Double-entry bookkeeping is based upon the principle of the dual effect.

5.4 The dual effect principle

The dual effect principle states that every financial transaction recorded will change the records of at least two items in the bookkeeping system, in other words, that is has two financial effects.

Let us consider some examples of dual effect in action!

(a)　If, for example, you spend £2,000 on a car and you pay by cheque, you will have £2,000 less money in the bank, but you will also have acquired an asset worth £2,000.

This can be viewed as:

Gained:　　　a £2,000 car

Lost:　　　　£2,000 in cash.

In the above example, the gain is that of a car, the loss is that of the money.

(The accounting terms used for this transaction are: **debit (gain)** and **credit (lose)**, and although you do need to know this terms for your Level 1 assessment, you should start thinking in these terms).

Using the accounting terminology, look at the example below:

(b)　If you buy from a supplier £100 of goods and send him a cheque for that amount, you will gain £100 worth of goods, but you will have £100 less money in the bank.

Gain　**£100** of goods (debit)

Loss　**£100** from the bank account (credit)

At first it can seem difficult, but break the transaction into two parts. Ask:

- What did I get? CAR/GOODS

- What did I lose? MONEY/MONEY

💡 Example

	Gain	Loss
a) Purchases goods for resale, paid £800.	Purchases	Bank
b) Pays rent for use of office of £500.	Rent	Bank
c) Buys a van, cost £2,000.	Van	Bank
d) Sells some of the goods for £600.	Bank	Sales GOODS
e) Sells some more of the goods for £700.	Bank	Sales GOODS
f) Purchases goods for resale for £1,000.	Purchases	Bank
g) Buys stationery for £200.	Stationery	Bank

Explanation for the above example follows:

a)　Gains goods to sell on, loses £800 of money from bank account

b)　Gains office space, but loses £500 of money from bank account

c)　Gains a van, but loses £2,000 of money from bank account

　　　　　　　　　KAPLAN PUBLISHING

d) Gains £600, which is paid into bank account, but loses some of the goods previously bought

e) Gains some money, £700, but more goods go out the door

f) Gains some more goods to sell on, but spends (loses) £1,000 from bank account

g) Gains some stationery to write on, but loses £200 from bank account.

Test your understanding 7

Jessica has been presented with the following cash transactions made by How Two Ltd. She has been asked how the accounts will be affected with regards to gains and losses (debits and credits).

In each case, state which account will show a gain and which will show a loss.

	Debit (gain)	Credit (loss)
Purchases goods for resale for £700.	PURCHASES GOODS	BANK
Customer entertainment £300 for a product launch.	CUSTOMER ENTERTAINMENT	BANK
Purchases three computers for £3,000.	COMPUTERS	BANK
Sells goods for £1,500.	BANK	SALES (GOODS)
Purchases goods for resale for £1,200.	PURCHASE GOODS	BANK
Pays telephone bill of £600.	SERVICE TELEPHONE	BANK
Receives telephone bill rebate of £200.	BANK	TELEPHONE REBATE
Purchases stationery for £157.	STATIONERY	BANK

refund or partial refund

não importa se tem dois serviços de débito no reembolso: o reembolso + o serviço. Sempre temos que ver a contrapartida

---

Case study

How Two Ltd purchase a new computer online using a faster payment. The money for this will leave the bank account immediately.

The dual effect of this transaction is that the bank account which is an asset will decrease because money has been paid out.

The second record that would change would be the computer equipment account which is an asset. The assets will increase as we have now added a new computer to them.

Many digital accounting systems will now automatically apply double entry bookkeeping principles, but users will still need to understand what is

ENTERTAINMENT

happening in the background of the digital system, and the impact of transactions on individual records within the accounts.

The individual accounting records are classified under the heading's assets, liabilities, income, expenses and capital.

5.5 What is capital?

> ### 🔍 Definitions
>
> **Capital** is the part of the business that belongs to the owner. It is an amount of money that the owner of a business puts in to start it up. Essentially the business owes that money back to the owner and therefore it is classed as a liability of the business.

For example, if the owner of a business initially pays £10,000 into the bank account to start up the business, this would be classified as capital. The business and the owner are separate entities; therefore, the business essentially owes the £10,000 back to the owner. For this reason, capital is classified as a liability of the business.

The amount of capital held in a business at any one time will fluctuate, due to the day to day transactions detailed within the accounting records. If a business makes a profit, the profit will increase the capital held. If a business makes a loss, the capital figure will decrease.

> ### 📝 Test your understanding 8
>
> Varun sets up his own business paying £20,000 into the business bank account.
>
> Select the correct dual effect of the transaction from the list below:
>
> | Options | ✓ |
> |---|---|
> | Increase asset £20,000 – Decrease Capital £20,000 | |
> | Increase asset £20,000 – Increase Capital £20,000 | ✓ |
> | Decrease asset £20,000 – Decrease Capital £20,000 | |
> | Decrease asset £20,000 – Increase Capital £20,000 | |

entity (noun) ·a thing with distinct and independent
entities (plural) existence. Organisation / Institution
                   · existence; being

Test your understanding 9

Varun pays the rent owing on his premises, of £900. *bank*

Select the correct dual effect of the transaction from the list below:

Options	✓
Increase asset £900 – Decrease Capital £900	
Increase income £12,000 – Decrease asset £20,000	
Decrease asset £900 – Increase expenses £900	
Decrease liabilities £900 – Increase expenses £900	✓

Test your understanding 10

Varun pays his cleaner's wages for the week.

State which of the following would increase and which would decrease:

Options	Increase/Decrease
Assets	*decrease*
Liabilities	
Income	
Expenses	*Increase*
Capital	

Test your understanding 11

Identify whether the following statements are true or false.

Statement	True/False
When a business makes a profit, it increases capital	TRUE
When a business makes a loss, it increases capital	FALSE
When a business makes a profit, it decreases capital	FALSE
When a business makes a loss, it decreases capital	TRUE

Case study

Jessica is discussing the dual effect principle with one of her colleagues, who is keen to help her progress in her role. They are looking a little further into the effects of transactions on the accounting records and are now considering credit transactions, using the real examples from the last month shown below to establish the dual effect on each.

As explained above, some transactions are for cash (immediate) and some are for credit. Credit means that money is owed to the business by a credit customer (a receivable – an asset) or that the business owes money to a supplier (a payable – a liability).

Similarly, if a credit customer returns goods, it will decrease the assets (receivables) because they do not owe as much money as they did on the original invoice. It will also decrease the income because the amount of money coming into the business will be less.

This works in exactly the same way for returns to a credit supplier (i.e. the amount owed to them is not as much). This would result in a decrease in liabilities and the amount of expenses would reduce as the value spent on purchases is smaller than stated on the original invoice.

		Effect 1	Effect 2
Nov 1	Started the business with £3,000 in the bank	Increase Assets	Increase Capital
Nov 3	Bought goods for cash £850	Increase Expenses	Decrease Assets
Nov 7	Bought goods on credit for £1,160	Increase Expenses	Increase Liabilities
Nov 10	Sold goods for cash £420	Increase Assets	Increase Income
Nov 14	Returned goods to a credit supplier for £100	Decrease Liabilities	Decrease Expenses
Nov 20	Paid a gas bill for £80 by direct debit	Increase Expenses	Decrease Assets
Nov 21	Returned goods to a credit supplier for £190	Decrease Liabilities	Decrease Expenses
Nov 24	Sold goods to a credit customer for £550	Increase Assets	Increase Income
Nov 25	Paid a credit supplier £500 from the bank via faster payment	Decrease Liabilities	Decrease Assets
Nov 31	A credit customer has returned goods worth £80	Decrease Income	Decrease Assets
Nov 31	Paid an electricity bill for £100 by direct debit	Increase Expenses	Decrease Assets

6 The accounting equation

6.1 The accounting equation

The dual effect will always impact on two accounting records. There is an equation that can be used to ensure the dual effect has taken place correctly.

The accounting equation is:

ASSETS – LIABILITIES = CAPITAL

The accounting equation will always balance and if it does not balance, something has gone wrong when applying the dual effect.

 Example

How Two Ltd has assets worth £168,000 and Liabilities of £128,000.

The accounting equation can be applied to calculate the capital.

Assets £168,000 – Liabilities £128,000 = Capital £40,000

6.2 Rearranging the accounting equation

The basic equation to remember is **ASSETS – LIABILITIES = CAPITAL**

To isolate 'ASSETS' you can move 'LIABILITIES' to the other side of the '=' sign. *ASSETS = CAPITAL + LIABILITIES.*

When this happens the 'minus' sign in front of 'LIABILITIES' changes to a 'plus' sign.

The equation can then be restated as **ASSETS = CAPITAL + LIABILITIES**

To isolate 'LIABILITIES' you can move 'CAPITAL' to the other side of the '=' sign. *LIABILITIES = ASSETS – CAPITAL*

When this happens the (invisible) 'plus' sign in front of 'CAPITAL' changes to a 'minus'.

The equation can then be restated as **ASSETS – CAPITAL = LIABILITIES**

dual effect → double entry bookkeeping system.

Método das partidas dobradas ou método veneziano. Cada transação financeira é registrada na forma de entradas em pelo menos duas contas, com sentido oposto (débitos e créditos), nas quais o total de débitos deve ser igual ao total de créditos. descrito por Luca Pacioli

This can be tested using some figures – see the example below.

 Example

Assets £50,000 – Liabilities £30,000 = Capital £20,000.

Tis the same as:

Assets £50,000 = Capital £20,000 + Liabilities £30,000

which is also the same as:

Assets £50,000 – Capital £20,000 = Liabilities £30,000.

However the accounting equation is written, it will always balance using the above calculations.

 Test your understanding 12

Identify whether the following statements are true or false.

Statement	True	False
The business and the owner are not separate entities		✓
When the owner of a business injects money into it, this is known as income	✓	✓
When the owner of a business injects money into it, this is known as capital	✓	
The accounting equation will always balance	✓	

 Test your understanding 13

A company has assets of £57,000 and liabilities of £23,000.

What is the value of the capital?

£ 34,000

CAPITAL = ASSETS – LIABILITIES

C = 57,000
 – 23,000
 + 34,000

Test your understanding 14

Pilgrim Sports and Leisure has assets of £125,900 and liabilities of £62,300.

What is the value of the capital?

£63,600

£125,900
− £62,300
63,600

Test your understanding 15

An online craft retailer has assets of £89,000 and liabilities of £34,000.

They then pay £5,000 out of the bank to a credit supplier.

How would the accounting equation be written?

ASSETS	MINUS	LIABILITIES	EQUALS	CAPITAL
89,000 − 5,000 = 84,000	− −	34,000 − 5,000 = 29,000	= =	55,000 55,000

reduz o ativo, e também o passivo
∴ retirou dinheiro do banco.

7 Summary and further questions

This chapter has introduced you to some important accounting terminology. You can distinguish between assets, liabilities, income and expenditure and understand how to use these terms when using the accounting equation.

You can also understand how the profit or loss of an organisation is calculated and that a business needs more income than expenses in order to operate profitably.

Finally you was introduced to the dual effect and you should now understand that every transaction recorded within the bookkeeping system increases/decreases at least two records.

Let us now return to the case study for some further practice questions to test your knowledge of this key bookkeeping terminology.

Case study activity 7

Jessica has been asked to define some key terms to help explain her e-mail to the managers. Choose the correct option in each statement:

a.   The sum of money spent in making sales is known as [sales/cost of sales]

b.   If total income is greater than the cost of sales plus other expenses the organisation has made a [profit/loss]

c.   If total income is less than the cost of sales plus other expenses the organisation has made a [profit/loss]

 Case study activity 8

Jessica has been given a list of terms which are commonly used every day in her department. She needs to decide if they are assets, liabilities, income or expenditure? Put a tick in the correct box.

	Asset	Liability	Income	Expenditure
Creditors		✓	✓	
Electricity bill				✓
Money in the bank	✓			
Bank overdraft		✓		✓
Sales to customers			✓	
Debtors	✓			
Office computers	✓			

Case study activity 9

Last month How Two Ltd's Head Office recorded income and expenditure in the table below:

Income and Expenditure	£
Sales	156,000
Cost of Sales	93,600
Wages	21,060
Administration Expenses	18,720
Selling Expenses	12,844

Jessica needs to use the income and expenditure figures to calculate the profit or loss and state underneath whether this would be a profit or loss.

Profit / Loss: £ 9,776 profit

income = 156,000
expenditure = -146,224
009,776

Case study activity 10

The following month's recorded income and expenditure is shown in the table below:

Income and Expenditure	£
Sales	152,880
Cost of Sales	91,728
Wages	20,640
Administration Expenses	18,350
Selling Expenses	12,590

Jessica needs to use the income and expenditure figures to calculate the profit or loss and state underneath whether this would be a profit or loss.

Profit / Loss: £ 9,572

Income = 152,880
Expenditure = 143,308
9,572

Case study activity 11

Jessica has then been given a list of recent transactions for How Two Ltd. For each, she needs to state the effects of each transaction on the assets, liabilities, income, expenses and capital.

Complete the table below.

	Effect 1	Effect 2
Sold goods for £500 and the customer pays cash	increase assets	increase income
Paid a gas bill for £90 by direct debit	increase expenses	decrease assets
Purchased goods from a credit supplier for £300	increase expenses	increase liabilities
Returned goods to a supplier for £50	decrease liabilities	decrease expenses
Sold goods to a credit customer for £800	increase income	increase assets
A credit customer returns goods worth £150	decrease income	decrease assets
Paid wages of £300 via a faster payment	increase expenses	decrease assets

 Case study activity 12

How Two Ltd. has assets of £120,000 and liabilities of £50,000.

They take out a bank loan of £10,000 which is paid into the business bank account.

Jessica has been asked to write out the accounting equation, taking into account the bank loan transaction.

ASSETS	MINUS	LIABILITIES	EQUAL	CAPITAL
120,000	–	50,000	=	70,000
130,000	–	60,000	=	70,000

Answers to chapter activities

Test your understanding 1

	Asset	Liability
Machinery	✓	
A bank loan		✓
A bank overdraft		✓
Inventory	✓	
Receivables	✓	
Payables		✓
A patent	✓	

Test your understanding 2

	Income	Expenditure
Payments to suppliers		✓
Electricity bill		✓
The cost of goods and services		✓
Cash sales	✓	
Sales of services	✓	
Telephone bill		✓
Water bill		✓

Test your understanding 3

	Profit	Loss
The business could fail		✓
The bank account is overdrawn		✓
A saving opportunity	✓	
There is an opportunity for growth	✓	
There is a high volume of sales	✓	
Money has been invested in new ventures	✓	
Not enough money to pay for purchases		✓
Suppliers withdraw their credit agreement		✓

Test your understanding 4

	£
Sales income	85,000
Cost of sales	-69,000
Other expenses	-18,000
	-2,000

This means that their sales income is lower than their expenses and therefore they have made **a loss of £2,000**.

Although this is a loss, it is £7,000 less than the loss in September.

Test your understanding 5

	£
Sales income	78,000
Cost of sales	-50,700
Wages	-7,500
Premises expenses	-1,750
Vehicle expenses	-2,000
	16,050

The company have made **a profit of £16,050** because their sales income is more than the total of their expenditure.

KAPLAN PUBLISHING

Test your understanding 6

As their sales income is lower than cost of sales plus expenses, the business has made a loss.

Test your understanding 7

	Gain (debit)	Loss (credit)
Purchases goods for resale for £700.	Purchases	Bank
Customer entertainment £300 for a product launch.	Entertainment	Bank
Purchases three computers for £3,000.	Computers	Bank
Sells goods for £1,500.	Bank	Sales
Purchases goods for resale for £1,200.	Purchases	Bank
Pays telephone bill of £600.	Telephone	Bank
Receives telephone bill rebate of £200.	Bank	Telephone
Purchases stationery for £157.	Stationery	Bank

Test your understanding 8

Options	✓
Increase asset £20,000 – Decrease Capital £20,000	
Increase asset £20,000 – Increase Capital £20,000	✓
Decrease asset £20,000 – Decrease Capital £20,000	
Decrease asset £20,000 – Increase Capital £20,000	

Test your understanding 9

Options	✓
Increase asset £900 – Decrease Capital £900	
Increase income £12,000 – Decrease asset £20,000	
Decrease asset £900 – Increase expenses £900	
Decrease liabilities £900 – Increase expenses £900	✓

Test your understanding 10

Options	Increase/Decrease
Assets	Decrease
Liabilities	
Income	
Expenses	Increase
Capital	

Test your understanding 11

Statement	True/False
When a business makes a profit, it increases capital	True
When a business makes a loss, it increases capital	False
When a business makes a profit, it decreases capital	False
When a business makes a loss, it decreases capital	True

Test your understanding 12

Statement	True	False
The business and the owner are not separate entities		✓
When the owner of a business injects money into it, this is known as income		✓
When the owner of a business injects money into it, this is known as capital	✓	
The accounting equation will always balance	✓	

Test your understanding 13

£34,000

Test your understanding 14

£63,600

Test your understanding 15

ASSETS	MINUS	LIABILITIES	EQUALS	CAPITAL
£84,000	-	£29,000	=	£55,000

Case study activity 7

a.   The sum of money spent in making sales is known as **cost of sales**

b.   If total income is greater than the cost of sales plus other expenses the organisation has made a **profit**

c.   If total income is less than the cost of sales plus other expenses the organisation has made a **loss**

Case study activity 8

	Asset	Liability	Income	Expenditure
Creditors		✓		
Electricity bill				✓
Money in the bank	✓			
Bank overdraft		✓		
Sales to customers			✓	
Debtors	✓			
Office computers	✓			

Case study activity 9

	£
Sales	156,000
Cost of Sales	-93,600
Wages	-21,060
Administration Expenses	-18,720
Selling Expenses	-12,844
	9,776

Profit / Loss: £ 9,776 Profit

KAPLAN PUBLISHING

Case study activity 10

	£
Sales	152,880
Cost of Sales	-91,728
Wages	-20,640
Administration Expenses	-18,350
Selling Expenses	-12,590
	9,572

Profit / Loss: £9,572 Profit

Case study activity 11

	Effect 1	Effect 2
Sold goods for £500 and the customer pays cash	Increase Assets	Increase Income
Paid a gas bill for £90 by direct debit	Increase Expenses	Decrease Assets
Purchased goods from a credit supplier for £300	Increase Expenses	Increase Liabilities
Returned goods to a supplier for £50	Decrease Liabilities	Decrease Expenses
Sold goods to a credit customer for £800	Increase Assets	Increase Income
A credit customer returns goods worth £150	Decrease Income	Decrease Assets
Paid wages of £300 via a faster payment	Increase Expenses	Decrease Assets

Case study activity 12

ASSETS	MINUS	LIABILITIES	EQUALS	CAPITAL
£130,000	-	£60,000	=	£70,000

Customer and supplier transactions

Introduction

owe = dever
owed = devido passado particípio.
alguém lhe deve.

As stated in the previous chapter, customer and supplier transactions are recorded so that organisations know how much money they are owed by customers, and how much they owe to suppliers.

Business documents are used to record these transactions and the documents are exchanged between the supplier and the customer so that both parties have a record of each transaction. It is important that both the supplier and the customer keep a copy of each of these documents. Mistakes can happen and each document is proof of each stage of the transaction.

The name of a document will depend on whether we look at it from the point of view of the seller or the purchaser. Thus an invoice may be called a 'sales invoice' for the seller but a 'purchase invoice' for the purchaser, although it is the same document.

Assim, por isso

KNOWLEDGE	CONTENTS
Process customer and supplier transactions	1 Cash and credit transactions
3.1 The buying and selling process	2 Sales documentation
3.2 Preparing sales invoices and credit notes	3 Purchases documentation
	4 Summary and further questions

1 Cash and credit transactions

1.1 Case study: an introduction

> ### 📖 Case study
>
> Having learnt about the double entry bookkeeping system, Jessica is now interested to know more about the nature of the transactions and documentation which are used in the business. To do so, she needs to understand the principles behind sales and purchases – and put the company's income and expenditure into context. She will need to understand who How Two Ltd's customers and suppliers are and the processes need for both.
>
> To get a better understanding, she has been tasked with looking through the different types of business documentation that she will come across on a day to day basis.
>
> She needs to establish what information is required on each document and then she will then be given the opportunity of completing some of these herself to be checked by her manager.
>
> Jessica also needs to demonstrate an understanding of the importance of working with accuracy when creating these documents and the impact that this has on the organisation if they are not completed correctly.

1.2 Sales of goods and services

As illustrated in the previous chapter, income is the amount of money received by an organisation from the sale of its goods or services. Returning to our case study, How Two Ltd sell computers and accessories to their customers; these would be classified as their sales of goods.

They also have a help desk that offer advice on technical issues or who deal with broken computers that customers bring into store to be fixed; this would be classified as their sales of services.

1.3 Cash and credit sales

As briefly covered in the previous chapter, **Cash Sales** is the term used to describe a payment at point of sale. The payment itself can be made by cash (currency), cheque, debit or credit card, or bank transfer. An example of a cash sale is when you go into a shop, choose the items you want to buy, and pay for them immediately.

Credit Sales are sales made where the goods or services will be paid later than the point of sale. Many organisations give credit to their regular trade customers so that one payment can be made for all the transactions made in each month. Credit sales are usually recorded by way of an invoice which will be covered in a later chapter.

1.4 Cash and credit customers

 Definitions

A **customer** is an individual or organisation to whom the goods or services have been sold. The organisation supplying the goods or services will then receive money in exchange.

A **trade receivable (also known as a debtor)** is a customer who has been sold goods on credit and who owes the business the money in respect of the sale.

With cash sales the organisation gets the money immediately from the customer and the relationship ends there. With credit customers, there is a risk to the organisation that the customer may not pay for the goods.

Therefore, before allowing customers to pay on credit the organisation will make certain checks to ensure that the customer can pay. If these checks identify that the customer has the ability to pay its debts, payment terms will be agreed with the customer and a credit account set up.

Payment terms usually state the length of time a customer has to pay for their goods and also a maximum amount that they are allowed to owe the business at any one time. The amounts outstanding from customers can be analysed so that a business can see at what point they can expect the money to come into their bank account.

If customers are taking longer to pay than expected, a business should chase for the outstanding monies to ensure a continual flow of cash moving through the organisation.

It is assumed that the money owed by credit customers will be paid and therefore they are classed as **trade receivables or receivables**. Receivables have the ability to be converted into cash and are therefore classed as assets of the organisation.

Test your understanding 1

Jessica has been asked to identify whether the following How Two Ltd transactions would be classified as a cash or credit transaction?

Put a tick in the correct box.

	Cash	Credit
A customer purchases a computer and pays by credit card	✓	
A customer buys a mouse mat, a mouse and a printer and pays by debit card	✓	
A customer buys 5 tablet computers, and pays in 30 days		✓

1.5 Cash and credit purchases

Definition

Purchases – to buy goods or services from an organisation in exchange for money.

Cash Purchases are when goods or services are paid for at the time of purchase.

Case study

How Two Ltd may purchase some stock and pay by 'cash'. Although the payment could be by cash (currency), credit card or debit card or bank transfer, if the payment is made immediately it is classed as a cash purchase.

Credit Purchases are when an organisation pays for the goods or services sometime after making the purchase. The money will be sent to the supplier after an agreed amount of time, for example, thirty days.

The supplier is now a payable of the organisation and as money is owed to the supplier in respect of the transaction, they are classed as a liability of the business.

Definition

A **supplier** is an individual or organisation providing goods or services to another in exchange for money.

A **trade payable** is a supplier who is owed money for goods purchased on credit.

 Test your understanding 2

Fill in the gaps below to complete the sentences. Choose from the Pick list provided.

When an organisation pays for items of expenditure at the time of purchase this is known as a _cash purchase._

When an organisation allows a customer to pay the amount they owe at a later date this is known as a _credit sale_.

Pick List

credit sale   cash sale   cash purchase   credit purchase.

Test your understanding 3

Match the definition with the correct term.

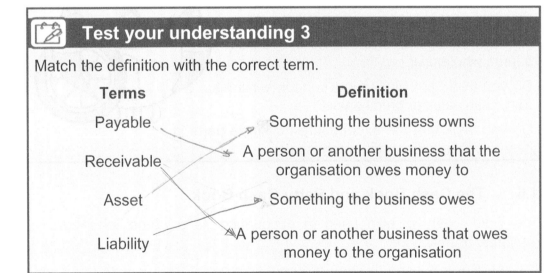

Terms	Definition
Payable	Something the business owns
Receivable	A person or another business that the organisation owes money to
Asset	Something the business owes
Liability	A person or another business that owes money to the organisation

Test your understanding 4

Jessica has been asked to identify whether the following How Two Ltd transactions would be classified as a cash or credit transaction?

Put a tick in the correct box.

	Cash	Credit
The Liverpool office purchases some inventory online and pays by bank transfer	✓	
The London office purchases some inventory and is issued an invoice from the supplier		✓
The Manchester office purchases a computer and pays by credit card	✓	

 Test your understanding 5

C Froome's Cycle World

Mr Froome has a small shop selling and repairing bicycles for individual customers.

He buys the spare parts that he needs from a large wholesaler.

Do you think that Mr Froome's income comes from cash sales or credit sales?

Do you think that the expenditure for spare parts is cash purchases or credit purchases?

1.6 The Cash Book and Petty Cash Book

The word 'cash' is also used in accounting as a name for recording monetary transactions.

A **Cash Book** is used to keep a record of most of the receipts of income and payments of expenses made by the organisation. The actual monies received and recorded may be by cash (currency), cheque, credit card or debit card, or bank transfer.

A **Petty Cash Book** is used to record small amounts of cash that most businesses hold in order to make small cash payments regularly. Petty cash systems and the management of petty cash are addressed further, later in this book.

deviation = desvio/ discrepância

2 Sales documentation

2.1 Offering credit and price quotations

Most transactions between business organisations will be on credit terms and this involves an element of risk. The goods are being taken away or delivered to the customer now with the promise of payment in the future. Therefore, suppliers must be confident that payment will be received.

In some organisations it is common practice to quote prices to customers over the telephone particularly if there is a catalogue or price list from which there are no deviations in price. However, some businesses will be prepared to offer certain customers goods at different prices and discounts may be offered and/or given to customers. Therefore, it is often the case that a price quotation is sent to a customer showing the price at which the goods that they want can be bought. The customer can then decide whether or not to buy the goods at that price. If they decide to purchase the goods upon receipt of the quotation, this can be used to generate the sales invoice later on in the sales process.

2.2 Purchase Order

If the customer is happy with the price quotation that they have received from the supplier then they will complete a purchase order for the goods or services required and send it to their supplier.

This document will state the details of the goods required, including:

- the quantity and description of the goods
- the price and other terms
- the supplier's code number for the items
- the date the order was placed.

When the supplier receives a purchase order, it is important for them to check all of the details carefully as it forms part of the sales contract.

- Is the price the same as the one which was quoted to the customer?
- Are the delivery terms acceptable?
- Are any discounts applicable?

Case study

An example of a purchase order received by How Two Ltd:

PURCHASE ORDER

IT Geeks Ltd.
11 Mountjoy Street
LONDON W12 6RS
Tel: 0208 741 2962
Fax: 0208 741 2963
Date: 17 March 2017
Purchase order no: P01562

To:	Delivery address
How Two Ltd.	(if different from above)
1 Baker Street	Four Hills Hotel
London	Park Lane
WC1 8QT	London
	W1 1UY

Product	Ref	Quantity	Price per unit (excl. VAT) £	Total (excl. VAT) £
Dall Touchpad 2	DTD2	7	250.00	1750.00

Signed: **J Belle**
Purchasing Manager

Notes:

a) The customer, IT Geeks Ltd. has placed an order with the supplier of computers, How Two Ltd.

b) The purchase order clearly states that the customer wants to purchase 7 Dall Touch Pad 2's at a price of £250.00 each.

c) The total amount that the customer wants to pay for the tablet computers is £1,750.00 (7 touchpads x £250.00 = £1,750.00).

d) If How Two Ltd. do not agree with any of these details, they will need to contact IT Geeks Ltd. immediately. The purchase order has been signed by J Belle, the authorised signatory. This is important to demonstrate that the process has been completed as required by the business.

Definition

An **authorised signatory** is an individual who has been given permission to sign an official document on behalf of an organisation.

2.3 Sales Order

The seller will create a sales order once both parties have agreed to a deal. The sales order is generated after the purchase order has been received to confirm that they agree to the terms set out in the purchase order.

A sales order will include the following details:

- Company name and contact information
- Customer name and contact information
- Customer reference/account number
- Customer billing information.
- Customer delivery address.
- Details of the products/services being supplied including quantities.
- Unit prices and total prices per product
- Total net price
- VAT amount
- Total price

2.4 Delivery note

When the goods or services are supplied, the supplier will prepare a delivery note to give to the customer. This document will show:

- The name and contact details of the seller
- Name and contact details of the customer
- Date of issue
- Date of delivery of the goods
- Delivery note number
- Purchase order number
- A description of the goods contained in the order
- The quantity of each type of goods

The delivery note will be signed by the customer upon receipt of the goods or services, so that the supplier has proof that the customer received them. This also ensures that there is a clear audit trail in case of any later queries.

2.5 The sales invoice

After the goods have been delivered, the supplier will request payment from the customer by sending an invoice.

The invoice will state the code, quantity, description and price of the goods. The invoice will also have a sequential number so that it can be filed in order.

The documentation used in order to generate this would include the quotation if there is one, a price list if it's a standard invoice and the delivery note.

Case study

An example of a sales invoice provided by How Two Ltd:

INVOICE

How Two Ltd.

1 Baker Street
London
WC1 8QT
Tel: 020 7890 1234
Fax: 020 7890 1235

Invoice no: 005673
Tax point: 25 March 2017
VAT reg no: 618 2201 63
Delivery note: DN00673
Account no: BEL65

To:	Delivery:	Delivery date:
IT Geeks Ltd.	Four Hills Hotel	25 March 2017
11 Mountjoy St	Park Lane	
London W12 6RS	London W1 1UY	

Date: 25 March 2017   **Sales order number:** 41161

Product	Quantity	Price per unit (£)	Total (£)
Dall Touchpad 2	7	250.00	1,750.00
		VAT 20%	350.00
		Total	2,100.00
Payment terms: 14 days net			

(handwritten margin notes:) order of a transaction: • purchase order • delivery note • invoice • payment

Notes:

This invoice confirms the price of the goods supplied to the customer

a)   7 Dall Touchpad 2's which have been supplied to the IT Geeks Ltd.

b)   The price for the goods is £1,750.00

c)   Value Added Tax (VAT) of 20%, £350.00 has been added to the cost of the goods.

d)   The amount of £2,100.00 is now due from the customer.

e)   The payment is due in 14 days from the date of the invoice.

2.6   Goods returned note

Upon receipt of goods, the customer may find that incorrect items have been delivered, some items are damaged, or they do not meet the required standard. In this case, the customer has the right to return the goods to the supplier. When a customer returns goods to a supplier, they complete a goods returned note.

A goods returned note is an important document as it will be used by the supplier to refund the customer or provide a replacement, depending on the circumstances surrounding the return.

The goods returned note will include the following details:

*   Customer name, reference and contact details
*   Contact details of the supplier
*   Quantities, description and price of goods returned
*   The reason for returning the goods
*   Condition of the goods returned
*   Date of the return
*   Name and signature of the person who received the goods.

2.7   Pricing and discounts

Unit prices for goods or services are kept in master files which must be updated regularly. If a price quotation has been sent to a customer then this must be used to determine the price to use on the invoice.

Trade discounts are a definite amount that is deducted from the list price of the goods for the supplies to some customers, with the intention of encouraging and rewarding customer loyalty. As well as checking the actual calculation of the trade discount on the face of the invoice, the supplier's file or the price quotation should be checked to ensure that the correct percentage of trade discount has been deducted.

Even if no trade discount appears on the purchase invoice, the supplier's file or price quotation must still be checked as it may be that a trade discount should have been deducted.

A **bulk discount** is similar to a trade discount in that it is deducted from the list price on the invoice. However, a bulk discount is given by a supplier for orders above a certain size.

A **prompt payment discount** is offered to customers if they settle the invoice within a certain time period. The discount is expressed as a percentage of the invoice total but is not deducted from the invoice total as it is not certain whether or not it will be accepted. Instead the details of the settlement discount will be noted at the bottom of the invoice.

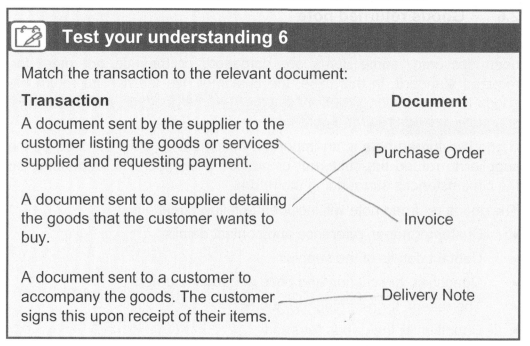

Test your understanding 6

Match the transaction to the relevant document:

Transaction	Document
A document sent by the supplier to the customer listing the goods or services supplied and requesting payment.	Purchase Order
A document sent to a supplier detailing the goods that the customer wants to buy.	Invoice
A document sent to a customer to accompany the goods. The customer signs this upon receipt of their items.	Delivery Note

2.8 VAT (sales tax)

VAT (Value Added Tax) also known as Sales Tax, is collected on behalf of HMRC (Her Majesty's Revenue and Customs) by companies in the UK.

VAT registered companies charge VAT on the supply of goods and services to their customers. They can claim back any VAT paid on their purchases.

The amount that gets paid to HMRC is the total amount of VAT charged to their customers minus the total amount of VAT that they can claim back on their purchases.

Definitions

Sales tax (VAT) is charged on the **taxable supply of goods and services** in the United Kingdom by a **taxable person** in the course of a business carried on by him.

Output tax is the tax charged on the sale of goods and services.

Input tax is the tax paid on the purchase of goods and services.

2.9 Rates of VAT (sales tax)

Taxable supply is the supply of all items except those which are **exempt.** Examples of exempt items are as follows:

- certain land and buildings, where sold, leased or hired
- insurance
- postal services

Input tax cannot be reclaimed where the trader's supplies are all exempt.

There are three rates of sales tax (VAT in the UK) on taxable supplies:

1. Some items are 'zero-rated' (similar to exempt except that input tax can be reclaimed), examples of which include:

   - water and most types of food
   - books and newspapers
   - drugs and medicines
   - children's clothing and footwear.

2. There is a special rate of 5% for domestic fuel and power

3. All other items are rated at the standard rate of 20%.

For the purpose of this assessment, you will normally be dealing with taxable supplies at the standard rate of 20%.

Therefore, if you are given the net price of goods, the price excluding VAT, then the amount of VAT is 20% or 20/100 of this price.

Note: VAT is always rounded down to the nearest penny.

sales tax

VAT = Value Added Tax / Value Added Tax

HMRC = Her Majesty Revenue and Customs
Her Majesty Revenue and Customs.

Example

A sale is made for £360.48 plus VAT. What is the amount of VAT to be charged on this sale?

Solution

VAT = £360.48 × 20/100 = £72.09

Remember to round down to the nearest penny.

An alternative way of calculating this would to be to multiply the net amount of £360.48 by 20% = £72.09.

If a price is given that already includes the VAT then calculating the VAT requires an understanding of the price structure where VAT is concerned.

	%
Selling price excl. VAT (net)	100
VAT	20
	———
Selling price incl. VAT (gross)	120
	———

 Example

How Two Ltd offer a small office starter pack, with a selling price of £3,000 **inclusive** of VAT. What is the VAT on the goods and the net price of these goods?

Solution

	£
Net price (£3,000 ÷ 120 x 100)	2,500
VAT (£3,000 ÷ 120 x 20)	500
	———
Gross price	3,000
	———

Test your understanding 7

Calculate the net, VAT and gross figures for the following transactions:

a)   A credit sale for £3,600 inclusive of VAT

b)   A cash sale for £2,800 exclusive of VAT

	a) Credit Sale	b) Cash Sale
Net	£ 3,000.00	£ 2,800.00
VAT	£ 600.00	£ 560.00
Gross	£ 3,600.00	£ 3,360.00

 Test your understanding 8

Alba works in the accounts office at NB Solutions Ltd. She has been asked to check three invoices relating to office supplies.

Invoice 1 – NB Solutions purchased 24 boxes of paper towels at £12.45 for each box. What is the total cost of the paper towels?

Invoice 2 – NB Solutions spent £250 excluding (or net of) VAT on stationery. How much VAT would be charged?

Invoice 3 – NB Solutions bought two new dishwashers for the staff kitchens, at a total cost of £480 including VAT. How much VAT would have been included in the cost?

Invoice 1 = 24 × £ 12.45 = £298.80
Invoice 2 = £250.00 × 20% = £50.00 VAT
Invoice 3 = £480.00 ÷ 120 × 20 = £80 VAT

2.10   Preparing a sales invoice

 Case study

As part of her role, Jessica deals with both sales and purchases.

How Two Ltd are a VAT registered IT and Computer Consumables company. Jessica prepares the sales invoices to be sent to the customer from the price list and a copy of the delivery note sent up to her by the sales department.

Today she has received the following delivery note from the sales department.

How Two Ltd.

Delivery note: 1036
Date of issue: 30ᵗʰ October 20X7
Purchase order number: PO1612

To: IT Crowd PLC.   From: How Two Ltd.
    19 Bond Street   1 Baker Street
    Chichester   London
    CH1 6MT   WC1 8QT

Delivery Address:
As Above

Delivery date: 31ˢᵗ October 20X7

Quantity	Code	DESCRIPTION	Size
10	CJA 991	**Codie Laptop**	12"
15	CJA 992	**Codie Laptop**	14"
5	CJA 994	**Codie Laptop**	15.7"

Received by: ....

Signature: ....   Date: ....

Code	Description	Screen Size	Unit price	VAT rate
CJA 991	Codie Laptop	12"	249.00	Standard
CJA 992	Codie Laptop	14"	279.00	Standard
CJA 993	Codie Laptop	15"	319.00	Standard
CJA 994	Codie Laptop	15.7"	349.00	Standard

The customer file shows that IT Crowd PLC's account number is ITC 4125 and that a trade discount of 10% is offered to this customer.

Jessica must now prepare the sales invoice. Today's date is 2nd November 20X7 and the last invoice issued was numbered 95123.

Solution

INVOICE

How Two Ltd.

Invoice to:
IT Crowd PLC.
19 Bond Street
Chichester
CH1 6MT

Deliver to:

As above

How Two Ltd
1 Baker Street
London
WC1 8QT

Tel: 0207 890 1234
Fax: 0207 890 1235

Invoice no: 95124
Tax point: 2nd November 17
VAT reg no: 618 2201 63
Delivery note no: 1036
Account no: ICT 4125

Code	Description	Quantity	VAT rate %	Unit price £	Amount net of VAT £
CJA 991	**Codie Laptop**	10	20	249.00	2,490.00
CJA 992	**Codie Laptop**	15	20	279.00	4,185.00
CJA 994	**Codie Laptop**	5	20	349.00	1,745.00
					8,420.00
Trade discount 10%					(842.00)
					7,578.00
VAT					1,515.60
Total amount payable					9,093.60

* Soma-se o total da quantidade dos produtos, no valor total, calcula-se o desconto, a partir do valor do desconto, calcula-se o VAT. O valor final total é o a ser cobrado.

How did Jessica do it?

Step 1   Enter today's date on the invoice and the invoice number which should be the next number after the last sales invoice number.

Step 2   Enter the customer details – name, address and account number.

Step 3   Refer now to the delivery note copy and enter the delivery note number and the quantities, codes and descriptions of the goods.

Step 4   Refer to the price list and enter the unit prices of the goods and the rate of VAT

Step 5   Now for the calculations – firstly multiply the number of each item by the unit price to find the VAT exclusive price – then total these total prices – finally calculate the trade discount as 10% of this total, £8,420.00 × 10% = £842.00 and deduct it.

Step 6   Calculate the VAT – in this case there is only standard rate VAT on the laptops but you must remember to deduct the trade discount (£8,420 – £842) before calculating the VAT amount £7,578 × 20% = £1,515.60 – add the VAT to the invoice total after deducting the trade discount.

Test your understanding 9

As mentioned in the example above, as part of her role as a bookkeeper at How Two Ltd, Jessica is required to generate sales invoices.

Today she has received the following delivery note from the sales department.

Delivery Note

How Two Ltd.

To: St Peter's Secondary School
191 St. Petersgate
Manchester
M2 6KS

From: How Two Ltd.
1 Baker Street
London
WC1 8QT

Delivery Address:
As Above

Delivery note: 1114
Date of issue: 30th October 20X7
Purchase order number: P6486

Delivery date: 31st October 20X7

Quantity	Code	DESCRIPTION	Size
5	SMG 121	Samsong HD Monitor	17"
12	SMG 123	Samsong HD Monitor	24"
8	SMG 124	Samsong HD Monitor	28"

Received by: ....

Signature: .... Date: ....

Code	Description	Screen Size	Unit price	VAT rate
SMG 121	Samsong HD Monitor	17"	69.99	Standard
SMG 122	Samsong HD Monitor	19"	99.99	Standard
SMG 123	Samsong HD Monitor	24"	129.99	Standard
SMG 124	Samsong HD Monitor	28"	149.99	Standard

The customer file shows that St. Peter's Secondary School's account number is SPS 1124 and that a bulk discount of 15% is offered to this customer.

She must now prepare the sales invoice and pass it back to Dave Woody to be checked. Today's date is 3rd November 20X7 and the last invoice issued was numbered 95156.

Solution

INVOICE

How Two Ltd.

Invoice to:

How Two Ltd
1 Baker Street
London
WC1 8QT

Tel: 0207 890 1234
Fax: 0207 890 1235

Deliver to:

Invoice no: 95157
Tax point: 3rd November 2017
VAT reg no: 618 2201 63
Delivery note no: 1114
Account no: SPS 1124

Code	Description	Quantity	VAT rate	Unit price	Amount net of VAT
			%	£	£
SMG 121	SAMSONG HD MONITOR 17"	5	20	69.99	349.95
SMG 123	SAMSONG HD MONITOR 24"	12	20	129.99	1,559.88
SMG 124	SAMSUNG HD MONITOR 28"	8	20	149.99	1,199.92
					3,109.75
Bulk discount 15%					(466.46)
					2,643.29
VAT 20%		VAT arredonda p/ men			528.65
Total amount payable					3,171.94

Test your understanding 10

You work for Cavalier Beds as a sales invoicing clerk. Your task is to prepare a sales invoice for each customer using the information below.

Today is 28 October, 20X6 and you have received the following delivery note from the sales department.

Use the information from the delivery note, the information from the customer file and the price list below to prepare an invoice for KP Furniture Ltd.

The last invoice issued was Invoice No. 67894.

Delivery Note:

Delivery note: 6785

To: KP Furniture Ltd
9 Paris Street
COLCHESTER
CF25 1XY

Cavalier Beds
3 Brussels Road
County Road
Gloucester
GL6 6TH
Tel: 01456 698271
Fax: 01456 698272

Delivery date: 27 October 20X6

Quantity	Code	DESCRIPTION	Size
5	MAT15K	Deluxe Mattress	King Size

Received by: ....

Signature: .... Date: ....

Customer File:

The customer file shows that KP Furniture Ltd's account number is KP12 and a trade discount of 10% is offered to this customer.

Price List:

Code	Description	Size	Unit price	VAT rate
MAT15S	Deluxe Mattress	Single	58.00	Standard
MAT15D	Deluxe Mattress	Double	74.00	Standard
MAT15K	Deluxe Mattress	King	98.00	Standard

Cavalier Beds
3 Brussels Road
County Road
Gloucester
GL6 6TH
Tel: 01456 698271   Fax: 01456 698272

Invoice to:		Invoice no:	67 895
KP FURNITURE LTD. 9 PARIS STREET COLCHESTER CF25 1XY		Date:	28/10/16
		VAT reg no:	488 7922 26
		Delivery note no:	6785
		Account no:	KP12

Code	DESCRIPTION	Quantity	VAT rate	Unit price £	Amount excl of VAT £
			20%	£	
MAT 15K	DELUXE MATTRESS KING	5		98.00	490.00
MAT 15 D	DELUXE MATTRESS				
MAT 15 K	DELUXE MATTRESS				
					490.00
Trade discount 10%					(49.00)
Subtotal					441.00
VAT					88.20
Total amount payable					529.20

2.11   Credit Notes

In some cases, the customer may want to return goods to the supplier. For example, if the goods are faulty. When this happens, the supplier will issue a credit note. This credit note will reduce the amount that the customer owes.

Common reasons for credit notes:

- when a customer has returned faulty or damaged goods

- when a customer has returned perfect goods by agreement with the supplier

- to make a refund for short deliveries

- to settle a dispute with a customer.

When a supplier receives returned goods they must be inspected, counted and recorded on receipt. They would normally be recorded on a goods returned note, as detailed earlier in the chapter.

All credit notes must be authorised by a supervisor prior to being issued to the customer.

Some credit notes may be issued without a goods returned note. For example, an error may have been made in pricing on an invoice but the customer is satisfied with the goods and does not need to return them.

These credit notes must be issued only after written authorisation has been received and must be reviewed and approved before being sent to the customer or recorded.

As credit notes look very similar to invoices, they are often printed in red to make it clear that it is not an invoice.

Credit Note

How Two Ltd.

1 Baker Street
London
WC1 8QT
Tel: 020 7890 1234
Fax: 020 7890 1235

Credit note no: CN 02542
Tax point: 30 November X7
VAT reg no: 618 2201 63
Invoice no: 95080
Account no: BEL65

CREDIT NOTE

Credit to:
Redshaw Cables
17 High Street
Manchester M1 6RS

Date: 30 November 2017

Description	Code	Quantity	Unit price £	Amount exclusive of VAT £
Epsan SXA Projector	ESXA14	1	300.00	300.00

VAT	60.00
Total amount of credit	360.00

Reason: Faulty

Notes

In this example, one of the Epsan SXA Projector's delivered to Redshaw Cables is faulty so they have requested a credit note.

When the replacement projector has been delivered, How Two Ltd. will raise another invoice for the replacement.

2.12 Remittance Advice

The final document in the process is the remittance advice. When the customer pays their outstanding balance, they will send a remittance advice to the supplier together with their payment.

The remittance advice will clearly show which invoices are being paid and the date of the payment.

If there are any credit notes, the customer will state which credit notes they are deducting from the payment.

📖 **Case study**

REMITTANCE ADVICE

To:	Company name:	Redshaw Cables
How Two Ltd.		17 High Street
1 Baker Street	Address:	Manchester
London		M1 6RS
WC1 8QT		

VAT reg no: 32141108
Date: 5/12/20X7

Date	Your ref	Amount	Discount taken	Paid
		£	£	£
5/11/X7	Invoice 95080	2,160.00	0	2,160.00
30/11/X7	CN 02542	360.00	0	(360.00)

Total paid £1,800.00

Cheque no 041261

Notes

In this example, on 5th December 20X7, Redshaw Cables paid £1,800.00 by cheque. This payment is £2,160.00 for Invoice No 95080 less £360.00 for Credit Note CN02542.

If customers do not send a remittance advice and there are a lot of transactions in the month, it would be difficult for the supplier to know which invoices and credit notes the payment relates to.

3 Purchases documentation

3.1 Payment terms

As mentioned previously, the majority of business transactions nowadays are conducted on credit terms. This applies to both sales and purchases.

When a credit account is set up with a supplier an agreement is put in place which states the point at which payment is to be made for goods and services, any conditions of payment and any discounts that may be applicable. This helps to ensure that suppliers are paid on time and to give them an idea of cash flows within the business i.e. at what point they can expect the money to come into their bank account.

Payment in advance

A payment in advance is where a payment for goods or services is made ahead of schedule. This is not uncommon when dealing with larger orders as it helps the supplier to cover any 'out of pocket' expenses or to pay for the materials required to produce the order if they don't have enough capital to fund the purchase.

A payment in advance also helps safeguard the supplier against customers who don't pay or those that cancel a large order at the last minute.

 Example – payment in advance

Where a supplier requests a 50% upfront payment from the buyer.

Payment on delivery

Payment on delivery is where the supplier will distribute goods to the customer and take payment for the goods upon delivery. If the customer does not pay for the goods, they are returned to the supplier.

Payment after invoice date

A payment after the invoice date gives the customer a certain number of calendar days to make payment 'after' the date of the invoice. The supplier can specify how many days this would be but quite commonly this is 10, 14, 30 or 60 days after the invoice date. This arrangement would be put in place as part of the supplier agreement.

Payment at the end of the month of invoice

A payment at the end of the month of invoice means that the supplier is expecting the money at the end of the month in which they have issued the invoice.

 Example – payment at the end of month

Where an invoice is issued on the 15th September, the supplier will be expecting payment by the 30th September.

3.2 The Purchasing Process

The flow chart on the following page demonstrates the process that How Two Ltd would follow when making a purchase.

Case study

How Two Ltd select a supplier

Some businesses will have an **approved supplier list**. This is a list of suppliers who are reliable and have the capacity to meet their customers needs. An approved supplier usually provides a consistent high level of service along with excellent quality standards of their products.

They then raise a purchase order and send to the supplier

The purchase order in the purchasing process is exactly the same as that in the sales process. The only difference is that we are effectively the customer and therefore we are the ones completing the document and sending it to the supplier.

How Two Ltd receive the goods or services from the supplier

How Two Ltd check the delivery note against the goods received and sign the delivery note to say that they agree that it matches

The delivery note contains details as stated in the Sales section above. If there are any differences between the delivery note and the goods received, How Two Ltd. makes a note of any differences and queries them with the supplier. This would be noted before the delivery note was signed because otherwise How Two Ltd. could be invoiced for goods that they have never actually received.

How Two Ltd complete a goods received note (GRN)

A **goods received note** is an internal document used to identify proof of goods actually received. See below for further explanation.

How Two Ltd receive an invoice from the supplier in respect of the purchase

How Two Ltd check the invoice received from the supplier against the purchase order, delivery note/goods received note to ensure that they have been invoice correctly

Once satisfied that they have been invoiced accurately for their purchase, How Two Ltd make a payment to the supplier and record the expenditure.

3.3 The Goods Received Note (GRN)

A goods received note is an internal document that is used to document the receipt of goods or services. Upon delivery, the goods received will be checked against the delivery note sent from the supplier. If everything is present and correct, the customer will sign the delivery note to be returned to the supplier and will generate a GRN as proof of what has been received. This is then compared to the purchase order and the supplier invoice before payment is made.

 Case study

You work for How Two Ltd. and have been asked to prepare a goods received note using the following information:

Today is 31st October 20X7, there has been a delivery of goods into the warehouse. Yacob Solvez has checked the goods received and agrees that the details on the following delivery note are correct.

Using the information in the delivery note below, prepare the goods received note as requested, ensuring all of the relevant details are entered.

Delivery Note	
To: How Two Ltd. 1 Baker Street London WC1 8QT	**From: PC's R Us Ltd.** 212 Wellington Street London WC12 8RD

Delivery Address:
1 Baker Street
London
WC1 8QT

Delivery note: 1056
Date of issue: 30th October 20X7
Purchase order number: PO5571

Delivery date: 31st October 20X7

Quantity	Code	DESCRIPTION
20	DKT476	Dall Laptop Model SKW665
25	ESMJA2	Epsan MJA2 projectors

Received by: ....

Signature: .... Date: ....

Goods Received Note

Goods Received Note		
Received From: PC's R Us 212 Wellington Street London WC12 8RD **GRN number: 102** **Date goods received: 31st October 20X7** **Delivery note number: 1056**		
Quantity	**Code**	**DESCRIPTION**
20	DKT476	**Dall Laptop Model SKW665**
25	ESMJA2	**Epsan MJA2 projectors**
Received by: *YACOB SOLVEZ*		
Signature: *Y. Solvez*................ Date: *31st October 20X7*		

Note:

The details entered include the dates that the goods have been received, a goods received note number, the delivery note number from the supplier (so that it can be matched up later), the supplier details, quantities, descriptions and codes of the goods received and then details of the person who has received the goods into store.

 Test your understanding 11

Jessica has been asked to prepare a goods received note using the following information:

Today is 31st October 20X7, there has been a delivery of goods into the warehouse.

Jessica has checked the goods received and agree that the details on the following delivery note are correct.

The last GRN created was number 123.

Delivery Note:

Delivery Note		
Delivery note: 2212		
Date of issue: 30th October 20X7		
Purchase order number: PO5589		
To: How Two Ltd.		**From: Tablet World**
1 Baker Street		477 High Street
London		Oxford
WC1 8QT		OX10 5WD

Delivery Address:
1 Baker Street
London
WC1 8QT

Delivery date: 31st October 20X7

Quantity	Code	DESCRIPTION
15	SSX52	Samsong SX52 9" Tablet computers
15	DL656	Dall MC656 8" Tablet computers

Received by: ....

Signature: .... Date: ....

Goods Received Note:

Goods Received Note		
Received From:		
TABLET WORLD		
477 HIGH STREET		
OXFORD		
OX10 5WD		

GRN number: 124
Date goods received: 31st OCTOBER 20X7
Delivery note number: 2212

Quantity	Code	DESCRIPTION
15	SSX52	SAMSONG SX52 9" TABLET COMPUTERS
15	DL656	DALL MC656 8" TABLET COMPUTERS

Received by: JESSICA HOWARD

Signature: Jessica H. Date: 31st October 20X7

3.4 Statement of Account

At the end of each month, the supplier will summarise all the transactions that have taken place with the customer. This could include invoices, credit notes, and any payments received from the customer.

The statement of account will show the outstanding balance owing from the customer at the end of the month.

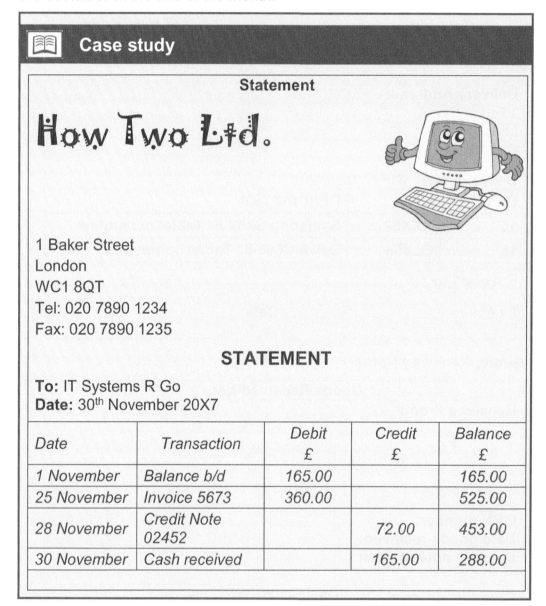

Case study

Statement

How Two Ltd.

1 Baker Street
London
WC1 8QT
Tel: 020 7890 1234
Fax: 020 7890 1235

STATEMENT

To: IT Systems R Go
Date: 30th November 20X7

Date	Transaction	Debit £	Credit £	Balance £
1 November	Balance b/d	165.00		165.00
25 November	Invoice 5673	360.00		525.00
28 November	Credit Note 02452		72.00	453.00
30 November	Cash received		165.00	288.00

Notes

a) 1st November IT Systems R Go owed £165.00 from last month;

b) 25th November Invoice No 5673 for £360.00 has been added to the £165.00 to show a balance owing of £525.00;

c) 28th November Credit note No 02452 for £72.00 has been deducted from the £525.00 to show a balance at that date of £453.00;

d) 30th November IT Systems R Go have paid the amount owing at the beginning of the month, leaving a balance outstanding of £288.00.

3.5 Overview of the flow of transaction

The diagram below shows the typical flow of a transaction including the documents involved.

Dependent on whether it is a credit sale or a credit purchase, we will be looking at it from the perspective of the business or customer.

Customer	Supplier
Purchase order ——————————————▶	
◀——————————————	Sends *delivery note* with
	goods supplied
Signs delivery note ——————————————▶	
◀——————————————	Sends *invoice*
Returns goods ——————————————▶	
◀——————————————	Sends *credit note*
◀——————————————	Sends *statement of account*
	(usually on a monthly basis)
(PG 95)	
Sends *remittance advice* ——————————▶	
with payment	

4 Summary and further questions

In this chapter we have both established who credit and cash customers/suppliers are and then looked in detail at the documents used to record transactions for both credit and cash customers and suppliers. You should now know what information is required for each of these documents and you should be able to accurately generate them from given information.

Let us return to the case study to see how Jessica uses some of the documents to record sales and purchases at How Two Ltd.

 Case study activity 13

Jessica needs to decide whether the following How Two Ltd transactions are cash or credit sales, or cash or credit purchases? Put a tick in the correct box.

	Cash Sale	Credit Sale	Cash Purchase	Credit Purchase
Printer paper bought from a supplier and paid for immediately.			✓	
Cables delivered to a customer who will pay at the end of the month.		✓		
Laptop components bought from a supplier on credit.				✓
A payment received from a customer for goods purchased online and paid for at the checkout.	✓			

Case study activity 14

Jessica has been given five pieces of paper:

- A delivery note
- A sales invoice
- A purchase order
- A remittance advice
- A statement

Match the document with the correct description to help Jessica understand how they relate to sales or purchases.

	Document
Sent by the customer to inform How Two Ltd that an invoice has been paid.	A REMITTANCE ADVICE
Summarises all transactions between a supplier and customer. It shows invoices and credit notes, payments and any outstanding balance.	A STATEMENT
Sent by the customer (How Two Ltd) to state which goods they want to purchase	A PURCHASE ORDER
Sent by the supplier to How Two Ltd with the goods when despatched	A DELIVERY NOTE
Sent by the supplier to How Two Ltd to inform them of how much the goods cost	A SALES INVOICE

Case study activity 15

Jessica has been asked to prepare a delivery note using the information below:

Today is 29th October 20X7 and the following purchase order has been processed with the goods ready to be despatched to the customer. The last delivery note issued was number 1026 and the goods are due to be delivered tomorrow.

Using the information above along with the purchase order below, prepare the delivery note as requested, ensuring all of the relevant details are entered.

PURCHASE ORDER

Redshaw Cables
17 High Street
Manchester M1 6RS
Tel: 0161 741 2962
Fax: 0161 741 2963
Date: 23rd October 20X7
Purchase order no: P01562

To:	Delivery address
How Two Ltd.	(if different from above)
1 Baker Street	Four Lane Ends
London	New Mills
WC1 8QT	SK22 4LG

Product	Ref	Quantity	Price per unit (excl. VAT) £	Total (excl. VAT) £
HDMI Cables	HDMI62	20	15.00	300.00
Epsan SXA projectors	ESXA14	5	300.00	1,500.00
Signed:	*J Johnson* Purchasing Manager			

Delivery Note:

Delivery Note

To: REDSHAW CABLES
17 HIGH STREET
MANCHESTER
M1 6RS

From: HOW TWO LTD.
1 BAKER STREET
LONDON
WC1 8QT

Delivery Address:

FOUR LANE ENDS
NEW MILLS
SK22 4LG

Delivery note: 1027
Date of issue: 29th OCTOBER 20X7
Purchase order number: PO1562

Delivery date: 30th OCTOBER 20X7

Quantity	Code	DESCRIPTION
20	HDM1 62	HDMI CABLES
5	ESXA 14	EPSAN SXA PROJECTORS

Received by: ....

Signature: .... Date: ....

Case study activity 16

Jessica is looking at the account of one of How Two Ltd's biggest customers, NB Solutions Ltd, to see how much money is owed.

During the last month, NB Solutions have been sent two invoices by How Two Ltd for computer equipment that has been supplied. The two invoices total £457.98 and £69.65.

NB Solutions have also received a credit note for some mouse mats ordered in error and returned to How Two Ltd. This credit note was for a total of £58.60.

During the month, NB Solutions paid £200.00 to How Two Ltd.

a) What is the balance outstanding on NB Solutions' account? £269.03

b) What is the name of the document which will be sent to the customer to show these transactions and the balance outstanding?
A STATEMENT OF ACCOUNT

 Case study activity 17

Jessica has also been tasked with finding out how much money How Two Ltd need to pay one of their suppliers, MMC Direct.

At the start of the month, How Two Ltd owes MMC Direct £1,250.

The following transactions take place throughout the month:

Invoice for £1,100   £1,250 + £1,100 + £3,250 – £500.00

Invoice for £3,250   + £2,225 – £225 = £7,100

Credit note for £500

Invoice for £2,225

Credit note for £225

a) What is the balance outstanding on How Two Ltd's credit account with MMC Direct? £7,100

b) What is the name of the document which Jessica should request is sent to How Two Ltd to show these transactions and the balance outstanding? STATEMENT OF ACCOUNT

Case study activity 18

Jessica has checked that the balance is owing to MMC Direct Ltd is correct and needs to arrange payment. If How Two Ltd want to settle their account in full, what is the name of the document which will be sent to the supplier along with the payment, to show which transaction(s) it relates to? REMITTANCE ADVICE

Case study Activity 16

a) £457.98 + £69.65 − £58.60 − £200.00 = £269.03

Answers to chapter activities

Test your understanding 1

	Cash	Credit
A customer purchases a computer and pays by credit card	✓	
A customer buys a mouse mat, a mouse and a printer and pays by debit card	✓	
A customer buys 5 tablet computers, and pays in 30 days		✓

Test your understanding 2

When an organisation pays for items of expenditure at the time of purchase this is known as a **cash purchase.**

When an organisation allows a customer to pay the amount they owe at a later date this is known as a **credit sale.**

Test your understanding 3

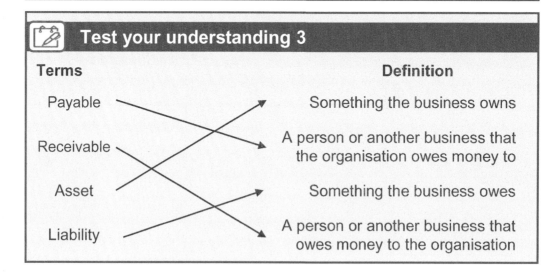

Terms	Definition
Payable	Something the business owns
Receivable	A person or another business that the organisation owes money to
Asset	Something the business owes
Liability	A person or another business that owes money to the organisation

Test your understanding 4

	Cash	Credit
The Liverpool office purchases some inventory online and pays by bank transfer	✓	
The London office purchases some inventory and is issued an invoice from the supplier		✓
The Manchester office purchases a computer and pays by credit card	✓	

Test your understanding 5

Mr Froome's income is most likely to be from cash sales. His customers are individuals who will probably pay when they come to pick up their bicycles. They are unlikely to be very regular customers.

His expenditure for the spare parts is likely to be a credit purchase. As Mr Froome will buy regularly from the supplier he may have been given credit so that he can make daily or weekly purchases and then pay for all he owes at a later date.

Test your understanding 6

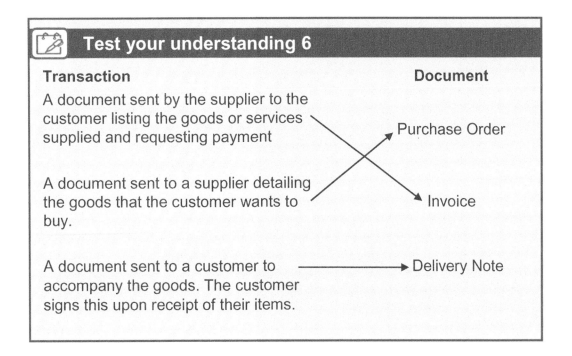

Transaction	Document
A document sent by the supplier to the customer listing the goods or services supplied and requesting payment	Purchase Order
A document sent to a supplier detailing the goods that the customer wants to buy.	Invoice
A document sent to a customer to accompany the goods. The customer signs this upon receipt of their items.	Delivery Note

Test your understanding 7

	a) Credit Sale	b) Cash Sale
Net	£3,000	£2,800
VAT	£600	£560
Gross	£3,600	£3,360

Workings:

a)   3,600 ÷ 120 x 100 = 3,000

      3,600 ÷ 120 x 20 = 600

b)   2,800 ÷ 100 x 20 = 560

      2,800 ÷ 100 x 120 = 3,360

Test your understanding 8

Invoice 1 – The cost of the paper towels is £298.80.

Invoice 2 – £250.00 × 20/100 = £50.00. Therefore the VAT would be £50.

Invoice 3 – £480.00/1.2 = £400. £480 - £400 = £80.00. Therefore the VAT would be £80.

Test your understanding 9

INVOICE

Invoice to:
St Peter's Secondary School
141 St Petersgate
Manchester
M2 6KS

Deliver to:

As above

How Two Ltd
1 Baker Street
London
WC1 8QT

Tel: 0207 890 1234
Fax: 0207 890 1235

Invoice no: 95157
Tax point: 3rd November 17
VAT reg no: 618 2201 63
Delivery note no: 1114
Account no: SPS 1124

Code	Description	Quantity	VAT rate %	Unit price £	Amount net of VAT £
SMG 121	Samsong HD Monitor	5	20	69.99	349.95
SMG 123	Samsong HD Monitor	12	20	129.99	1,559.88
SMG 124	Samsong HD Monitor	8	20	149.99	1,199.92
					3,109.75
Bulk discount 15%					(466.46)
					2,643.29
VAT					528.65
Total amount payable					3,171.94

Test your understanding 10

Cavalier Beds
3 Brussels Road
County Road
Gloucester
GL6 6TH
Tel: 01456 698271   Fax: 01456 698272

Invoice to:			
	Invoice no:	67895	
KP Furniture Ltd	Date:	28/10/X6	
9 Paris Street	VAT reg no:	488 7922 26	
COLCHESTER	Delivery note no:	6785	
CF25 1XY	Account no:	KP12	

Code		Quantity	VAT rate	Unit price £	Amount excl of VAT £
MAT15K	Deluxe Mattress	5	20%	98.00	490.00
Trade discount 10%					49.00
Subtotal					441.00
VAT					88.20
Total amount payable					529.20

Test your understanding 11

Goods Received Note

Goods Received Note		
GRN number: 124		
Date goods received: 31st October 20X7		
Delivery note number: 2212		
Received From:		
Tablet World		
477 High Street		
Oxford		
OX10 5WD		
Quantity	**Code**	**DESCRIPTION**
15	SSX52	Samsong SX52 9" Tablet computers
15	DL656	Dall MC656 8" Tablet computers
Received by: *JESSICA HOWARD*		
Signature: *J. Howard*............ Date: *31st October 20X7*..........		

Case study activity 13

	Cash Sale	Credit Sale	Cash Purchase	Credit Purchase
Printer paper bought from a supplier and paid for immediately.			✓	
Cables delivered to a customer who will pay at the end of the month.		✓		
Laptop components bought from a supplier on credit.				✓
A payment received from a customer for goods purchased online and paid for at the checkout.	✓			

Case study activity 14

	Document
Sent by the customer to inform How Two Ltd that an invoice has been paid.	**A remittance advice**
Summarises all transactions between a supplier and customer. It shows invoices and credit notes, payments and any outstanding balance.	**A statement**
Sent by the customer (How Two Ltd) to state which goods they want to purchase	**A purchase order**
Sent by the supplier to How Two Ltd with the goods when despatched	**A delivery note**
Sent by the supplier to How Two Ltd to inform them of how much the goods cost	**A sales invoice**

Case study activity 15

Delivery Note

To: Redshaw Cables
17 High Street
Manchester
M1 6RS

From: How Two Ltd.
1 Baker Street
London
WC1 8QT

Delivery Address:
Four Lane Ends
New Mills
SK22 4LG

Delivery note: 1027
Date of issue: 29ᵗʰ October 20X7
Purchase order number: PO1562

Delivery date: 30ᵗʰ October 20X7

Quantity	Code	DESCRIPTION
20	HDMI62	HDMI Cables
5	ESXA14	Epsan SXA projectors

Received by: ....

Signature: .... Date: ....

Case study activity 16

a) What is the balance outstanding on NB Solutions' account?

£269.03

b) What is the name of the document which will be sent to the customer to show these transactions and the balance outstanding?

Statement of Account

Case study activity 17

a) What is the balance outstanding on How Two Ltd's credit account with MMC Direct?

   £7,100

b) What is the name of the document which Jessica should request is sent to How Two Ltd to show these transactions and the balance outstanding?

   Statement of Account

 Case study activity 18

A remittance advice is the document to be sent with the payment.

Checking documentation

4

Introduction

In the previous chapter we looked at the different types of business documentation used by a bookkeeper and the purposes for each. Here, we will establish the importance of ensuring that these documents are accurate. We will compare documents in the purchasing process to ensure that they are accurate.

We will also look at the different types of errors that could occur and what action should be taken should this happen.

KNOWLEDGE
Understand the role of a bookkeeper
1.2 The importance of timely and accurate information
Process customer and supplier transactions
3.3 Check purchase invoices and credit notes

CONTENTS

1 Business procedures
2 Checking documents
3 Summary and further questions

1 Business procedures

1.1 Case study: an introduction

 Case study

Jessica is now feeling very confident about her bookkeeping skills and has been working on processing sales and purchasing documentation for a few days now. She feels as though she is really starting to understand the systems and processes around this.

Jessica is keen to continue looking at How Two Ltd's finances and helping to balance the books. Her manager makes Jessica aware of the impact it could have on the organisation if these documents are not accurate and the consequences as a result of them being incorrect.

Therefore it is vital that Jessica understands the importance of checking all business documentation before processing it. As a result, Jessica is now going to explore in more detail how to check business documents for accuracy and what to do if she discovers discrepancies or errors.

1.2 The need to follow business procedures

It is essential to follow business procedures when dealing with sales and purchases. This will ensure that the processes are completed fully and accurately as required by the organisation. Failure to do so could result in deadlines being missed, which ultimately causes issues for the business.

For example, if goods are not checked properly upon receipt this could lead to the company creating a goods received note for incorrect items of stock and they could be charged incorrectly for items that they have never received.

If there are many queries raised in relation to goods received, this could lead to further complications when it comes to the payment run, and could result in the internal deadline being missed. If this was the case, the supplier may not receive their payment on time which could damage the business relationship with the supplier.

It is important to follow the correct procedures for the following reasons:

*   It helps to avoid errors – if the process of completing business documents is followed properly, the number of errors made will be minimal. Examples of such errors are provided below.

- It helps to avoid missing internal or external deadlines – this is key to the smooth operation of the sales and purchasing departments. If deadlines are missed, a backlog of work will be created. If you get behind with your work, you could rush to try to get back on top of it which creates a risk of errors being made.

- It ensures processes are completed as required by the business – every business has different needs and requirements from business documents. Invoices, credit notes, purchase orders, delivery notes, goods returned notes and goods received notes will look different depending on the company that has created them. The basic information within these documents however, will remain the same.

- It maintains good business relationships with customers and suppliers – if procedures are followed accurately then the number of errors or queries will be minimal, payments will be made on time and therefore business relationships will remain positive.

 Example

When processing sales invoices, it is important to ensure the figures processed are a true reflection of the customer's order.

If the figures are overstated, this could lead to customers being chased for more money than they actually owe. As a result, the customer would dispute the amount owed and it would take time for the discrepancy to be investigated and corrected.

Not only could this damage the businesses reputation with the customer, but the receipt of money owed would be delayed which could result in cash flow issues.

 Example

When processing purchase invoices or making payments to suppliers, it is important to review the accounting records for accuracy. Failure to do so could result in an overpayment/underpayment, ultimately leading to further errors in the accounting records.

If the business overpays them or makes duplicate payments to the supplier, this could lead to cash flow problems for the business.

As a result, the business may find that they don't have enough money to pay other suppliers and could therefore either face operational/ production delays or have to source money from elsewhere (e.g. a loan or overdraft). This is an expensive option for the business and could have a negative effect on the overall profit or loss.

> ### Example
>
> Likewise, if an underpayment is made, this could lead to a lack of trust between the supplier and the business, making future the partnership between the organisations, and any future commercial arrangements, more difficult.
>
> It could also result in the supplier putting the account on hold and refusing to process any further orders of inventory. This would cause delays in supplies, leading to problems with business operations and fulfilling customer orders in a timely fashion, therefore having a negative impact on both the customer and supplier relationship.

1.3 Ensuring procedures are followed correctly

Following procedures correctly is of paramount importance to the smooth operation of an organisation.

The following steps give you an idea of how to ensure that you are performing work-related tasks correctly to prevent wasting time tracing and correcting errors.

- Ensure that business documentation is completed fully and accurately – make sure that all quantities, prices and discounts are cross checked for accuracy and that all item codes, customer or supplier codes and document reference number e.g. PO numbers or delivery note numbers are correct too.

- Complete all documents on time – within the sales and purchasing departments there will be deadlines that need to be met. It is highly likely that someone else within the department is relying on the completion of your work before they can complete theirs. Failure to meet deadlines will cause delays in sales invoices being sent out to the customer and therefore will delay the payment coming in from the customer. It could also create delays in payments to suppliers which could cause issues in terms of receiving stock to fulfil customer orders. This will have a negative effect of business relationships with both customers and suppliers.

- Ensure that the correct authorisation has been obtained – not having the correct authorisation before sending out documents or processing documentation can lead to errors being made within the system. Obtaining authorisation means that your work has been checked and it has been agreed with someone more senior who has the ability to make business decisions. Failure to do so could lead to incorrect information being entered into the accounts.

- An overstatement or understatement of figures within the accounting records could lead to incorrect profit or loss figures being recorded. It is imperative that this is accurate for accurate business decisions to be made. For example, if a profit figure is overstated, the director could start thinking about expansion plans for the business. If the business doesn't have the correct resource to be able to put this into place then this could lead the business to fail.

Test your understanding 1

Which ONE of the following is a likely outcome of procedures NOT being followed correctly?

Options	✓
Deadlines being met	
Greater customer satisfaction	
Increased profits	
Errors when completing documentation and/or payments	✓

---

2   Checking documents

2.1   Dealing with common errors and discrepancies

If there are errors when checking purchasing documentation, it depends on what the error is as to how it should be dealt with.

There are many different errors or discrepancies that may be found when checking documents but the main ones that you will come across on an invoice might include:

- calculation errors
- incorrect VAT calculations
- incorrect type/quantity of goods
- incorrect prices being charged for the goods.

If this is the case then the invoice should be rejected and a dispute raised with the supplier.

Another common example of discrepancies involves the goods themselves. If the goods are damaged or the incorrect goods have been delivered then the buyer will return the goods to the supplier with a goods returned note, requesting a credit note to be issued from the supplier. Upon receipt of the credit note, the buyer would need to check the goods returned note against the credit note to make sure that there are no discrepancies.

The following information should be checked:

- Do the purchase order numbers match?

- Do the details of the goods returned match, including, the quantity, price and description?

- Have the same % of discounts been applied to the credit note?

- Has the VAT been calculated correctly?

If an error or discrepancy is discovered on a credit note or goods returned note, the issue should be raised and the credit note should not be recorded or processed in the accounts.

📝 Test your understanding 2

Which of the following should be checked on documentation relating to sales and purchases to identify potential errors? (Tick ALL correct answers).

Options	✓
Purchase Order number	✓
Quantity of goods supplied	✓
Prices of goods supplied	✓
VAT calculation on goods supplied	✓
Registered charity no of supplier	
Company logo of supplier	
Discount given by supplier	✓

2.2   Case study: an example of checking documents

 Case study

Jessica has been asked to check the following documentation to see whether there are any discrepancies.

PURCHASE ORDER				

How Two Ltd.
1 Baker Street
London
WC1 8QT
Tel: 0207 3972 226

Date: 25th October 20X7
Purchase order no: P01671

To: MMC Direct 12 Saunders Street London, WC4 VCV Tel: 0207 3972 226	Delivery address (if different from above) **As above**

Product	Ref	Quantity	Price per unit (excl. VAT) £	Total (excl. VAT) £
Koduk SNS200 Printer	SNS200	10	99.99	999.99
Koduk SNS400 Printer	SNS400	15	149.99	2,249.85
Epsan EPS500 Printer	EPS500	20	109.00	2,810.00
Signed: **A Khan** Purchasing Manager				

Delivery Note:

Delivery Note		
To: How Two Ltd.		**From:** MMC Direct

To: How Two Ltd.
1 Baker Street
London
WC1 8QT

From: MMC Direct
12 Saunders Street
London
WC4 VCV

Delivery note: 2331   **Date of issue:** 30th October 20X7
Purchase order number: PO1671

Delivery Address:
12 Saunders Street
London
WC4 VCV

Delivery date: 31st October 20X7

Quantity	Code	DESCRIPTION
15	SNS201	Koduk SNS201 Printer
10	SNS400	Koduk SNS400 Printer
15	EPS500	Epsan EPS500 Printer

Received by: ....

Signature: .... Date: ....

Goods Received Note:

Good Received Note

Received From:
MMC Direct
12 Saunders Street
London
WC4 VCV

Delivery note number: 2333
Purchase order number: PO1671

Quantity	Code	DESCRIPTION
15	SNS200	Koduk SNS200 Printer
10	SNS400	Koduk SNS400 Printer
15	EPS500	Epsan EPS500 Printer

Received by: *YACOB SOLVEZ* ....

Signature: *Y. Solvez*............... Date: *31st October 20X7* ....

When checking the documents for accuracy the following errors have been identified:

- When checking the calculations of prices on the PO the total price for the Epsan EPS500 Printer is incorrect. The order states 20 @ £109.00 which equals £2,180.00. The total price on the order has been entered as £2,810. This has been signed by A Khan (Purchasing Manager) to say that it is correct.

- The incorrect quantities have been delivered.

  The PO states:

  - 10 x Koduk SNS200 Printers

  - 15 x Koduk SNS400 Printers

  - 20 x Epsan EPS500 Printers

  The delivery note states:

  - 15 x Koduk SNS201 Printers

  - 10 x Koduk SNS400 Printers

  - 15 x Epsan EPS500 Printers

- Some incorrect items have also been delivered. How Two Ltd. ordered 10 x Koduk SNS200 Printers but 15 x Koduk SNS201 Printers have been delivered.

- The supplier address has been entered as the delivery address on the delivery note. This should be the address of How Two Ltd.

- Yacob Solvez has completed a GRN even though the items delivered do not match the PO.

- Yacob has entered the delivery note number incorrectly on the GRN which will cause issues when dealing with the queries.

- On the GRN Yacob states that 15 x Koduk SNS200 Printers have been received when in actual fact it was 15 x Koduk SNS201 Printers. This is the wrong item and therefore should not be accepted. If he has signed to say that the correct item has been received this could cause issues when raising a query with the supplier.

As all of the above is incorrect, this should be referred back to the Purchasing Manager to resolve.

3 Summary and further questions

In this chapter we have looked at how invoices and credit notes should be checked in business. You should now be able to check the relevant purchasing documentation for errors and you should understand why this is important. You should know what to do if you discover any discrepancies within a place of work and how these should be dealt with.

We will return to the How Two Ltd case study to further practice checking documentation.

Case study activity 19

Jessica has been asked to review the following price list and check whether the Purchase Order has been completed correctly.

She has then been asked to check the additional documentation to see whether there are any discrepancies between the PO, delivery note and GRN.

Price List		
Item description	**Item Code**	**Price (excluding VAT)**
HT Notebook	HT477	345.00
Dall Notepad	DL90X	350.00
Tashibo Note Perfect	TNP450	295.00
Micrasaft Touch Pro	MTP225	399.00

PURCHASE ORDER

How Two Ltd.

1 Baker Street

London

WC1 8QT

Tel: 0207 890 1234

Date: 29th October 20X7
Purchase order no: P01682

To: Tech Unlimited 427 Lever Street Manchester, M1 2LF Tel: 0161 484 7711	Delivery address (if different from above) **As above**

Product	Ref	Quantity	Price per unit (excl. VAT) £	Total (excl. VAT) £
HT Notebook	HT477	5	354.00 ① _345.00_	1,770.00 _1,725.00_ ②
Micrasaft Touch Pro	MTP225	7	399.00	2,793.00
Dall Notepad	DL90X	8	350.00	2,400.00 _2,800.00_ ③

Signed:	**A Khan**
	Purchasing Manager

Delivery Note:

Delivery Note		
To: How Two Ltd. 1 Baker Street London WC1 8QT	**From:** Tech Unlimited 427 Lever Street Manchester M1 2LF	

Delivery note: 2401   **Date of issue:** 31st Oct 20X7

Purchase order number: PO1682

Delivery Address:
1 Baker Street
London
WC1 8QT

Delivery date: 1st November 20X7

Quantity	Code	DESCRIPTION
5 (4)	HT478 7	HT Notebook
8 7 (5)	MTP225	Micrasaft Touch Pro
7 8 (6)	DL90X	Dall Notepad

Received by: ....

Signature: ....   Date: ....

Goods Received Note:

Good Received Note		
Received From: MMC Direct 12 Saunders Street London WC4 VCV	TECH UNLIMITED 427 LEVER STREET (x) MANCHESTER M1 2LF (1)	

Delivery note number: 2401

Purchase order number: PO1682

Quantity	Code	DESCRIPTION
5	HT477	HT Notebook
7	MTP225	Micrasaft Touch Pro
8	DL90X	Dall Notepad

Received by: *YACOB SOLVEZ* ....

Signature: *Y. Solvez*...............   Date: *31st October 2017*

Case study activity 20

Jessica has been asked to review the following goods returned note and check whether the credit note has been completed correctly.

Good Returned Note			
MMC Direct 12 Saunders Street London WC4 VCV VAT Number: 231 7787 543		**To: How Two Ltd.** 1 Baker Street London WC1 8QT	

Goods returned note number: 1023
Purchase order number: PO193

Date: 31st October 2017

Quantity	Code	DESCRIPTION	£
1	HT477	HT Notebook	225.00
2	MTP225	Micrasaft Touch Pro	500.00
1	DL90X	Dall Notepad	200.00

Received by: *YACOB SOLVEZ*...

Signature: *Y. Solvez*................. Date: *31st October 2017*..........

Credit Note			
How Two Ltd. 1 Baker Street London WC1 8QT		MMC Direct 12 Saunders Street London WC4 VCV	

Date: 5th November 2017
Credit note number: CN440
Purchase order number: PO182 / *PO193*

Quantity	Code	DESCRIPTION	£
1 *HT477* HP499		HP Notebook	225.00
✗ 2	MTP225	Micrasaft Touch Pro	⟨500.00⟩
1	DL90X	Dall Notepad	200.00
		Net	925.00
		VAT	~~155.00~~ *185.00*
		Total	~~1,080.00~~ *1,110.00*

Answers to chapter activities

Test your understanding 1

Options	✓
Deadlines being met	
Greater customer satisfaction	
Increased profits	
Errors when completing documentation and/or payments	✓

Test your understanding 2

Options	✓
Purchase Order number	✓
Quantity of goods supplied	✓
Prices of goods supplied	✓
VAT calculation on goods supplied	✓
Registered charity no of supplier	
Company logo of supplier	
Discount given by supplier	✓

Case study activity 19

The following errors and discrepancies can be identified:

- The HT Notebook has been priced at £354 on the purchase order instead of £345.

- The total of the HT Notebooks should be £1,725 if the correct price of £345 had been stated however £1,770 has been entered on the PO.

- The total of the Dall notepads should be £2,800 but £2,400 has been entered on the PO.

- The incorrect product code has been entered on the delivery note for the HT Notebook.

- The incorrect quantities have been entered on the delivery note for the Micrasaft Touch Pro and the Dall Notepad, 7 Micrasaft Touch Pros had been ordered but the delivery note states 8 have been delivered and 8 Dall Notepads had been ordered but the delivery note states that 7 have been delivered.

- The goods received note matches the purchase order but due to the discrepancies on the delivery note this does not match the goods received note.

 Case study activity 20

The following errors and discrepancies can be identified:

- The incorrect purchase order number has been stated on the credit note

- The incorrect product code has been stated on the credit note for the HP Notebook, this should be HT477 not HP499

- The goods returned note states that 2 Micrasaft Touch Pros have been returned but only one has been credited

- 2 Micrasaft Touch Pros have been returned which in total come to £500. Only 1 has been entered on the credit note but the price state is still £500

- The VAT has been calculated on the credit note. It should be £185 not £155.

- The total of the credit note is incorrect, this should be £1,110 not £1,080.

Books of prime entry

5

Introduction

In the previous chapter you looked at the documents that are used in cash and credit transactions. These documents now need to be summarised in **books of prime entry**. As the documents are recorded regularly, these books are also known as **day books.**

We will look at how these are created and which documents are required. Having done so, we will also establish how these records can also be used to identify the amounts owed to the business by individual customers, and in turn, the amount they have outstanding to their suppliers.

KNOWLEDGE	CONTENTS
Process customer and supplier transactions	1 Documents used to record transactions with customers
3.4 Record sales and purchase invoices and credit notes in the books of prime entry	2 Documents used to record transactions with suppliers
3.4 Identify outstanding amounts for individual customers and suppliers	3 Calculating opening and closing balances for credit accounts
	4 Summary and further questions

1 Documents used to record transactions with customers

1.1 Introduction: case study and overview

 Case study

Having looked at the documents used in cash and credit transactions, Jessica has gained a greater awareness of how important accuracy is when dealing with business documentation and also the need to check them carefully to ensure that there are no errors.

Extremely happy with Jessica's progress, her manager now feels that she is competent to accomplish bookkeeping tasks and is ready to move on to the next stage. To do so, Jessica now needs to learn how to summarise the documents she has encountered into the books of prime entry, also known as day books.

Her manager provides her with an overview of the different day books she needs to learn to use to record transactions with customers (below).

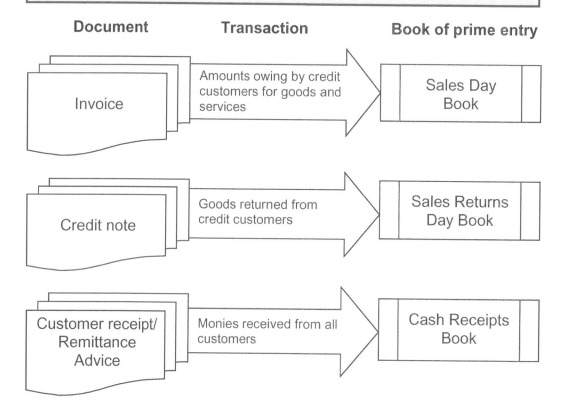

Document	Transaction	Book of prime entry
Invoice	Amounts owing by credit customers for goods and services	Sales Day Book
Credit note	Goods returned from credit customers	Sales Returns Day Book
Customer receipt/ Remittance Advice	Monies received from all customers	Cash Receipts Book

1.2 The sales day book (SDB)

The sales day book records individual invoices issued to credit customers within one day, week or month. It is basically a list which is totalled at the end of the specified period to indicate how much a company has made in sales, how much VAT they owe to HMRC in respect of those sales and how much they are owed in total by their customers. It will then be used to perform double entry bookkeeping, which you will learn about in the AAT Foundation Certificate.

Example

SALES DAY BOOK

Date	Customer	Reference	Invoice number	Total £	VAT £	Sales £
1 July	Althams Ltd	ALT01	45787	120.00	20.00	100.00
2 July	Broadhurst plc	BRO02	45788	240.00	40.00	200.00
			TOTALS	360.00	60.00	300.00

Notes

- The reference number is the code number of the customer's account in the sales ledger this information can be found on the invoice.
- The invoice number is the number of the invoice issued for each sale.
- The Sales column is the total value of the goods sold as shown on the invoice after deducting trade discount, i.e. net of VAT.
- The amount of VAT is recorded in a separate column to show the amount owing to HMRC for these invoices.
- The Total column shows the total amount due from credit customers (Receivables).

Example

Farley's AV Supplies sell a variety of audio visual products for both business customers and online for the general public.

On 3rd January, they have recorded two trade sales to customers on account.

Invoice number 365 to JBU Wines is made up as follows:

	£
Sale of 20 AV lead packs at £5 per unit	100.00
Less: 20% trade discount	(20.00)
	80.00
VAT (£80 × 20%)	16.00
Total invoice value	96.00

Invoice number 366 to Stop-it Holidays is made up as follows:

	£
Sale of 5 headphone & charger sets at £30 per unit	150.00
Less: 10% trade discount	(15.00)
	135.00
VAT (£135.00 × 20%)	27.00
Total invoice value	162.00

Farley AV Supplies' sales day book would therefore look like this:

Date	Customer	Reference	Invoice number	Total £	VAT £	Sales £
3/1	JBU Wines	JBU1708	365	96.00	16.00	80.00
3/1	Stop-it Holidays	STO1999	366	162.00	27.00	135.00
			TOTALS	**258.00**	**43.00**	**215.00**

1.3 The sales returns day book = *credit notes*

Credit notes, also known as sales returns, are usually entered in a 'sales returns day book'.

This is similar to the sales day book, and the columns are used in the same way. The only difference is that instead of having a column for the invoice number, there is a column for the 'credit note number'. This is because when the goods are returned by customers a credit note is issued.

💡 Example

Farley's AV Supplies receive two returns from customers in the first week of May.

Credit note number 072 for Pilgrim Sports and Leisure on 1st May is made up as follows:

	£
Return of 2 faulty television stands at £55 each	110.00
VAT (£110 × 20%)	22.00
Total credit note value	132.00

Credit note number 073 for Crabtree's Circus on 3rd May is made up as follows:

	£
Return of 4 large venue speakers at £195 each	780.00
VAT (£780 × 20%)	156.00
Total credit note value	936.00

Farley AV Supplies' sales returns day book would therefore look like this:

SALES RETURNS DAY BOOK

Date	Customer	Reference	Credit note number	Total £	VAT £	Sales returns £
1/5	Pilgrim Sports and Leisure	PSLR04	072	132.00	22.00	110.00
3/5	Crabtree's Circus	CCR05	073	936.00	156.00	780.00
			TOTALS	**1,068.00**	**178.00**	**890.00**

In some businesses the level of sales returns are fairly low and therefore it is not justified to keep a separate sales returns day book. In these cases any credit notes that are issued for sales returns are recorded as negative amounts in the sales day book.

For the purpose of this assessment, a sales returns day book will be used to record credit note transactions.

2 Documents used to record transactions with suppliers

2.1 Introduction: case study and overview

📖 **Case study**

As Jessica has understood the different day books used for customer transactions, her manager now provides an overview of those to record transactions with suppliers (below).

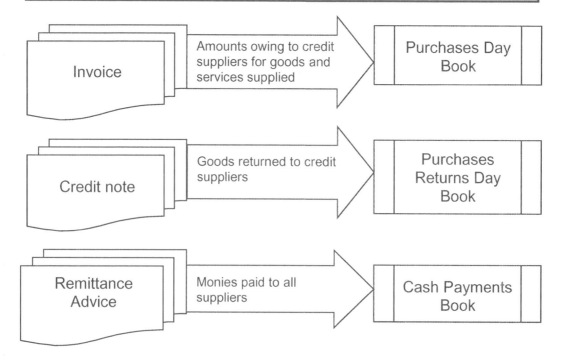

2.2 The purchases day book

As seen earlier in the chapter, credit sales are recorded in the 'sales day book'. In the case of credit purchases, we have the 'purchases day book'.

The purchases day book is simply a list of the purchases invoices that are to be processed for a given period (e.g. a week).

In its simplest form, the purchases day book will comprise just the names of the suppliers and the amount of the invoices received in the week.

Example

PURCHASES DAY BOOK

Date	Supplier	Reference	Invoice number	Total £	VAT £	Purchases £
1 Sept 17	W E L Ltd	Q73243	56712	1,800	300	1,500
3 Sept 17	Vivalitee plc	L73244	AV942	402	67	335
			TOTALS	2,202	367	1,835

Purchases returns are entered in a 'purchases returns day book'. This looks similar to the purchases day book, and the columns are used in the same way. The only difference is that instead of having a column for the invoice number, there is a column for the 'credit note number'. This is because when the goods are sent back the business will receive a credit note from the supplier.

Example

PURCHASES RETURNS DAY BOOK

Date	Supplier	Reference	Credit note number	Total £	VAT £	Purchases returns £
1 Sept 17	Lazza & Co	RET732	AR678	360	60	300
4 Sept 17	BFBC	RET733	09132	222	37	185
			TOTALS	582	97	485

In some businesses the level of purchases returns are fairly low and therefore it is not necessary to keep a separate purchases returns day book.

In these cases any credit notes that are received for purchases returns are recorded as negative amounts in the purchases day book.

Example

You work in the accounts department of R Porte Manufacturing Ltd and one of your tasks is to sort the documents before they are entered in to the correct books of prime entry.

From the following documents, identify which book of prime entry it should be recorded in.

Document 1

R Moore Fashions

12 Dutch Corner
High Wycombe
HG4 7NQ

Invoice no: 005673
Tax point:14 July 2018

INVOICE

**To: R Porte Manufacturing Ltd
    5 Ventoux Crescent, Cardiff, CA2 3HU**

Product	Quantity	Price per unit	Total
		£	£
Cargo pants	5	25.00	125.00
T-shirts	10	15.00	150.00
			275.00
		VAT 20%	55.00
		Total	330.00
Payment terms: 30 days net			

Answer: You are dealing with documents for R Porte Manufacturing.

This invoice is sent **to** you at R Porte Manufacturing, so you have received it from R Moore Fashions, who must be the supplier.

Therefore, this is a supplier invoice and should be entered into the **purchases day book.**

The entry would appear as follows:

Date	Supplier	Reference	Invoice number	Total £	VAT £	Purchases £
14 July 18	R Moore Fashions	MORS78	005673	330	55	275
			TOTALS	330	55	275

Document 2

R Porte Manufacturing Ltd

5 Ventoux Crescent

Cardiff

CA2 3HU

Credit Note no: 05876

Tax point: 16 July 2018

CREDIT NOTE

To: Birnies Biscuits
 Elysee Avenue, Mitcham, MA3 6ZT

Product	Quantity	Price per unit (£)	Total (£)
Packing cases	4	5.00	20.00
		VAT 20%	4.00
		Total	24.00

Payment terms: 30 days net

Answer: Remember, you are dealing with documents for R Porte Manufacturing.

This credit note is sent **to** Birnies Biscuits, so they must be the customer.

Therefore, this is a customer credit note and should be entered into the **sales returns day book.**

The entry would appear as follows:

Date	Customer	Reference	Credit note no	Total £	VAT £	Sales return £
16 July 18	Birnies Biscuits	BIR732	05876	24.00	4.00	20.00
			TOTALS	**24.00**	**4.00**	**20.00**

Test your understanding 1

Jessica has been asked to match the following documents to the relevant book of prime entry.

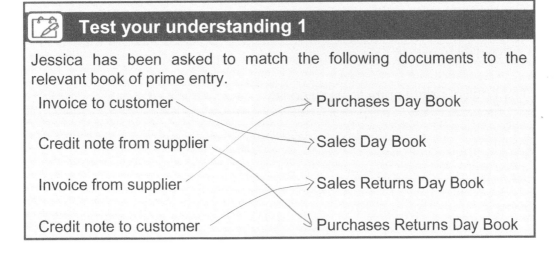

Invoice to customer → Purchases Day Book

Credit note from supplier → Sales Day Book

Invoice from supplier → Sales Returns Day Book

Credit note to customer → Purchases Returns Day Book

Test your understanding 2

Fill in the gaps below to complete the sentences. Choose from the Pick list provided.

The _Sales day book_ is used to record invoices to customers.

The _Sales return day book_ is used to record credit notes to customers.

The _Purchaser day book_ is used to record invoices from suppliers.

The _Purchases returns day book_ is used to record credit notes from suppliers.

Pick List

Sales returns day book	Sales day book
Purchases day book	Purchases returns day book

 Test your understanding 3

You work in the accounts department of Armistead & Co and one of your tasks is to sort the documents before they are entered in to the books of prime entry.

Armistead & Co	
Ryan's Close Lower Meltham MT4 3SQ	Invoice no: 59870 Tax point: 1 July 2016

INVOICE

To: **Pendleton Prisms**
   Stuart Street, Bristol, BR1 JQ8

Product	Quantity	Price per unit	Total
Anti-rust bike chain	100	£3.99	£399.00
Chainset and cable kit	5	£25.00	£125.00
			£524.00
		VAT 20%	£104.80
		Total	**£628.80**
Payment terms: 15 days net			

The book of prime entry to be used is: _Sales day book_

🔍 Test your understanding 4

You work in the accounts department of Foe & Co and one of your tasks is to sort the documents before they are entered in to the books of prime entry.

Foe & Co	
Middlebrow	Invoice no: 598
MI4 3SQ	Tax point: 18 July 20X6

Credit Note

To: Fi and Fun
   Rose Avenue, Cardiff, CT1 JQ8

Product	Quantity	Price per unit	Total
KBM15	1	£35.99	£35.99
		VAT 20%	£7.19
		Total	**£43.18**

Payment terms: 15 days net

Which daybook should this document be entered in? *sales returns day book.*

---

3 Calculating opening and closing balances

3.1 Calculating amounts owed by credit customers

You should now know that when providing goods/services to credit customers there will be monies due to the organisation. This chapter has looked at how the amounts due from sales invoices are recorded in the sales day book. When a customer returns goods to the organisation, credit notes are recorded in the sales returns day book.

Customers will pay amounts due on a regular basis, this will depend on the credit terms agreed i.e., 10 days, 14 days, 30 days etc. Cash flow is important to the successful operation of an organisation, therefore it is important that individual customer records are monitored closely and any amounts due are paid on time. If a credit customer does not pay their outstanding account balances, the organisation will chase them for any amounts due.

Example

L Riley & Co are a credit customer of How Two Ltd.

At the beginning of July, they had an opening balance of amounts due of £432.59. They have since been issued with additional invoices amounting to £751.23.

Upon receipt of their last order, some of the items were damaged and returned to How Two Ltd. A credit note for £126.88 was issued to L Riley & Co.

During July, L Riley & Co paid £350.00 to How Two Ltd via a Faster Payment which was received into the bank account. How Two Ltd received a remittance advice from L Riley & Co to accompany this payment.

To calculate the amount due to How Two Ltd at the end of July, the following calculation would be performed:

Opening balance	£432.59
Plus Invoices due	£751.23
Less Credit notes issued	(£126.88)
Less Payment/remittance received	(£350.00)
Amount owed at the end of July	£706.94

3.2 Calculating amounts due to credit suppliers

Calculating amounts due to credit suppliers is the same process as with calculating amounts owed from credit customers. This chapter has looked at how the amounts due to received suppliers are recorded from invoices received. It is essential that the relevant documentation is checked for accuracy before any payments are made, otherwise the business may pay for goods that have never been received. You should now know that purchase invoices are recorded in the purchases day book and credit notes received are recorded in the purchases returns day book.

Payments will be made to credit suppliers on a regular basis, again this will depend on the credit terms agreed i.e., 10 days, 14 days, 30 days etc. As mentioned previously, cash flow is important to the successful operation of an organisation, you do not want to pay invoices too soon as there may not be enough cash available to pay everything at once, therefore it is beneficial to make the most of the credit terms available.

Most businesses will prepare payment to suppliers on a weekly basis, others may do it fortnightly or monthly. Timescales and processes for doing this will differ slightly dependant on the organisation you work for, but the principles remain the same.

Example

How Two Ltd have 30 day credit terms with Inked Up Ltd. At the beginning of July, they had an opening balance of amounts owing of £326.89.

How Two Ltd have since received additional invoices amounting to £525.11, these were checked against the relevant documentation and it was discovered that an incorrect batch of ink was received amounting to £98.50.

Inked Up Ltd investigated this and issued a credit note to How Two Ltd for these goods.

To calculate the amount owing to Inked Up Ltd. at the end of July, the following calculation would be performed:

Opening balance	£326.89
Plus Invoices due	£525.11
Less Credit notes issued	(£ 98.50)
Amount owed at the end of July	£753.50

At the end of July, a payment was made to Inked Up Ltd. to clear the amount outstanding at the beginning of the month. The payment was made by debit card for £326.89.

The amount due at the end of July would be £753.50 - £326.89 = £426.61

The payment made to Inked Up Ltd. would be a **bank payment** and would be entered into the **payments** side of the **cash book.**

 Test your understanding 5

JBU Wines has the following information related to one of its credit customers for April:

	Amount £
Opening balance	1,287.64
Invoice 2410	541.22
Credit note 376	220.99
Invoice 2489	421.75
Amount from cash receipts listing	787.64
Credit note 410	125.20

Complete the table below to show the amount owing from JBU Wines at the end of April. Show any negative amounts using a minus sign or brackets.

	£
Opening Balance	1,287.64
Total of invoices	962.97
Total of credit notes	(346.19)
Cash receipts	+ (787.64)
Closing balance	1,116.78

📝 Test your understanding 6

JBU Wines has the following information related to one of its credit suppliers Bee Happy Ltd for April:

	Amount £
Opening balance	822.45
Invoice 789Y	264.78
Invoice 1023X	455.87
Amount from cash payments listings	522.45
Invoice 1114Y	198.79
Credit note 99	89.87

Complete the table below to show the amount owing to Bee Happy Ltd at the end of April. Show any negative amounts using a minus sign or brackets.

	£
Opening Balance	822.45
Total of invoices	919.44
Total of credit notes	(89.87)
Cash payments	− (522.45)
Closing balance	1,129.57

4 Summary and further questions

In this chapter you learnt about the different day books used to keep of a record of the documents used in accounting transactions.

You should now understand which day books should be used for different transactions in the sales and purchasing processes. We have also detailed how to calculate opening and closing balances for suppliers and customers.

Let us now return to the How Two Ltd case study to apply this knowledge in context.

 Case study activity 21

Jessica has been asked to enter the invoice below into the sales day book.

How Two Ltd	
1 Baker Street London WC1 8QT	Invoice no: 5698 Tax point: 26 Nov 2017

INVOICE

To: G Thomas (A/C Ref TH02)
5 Holland Crescent, Chesham CA2 3HU

Product	Quantity	Price per unit	Total
Goods (Deluxe Laptop Case)	5	£50.12	£250.60
		VAT 20%	£50.12
		Total	£300.72
Payment terms: 30 days net			

Complete the Sales Day Book below with the correct information:

_Date	Customer	Reference	Invoice No	Total £	VAT £	Net £
26/11/17	G. Thomas	TH 02	5698	300.72	50.12	250.60

Case study activity 22

Jessica works for How Two Ltd. Given the document below, which day book should Jessica enter this document into?

King & Co

Highbrow
HI4 3SQ

Invoice no: 2867
Tax point: 18 June 20X6

Invoice

To: How Two Ltd
   1 Baker Street, London WC1 8QT

Product	Quantity	Price per unit	Total
Item 5	10	£35.50	£355.00
		VAT 20%	£71.00
		Total	£426.00
Payment terms: 15 days net			

Purchases day book

 Case study activity 23

Jessica needs to sort the documents received by How Two Ltd this week before they are entered in to the correct books of prime entry.

Which book of prime entry should be used for the following document?

Drake Kelleher Manufacturing

Unit 4 Appletree Industrial Estate
Merthyr Tydfil
CA99 9ZZ

Credit Note no:
05876
Tax point: 16 July
2016

CREDIT NOTE

To: How Two Ltd
   1 Baker Street, London WC1 8QT

Product	Quantity	Price per unit (£)	Total (£)
Packing cases	4	5.00	20.00
		VAT 20%	4.00
		Total	24.00
Payment terms: 30 days net			

Purchases returns day book.

Answers to chapter activities

 Test your understanding 1

Invoice to customer	=	Sales Day Book
Credit note from supplier	=	Purchase Returns Day Book
Invoice from supplier	=	Purchases Day Book
Credit note to customer	=	Sales Returns Day Book

 Test your understanding 2

The **Sales day book** is used to record invoices to customers.

The **Sales returns day book** is used to record credit notes to customers.

The **Purchases day book** is used to record invoices from suppliers.

The **Purchases returns day book** is used to record credit notes from suppliers.

 Test your understanding 3

You are dealing with documents for Armistead & Co. This invoice is **to** Pendleton Prisms, so they must be the customer.

Therefore, this is a customer invoice and should be entered into the sales day book.

 Test your understanding 4

You are dealing with documents for Foe & Co. This credit note is **to** Fi and Fun, so they must be the customer.

Therefore, this is a credit note sent to a customer and should be entered into the sales returns day book.

Test your understanding 5

	£
Opening Balance	1,287.64
Total of invoices	962.97
Total of credit notes	(346.19)
Cash receipts	(787.64)
Closing balance	1,116.78

Test your understanding 6

	£
Opening Balance	822.45
Total of invoices	919.44
Total of credit notes	(89.87)
Cash payments	(522.45)
Closing balance	1,129.57

Case study activity 21

Date	Customer	Reference	Invoice No	Total £	VAT £	Net £
26 Nov 2017	G Thomas	TH02	5698	300.72	50.12	250.60

 Case study activity 22

This invoice is sent from King and Co who must be the supplier of the goods. Therefore, this is an invoice received by How Two Ltd from a supplier and should be entered into the **purchases day book.**

 Case study activity 23

Jessica is dealing with documents for How Two Ltd. This credit note is **from** Drake Kelleher Manufacturing, so they must be the supplier.

Therefore, this is a supplier credit note and should be entered in the **purchases returns day book.**

Processing receipts and payments

Introduction

Having looked at how sales and purchase invoices are entered into books of prime entry in the previous chapter, we will now look at how receipts and payments are recorded, in the cash book.

This chapter covers the different types of payment which can be received and the types of documents which can be used to record them. We will look at the management of cash in hand and how batch control can be used to simplify processing.

KNOWLEDGE	CONTENTS
Process receipts and payments	1 Receipts and payments
4.1 Enter receipts and payments into a cash book	2 The cash book
	3 The petty cash book
4.2 Use the cash book to calculate closing amounts of cash in hand and cash in the bank	4 Batch control
	5 Calculating opening and closing balances
4.4 Identify outstanding amounts for individual customers and suppliers	6 Summary and further questions

1 Receipts and payments

1.1 Case study: an introduction

 Case study

Jessica has a good knowledge of business documents and the books of prime entry used to record them.

As she has now taken on the role of junior bookkeeper, she now needs to also understand more about the payments the business both makes and receives, and in particular how cash is handled.

She has been asked to help with the petty cash book and look at some cheques which have been received, as a way of seeing how these processes work.

Her manager has also said that Jessica can help her to complete the Cash Book, although Jessica is currently unaware of the format it takes.

1.2 Cash receipts and payments

There are many different ways a business can make and receive payments. A lot of businesses make electronic payments; however, many customers still pay in cash or by writing a cheque. When physical payments are received by an organisation, the monies will need to be paid into the business's bank account.

In a cash sale or purchase, the transaction is much simpler. The customer will probably place an order verbally and payment is always made as soon as the customer receives the goods or services. Payment for cash sales or purchases are usually made by cash, credit or debit card.

The customer will need a copy of the sales receipt in case they need to return them to the supplier.

 Definition

Monies – A term used to describe all types of payments and receipts including cash, cheques and direct bank transfers.

1.3 Paying-in slips

All business organisations are provided with a paying-in book by the bank. Each paying-in book contains paying-in slips. When money is received from customers in cash or by cheque, it is paid into the bank and is accompanied by one of the completed paying-in slips.

If your job is to pay money into the bank, you will need to complete and sign the bank paying-in slip taken from the paying-in book. The paying-in slip is then given to the bank cashier who will check it against the monies being paid in to the bank.

You only need to enter the number of cheques being paid in and the total amount on the front of the paying in slip. On the back of the paying in slip you should write a list of the cheques being paid in.

The paying-in stub is the part of the paying-in slip which stays in the paying-in book and is a record for the organisation of the amounts paid into the bank. Sometimes a business may keep a separate list of monies received so that they can cross reference it the bank statement to ensure the correct amount has been paid in, or with the paying in slip should issues arise further on down the line.

1.4 Example of a paying-in slip

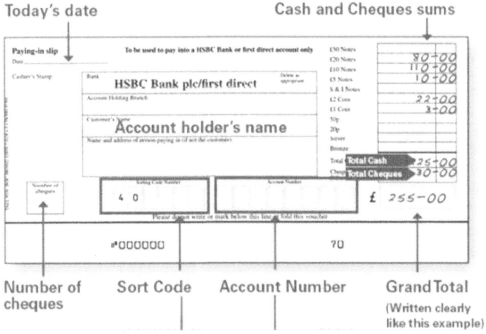

(Source: www.hsbc.co.uk)

Test your understanding 1

Today's date is 19 November 2017.

Jessica has been asked to complete a bank paying-in slip for the money received today, which is as follows:

Notes	Coins	Cheques
3 x £20 notes	25 x £1 coins	Thomas £1,500.00
15 x £10 notes	8 x 50p coins	Friebe £ 750.00
20 x £5 notes	20 x 10p coins	

Complete the paying-in slip below:

Date: 19 November 2017	ABC Bank plc Manchester	£50 notes	–
		£20 notes	60 .00
		£10 notes	150 .00
	Account How Two Ltd	£5 notes	100 .00
		£2 coin	–
		£1 coin	25 .00
No of cheques 2	Paid in by *Jessica Howard*	Other coin	6 .00
		Total cash	341 .00
	Sort Code Account No	Cheques	2,250 .00
	25-22-78 30087251	Total £	2,591 .00

 Test your understanding 2

When Jessica asked her manager to check over the paying in slip to ensure that she had completed it correctly before taking it to the bank, she was asked why it is important that the paying-in slip is signed and dated.

What would Jessica's response have been? *Bank can contact the person who made the payment in case there are any queries.*

1.5   The use of cheques

When a person (or organisation) writes a cheque they are instructing their bank to transfer a specified amount of money from their bank account to the bank account of the recipient of the cheque – the payee.

If the cheque hasn't been completed correctly the bank may return it to the payee. The payee will then have to ask for a replacement cheque from the organisation.

As this causes delays in the payment process, it is important that the cheque is completed correctly in the first place.

1.6 Cheque requirements

For a cheque to be valid it should include:

- **Payee name** The payee is the person or organisation to whom the cheque is written. The payee's name should exactly match the name on their bank account.

- **Date** The date that the cheque is written must include the day, month and the year. A cheque that is more than 6 months old is invalid and the bank will not accept the cheque.

- **Words** The pounds part of the amount being paid must be written in words but the pence part can be written in numbers. If the amount is a whole number of pounds then you should write 'ONLY' after the amount to prevent someone changing the figure.

- **Numbers** The amount being paid should be written in numbers in the box on the right hand side of the cheque. The amount in numbers should exactly match the amount written in words.

- **Signature** The cheque should be signed by an authorised signatory of the organisation.

🔍 Definition

Signatories – a person or persons who are authorised to sign cheques on behalf of an organisation.

💡 Example

ABC Bank PLC	Date: 30th January 20X7
Payee: *Mr John Smith*	
	£350.00
Three hundred and fifty pounds only	MISS ANNE JONES

CHEQUE NO	SORT CODE	ACCOUNT NO
00017	32-32-68	5552222

Test your understanding 3

Today's date is 29th November 2017 and Jessica has been given the following cheques to complete.

Fill in the gaps using the correct numbers, words and/or date.

Cheque A

ABC Bank PLC	Date: 29th November, 2017
Payee: *NB Solutions Ltd*	
	500.00
Five hundred pounds ONLY	on behalf of How Two Ltd
	J Howard

CHEQUE NO	SORT CODE	ACCOUNT NO
04312	25-22-78	30087251

Cheque B

ABC Bank PLC	Date: 29th November, 2017
Payee: *Armistead & Co*	
	£ 250.50
TWO HUNDRED AND FIFTY POUNDS AND 50p	on behalf of How Two Ltd
	J Howard

CHEQUE NO	SORT CODE	ACCOUNT NO
04313	25-22-78	30087251

Cheque C

ABC Bank PLC	Date: 29th NOVEMBER, 2017
Payee: *Mr P Sagan*	
	£ 25.20
Twenty five pounds and 20p ~~only~~	on behalf of How Two Ltd
	J Howard

CHEQUE NO	SORT CODE	ACCOUNT NO
04314	25-22-78	30087251

Test your understanding 4

Cheques can be signed by anyone in an organisation. True or False?

1.7 Cheque stubs

When cheques are paid out, the person who writes the cheque will fill in the cheque book stub. This contains details of the date the cheque was written out, who the cheque was sent to and the amount paid.

The bookkeeper uses the cheque book stub to update the accounting records, to show the payments made.

They will then cross reference the cheque number to the bank statement to ensure the correct amount of money has been paid out of the bank. This will be covered in more detail in the next chapter.

1.8 Direct debits and standing orders

A **direct debit** is an electronic payment set up by you. You instruct your bank or building society to allow a third party to take money from your bank account at a specified time.

The amounts paid could vary in amount but you will have been informed of how much this will be and when the money will be taken, by the company you are making payment to.

An example of this might be when you are paying your gas or electric bill. The total of the bill will vary from month on month depending on how much gas and electric you use; however, you will have been sent the bill in advance of the money being taken from your bank and this will advise you of the date on which the money will be taken.

A **standing order** is where you set up a regular automated payment to be taken from your bank at a specified time in the month e.g. the 1st of every month. With a standing order, the amounts to be paid are fixed for a certain amount of time. An example of this might be when you are paying your rent. Payments of rent will be the same amount to be paid at the same time each month, in this case, a standing order would be the most suitable method of payment. Standing orders can be amended or cancelled at any time.

Usually, a business will have a direct debit or standing order schedule set up which is basically list of payments that they are expecting to go out of their bank account. This helps them to cross reference payments on their bank statement to ensure the correct ones have been made.

Bankers Automated Clearing Systems

1.9 BACS and faster payments

A **BACS** payment is an automated system that is used to make payment from one bank to another. They are mainly used for direct debits so once you have given permission for an organisation to take payment from your bank account, they will usually do this via the BACS system. A BACS payment takes 3 days to clear in a bank account so if payment was made on Monday, it wouldn't appear in the recipient's bank until Wednesday.

A **faster payment** is an electronic payment that can be made online via internet banking or over the phone. A faster payment is usually made within two hours of making the payment meaning that the money will clear in the recipient's bank account the same day. Both banks have to be part of the faster payments service for this method of payment to be an option however nowadays this is a common service used by businesses to make quick payments to suppliers of goods or services.

Bank Statements are sent from the bank in paper format or can be downloaded from the online banking system. Bank statements show the monies paid in or out of the business bank account and can be used to identify transactions that have not been processed in the accounting software.

As a bookkeeper, it is important that an amount showing on the bank statement that has not been recorded in the accounting software are fully investigated and evidence of the transaction is located to ensure there is an audit trail. For example, a director may have paid for a meal out with a client using the business debit card but may not have provided a receipt for the transaction. The bookkeeper has a duty to investigate this and locate a copy of the receipt for the accounting records before processing the transaction on the system. Bank statements will be covered in more detail in a later chapter.

Automatic Bank Feeds are where the accounting software is directly linked to the business bank account. The technology surrounding automatic bank feeds allows the software to automatically allocate amounts to the relevant accounting records within the system. These are then reviewed and agreed to ensure the information has been transferred accurately.

Automating large proportions of manual bookkeeping transactions, saves time manually entering transactions which helps to increase efficiency and productivity. It also helps reduce the risk of human error and in turn increases the accuracy of financial data.

Chaps – Clearing house automated Payment System. (Related to FP) earlier than CHAPS

Test your understanding 5

Match the definitions with the correct words used in banking

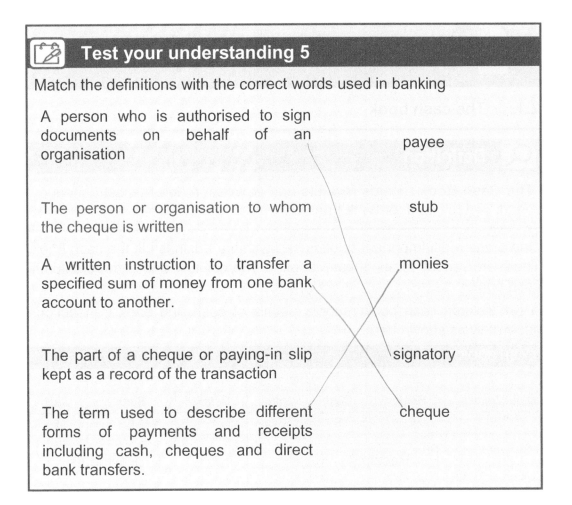

A person who is authorised to sign documents on behalf of an organisation	payee
The person or organisation to whom the cheque is written	stub
A written instruction to transfer a specified sum of money from one bank account to another.	monies
The part of a cheque or paying-in slip kept as a record of the transaction	signatory
The term used to describe different forms of payments and receipts including cash, cheques and direct bank transfers.	cheque

2 The cash book

2.1 The cash book

> ### 🔍 Definition
>
> **The Cash Book** records receipts and payment made by cash, cheque, credit or debit card, or bank transfer.

One of the most important books used within a business is the cash book. There are various forms of cash book, a 'two column' and a 'three column' cash book.

A two column cash book records details of cash and bank transactions separately as shown here:

CASH BOOK							
Date	Details	Bank	Cash	Date	Details	Bank	Cash
		£	£			£	£
		Receipts				Payments	

Notes

- The left hand side of the cash book represents the debit side – money received. Often the paying in slips, remittance advices received from customer and lists of receipts will be used to update this side of the cash book.

- The right hand side of the cash book represents the credit side – money paid out. Often the list of payments, direct debit/standing order schedules and cheque book stubs are used to update this side of the cash book.

- In practice, there is usually a column on both the debit and the credit side for the date.

- The details column describes the transactions – typically the name of the customer or supplier.

- The bank column on the debit side represents money received (by cheque or other bank payment) whereas the bank column on the credit side represents money paid (by cheque or other bank payment).

- The cash column on the debit side represents cash received whereas the cash column on the credit side represents cash paid out in respect of purchases or other expenses.

Some organisations keep separate cash books to record receipts and payments. These are known as the cash receipts book and cash payments book, respectively.

 Test your understanding 6

Alba works in the accounts department at NB Solutions Ltd. She has been asked to complete a two column cash book by recording transactions from today.

For each of the following, indicate whether they should be on the left or right hand side of the Cash Book.

	Left / right
Money received	LEFT
Money paid out	RIGHT
Credit	RIGHT
Debit	LEFT
£220 cash to pay for catering at NB Solutions event	RIGHT
Bank transfer from a one-off customer for £150	LEFT
Cheque from Miss B Craven for £232	LEFT
Cheque payable to How Two Ltd for £459	RIGHT

2.2 The cash receipts book

Example

CASH RECEIPTS BOOK

Date	Details	Bank	VAT	Sales	Receivables	Bank Interest Received
		£	£	£	£	£
20/11	ABC Ltd.	1,350			1,350	
20/11	Cash Sale	660	110	550		
21/11	Interest	50				50
	Totals	**2,060**	**110**	**550**	**1,350**	**50**

In the example above, you can see that the company have used analysis columns to analyse the receipts so that they know what they represent. Most companies would do this in order to make it easier to perform the double-entry bookkeeping into the general ledger accounts. As mentioned previously, you will learn about this in the AAT Level 2 qualification.

It is important to cross-cast your total figures at the bottom to ensure that what you have entered into the cash book is accurate.

 Example

Using the previous example:

110 + 550 + 1,350 + 50 = 2,060

You can see from this example that by adding up the totals of the analysis columns, you can be confident that you have accurately recorded money received into the cash book.

Cross-casting helps to ensure that the figures being transferred into the accounts are accurate and free from misstatement. This contributes to the accurate calculation of the company's profit or loss figure.

Incorrect entries being recorded in any of the day books can lead to false information being reported to management.

For example, if you don't cross-cast your total figures in the sales day book to make sure that the total of the net and VAT columns equal the total of the receivables column, then the incorrect figures would be transferred to the accounts in the ledgers.

Not only would this mean wasting time trying to trace the figure before being able to correct it, there is also a danger that errors could go unnoticed.

If this was to happen, the sales figures within the management reports could be wrong. Management might think that the sales figures were down and could try to solve the issue, when in actual fact there was no issue in the first place. This is inefficient working and could result in loss of earnings for the company.

2.3   The cash payments book

Example

CASH PAYMENTS BOOK

Date	Details	Bank	VAT	Stationery	Payables
		£	£	£	£
20/11	Lazza & Co	1,050			1,050
20/11	Stationery	420	70	350	
21/11	BNM	800			800
	Totals	**2,270**	**70**	**350**	**1,850**

The cash payments book works in exactly the same way as the cash receipts book, the only difference is that it is recording the monies paid out of the business.

Again, analysis columns may be used to analyse the expenditure to save time when posting the double-entry to the general ledger.

Example

Using the previous example, cross casting to check for accuracy:

70 + 350 + 1,850 = 2,270

Test your understanding 7

Fill in the gaps below to complete the sentences. Choose from the Pick list provided.

The _Cash receipts book_ is used to record monies received from customers.

The _Cash payment book_ is used to record monies paid to suppliers.

Pick List

Cash receipts book	Sales day book
Cash payments book	Sales returns day book

3 The petty cash book

3.1 What is petty cash?

> ### 🔍 Definition
>
> **Petty cash** is the small amount of cash that most businesses hold in order to make small cash payments, such as payment for coffee and milk for the staff kitchen.

3.2 Petty cash box

Holding cash on business premises is a security risk and therefore it is important that the petty cash is secure. It should be kept in a locked petty cash box and usually this itself will be held in the safe.

Only the person responsible for the petty cash should have access to the petty cash box.

3.3 Payment of petty cash

Petty cash is usually reimbursed to employees who have already incurred a small cash expense on behalf of the business. These payments should be made for valid business expenses only.

For this reason, the petty cashier should pay out to the employee on receipt of an authorised petty cash voucher and, where appropriate, VAT receipt.

> ### 🔍 Definition
>
> A **petty cash voucher** is an internal document that details the business expenditure that an employee has incurred out of his own money.

This voucher must be authorised by an appropriate person before any amounts can be paid to that employee out of the petty cash box.

A typical petty cash voucher is shown below.

	PETTY CASH VOUCHER			
Authorised by F R Clarke	Received by L Kent		No	4173
Date	Description		Amount	
4 April 20X7	Train Fare		12	50
	Total		12	50

Signature of person authorising voucher →

Signature of claimant ←

Details of expenditure including the date and the nature of the expense →

Sequential voucher number ←

Total paid to employee ←

3.4 Maintaining petty cash records

The cashier, on receipt of the petty cash voucher should check that the receipt is genuine and that the voucher amounts add up to the total. Once the petty cash vouchers have been received, checked, authorised and the employee reimbursed, the details are recorded in the petty cash book.

3.5 Writing up the petty cash book

The petty cash book is normally set out as a large ledger account with a small receipts side and a larger analysed payments side.

A typical petty cash book is set out below:

Example

Receipts			Payments							
Date	Narrative	Total	Date	Narrative	Voucher no	Total	Postage	Cleaning	Tea & Coffee	VAT
						£	£	£	£	£
1 Nov	Bal b/f	35.50								
1 Nov	Bank	114.50	1 Nov	ASDA	58	23.50			23.50	
			2 Nov	Post Office	59	29.50	29.50			
			2 Nov	Cleaning materials	60	15.07		12.56		2.51
			3 Nov	Postage	61	16.19	16.19			

When cash is paid into the petty cash book it will be recorded on the receipts side (debit side) of the petty cash book.

Each petty cash voucher will then in turn be written up in the petty cash book on the payments (credit) side.

To ensure that no vouchers have been mislaid, petty cash vouchers are pre-numbered sequentially.

Each voucher is then entered into the petty cash book in the correct order, with each item of expenditure being recorded in the correct expense analysis column.

The receipts side of the petty cash book only requires one column, as the only receipt into the petty cash box is the regular payment of cash drawn out of the bank account to top up the tin.

From the example of a typical petty cash book (above), we can see that the balance brought forward was £35.50. This means that at the beginning of November, there was £35.50 in the tin. The petty cash has then been restored up to £150 by paying in an additional £114.50 which was drawn out of the bank and placed in the tin.

Payments out of the petty cash box will be for a variety of different types of expense and an analysis column is required for each type of expense in the same way as the cash payments book is analysed. The example (above) has split the expenses into postage, cleaning, tea & coffee and sundry expenses. Note that a column is also required for VAT, if a petty cash expense includes VAT this must also be analysed out.

3.6 Procedure for balancing the petty cash book

An organisation needs to know how much it has spent, and on what. In order to gain that information a balance of the petty cash book needs to be calculated:

This is done as follows:

Step 1 Total both the debit and the credit side of the petty cash book and make a note of each total.

Step 2 Insert the higher of the two totals as the total on both sides of the petty cash book leaving a line beneath the final entry on each side of the cash book.

Step 3 On the side with the smaller total insert the figure needed to make this column add up to the total. Call this figure the balance carried down (or 'Bal c/d' as an abbreviation).

Step 4 On the opposite side of the petty cash book, below the total insert this same figure and call it the balance brought down (or 'Bal b/d' as an abbreviation). *balance brought down = B/D.*

Here is an example of this method.

 Case study

The petty cash book of How Two Ltd. has the following entries:

Petty Cash Book				
	Debit			Credit
	£			£
Balance b/d	100	Tea & Coffee		5
Bank	100	Postage		10
		Taxi Fare		25

Calculate the balance on the account and bring the balance down as a single amount.

Step 1 Total both sides of the account and make a note of the totals. (Note that these totals that are asterisked below would not normally be written into the ledger account itself.)

Petty Cash Book				
	Debit			Credit
	£			£
Balance b/d	100	Tea & Coffee		5
Bank	100	Postage		10
		Taxi Fare		25
*Sub-total debits**	200	*Sub-total credits**		40

Step 2   Insert the higher total as the total of both sides.

Petty Cash Book				
	Debit			Credit
	£			£
Balance b/d	100	Tea & Coffee		5
Bank	100	Postage		10
		Taxi Fare		25
	———			———
*Sub-total debits**	200	*Sub-total credits**		40
	———			———
Total	200	Total		200
	———			———

Step 3   Insert a balancing figure on the side of the account with the lower sub-total so that both sides total the same. This is referred to as the 'balance carried down' or 'bal c/d' for short.

Petty Cash Book				
	Debit			Credit
	£			£
Balance b/d	100	Tea & Coffee		5
Bank	100	Postage		10
		Taxi Fare		25
		Balance c/d		160
	———			———
*Sub-total debits**	200	*Sub-total credits**		40
	———			———
Total	200	Total		200
	———			———

Step 4 Insert the balance carried down figure beneath the total on the other side of the account. This is referred to as 'bal b/d' for short.

Petty Cash Book			
	Debit		Credit
	£		£
Balance b/d	100	Tea & Coffee	5
Bank	100	Postage	10
		Taxi Fare	25
		Balance c/d	160
	____		____
*Sub-total debits**	200	*Sub-total credits**	40
	____		____
Total	200	Total	200
	____		____
Balance b/d	160		

The closing balance carried down at the end of the period is also the opening balance brought down at the start of the next period. This opening balance remains in the account as the starting position and any further transactions are then added into the account. In this case the balance brought down is a debit balance as there is money in the bank account making it an asset.

Test your understanding 8

A business has just started to run a petty cash system with an amount of £100. £100 is withdrawn from the bank account and paid into the petty cash box on *3 April 20X7*.

During the first week the following authorised petty cash vouchers were paid.

You are required to record these transactions in the petty cash book and total the columns appropriately. How much (if anything) would be left in the cash tin?

PETTY CASH VOUCHER

Authorised by T Smedley	Received by P Lannall	*No*	0001
Date	Description	Amount	
3 April 20X7	Tea/coffee/milk	4	73
	Total	4	73

PETTY CASH VOUCHER

Authorised by T Smedley	Received by R Sellers	*No*	0002
Date	Description	Amount	
3 April 20X7	Train fare	14	90
	Total	14	90

PETTY CASH VOUCHER

Authorised by T Smedley	Received by F Dorne	*No*	0003
Date	Description	Amount	
4 April 20X7	Stationery	4	00
	VAT	0	80
	Total	4	80

PETTY CASH VOUCHER			
Authorised by T Smedley	Received by P Dent	No	0004
Date	Description	Amount	
5 April 20X7	Postage costs	16	35
	Total	16	35

PETTY CASH VOUCHER			
Authorised by T Smedley	Received by H Polly	No	0005
Date	Description	Amount	
7 April 20X7	Train fare	15	30
	Total	15	30

PETTY CASH VOUCHER			
Authorised by T Smedley	Received by P Lannall	No	0006
Date	Description	Amount	
8 April 20X7	Milk/biscuits	3	85
	Total	3	85

Answer

Petty cash book											
Receipts			Payments								
Date	Narrative	Total	Date	Narrative	Voucher no	Total	Postage	Travel	Tea & coffee	Sundry	VAT
20X7		£	20X7			£	£	£	£	£	£
3 APRIL	CASH	100	3 April	TEA/COFFEE/M.	0001	4.73			4.73		
			3 APRIL	TRAIN FARE	0002	14.90		14.90			
			4 APRIL	STATIONERY	0003	4.80				4.00	0.80
			5 APRIL	POSTAGE	0004	16.35	16.35				
			7 APRIL	TRAIN FARE	0005	15.30		15.30			
			8 APRIL	MILK/BISCUIT	0006	3.85		3.85			
						59.93	16.35	30.20	8.58	4.00	0.80

100.00
– 59.93
40.07

Would be left £40.07 in the cash tin.

4 Batch control

4.1 Batch processing

A busy accounts office will need to record a lot of transactions and it is important that all the information is entered quickly and accurately into the correct book of prime entry.

Batch processing is a method of entering batches of similar transactions all together rather than individually. Using this method, all customer invoices, credit notes and receipts and all supplier invoices, credit notes and receipts will be sorted into separate piles before being entered into the relevant book of prime entry.

4.2 Benefits of batch processing

Batch processing will help to save time as it means that accounting staff can concentrate on one task at a time can be rather than swapping between different documents and books of prime entry. By focusing on one task at a time, it also means that fewer mistakes will be made.

Cheques and cash paid listings can be used to quickly record all the money paid out by the organisation each day. The total amount is then entered into the cash payments book.

Cheques and cash received listings can be used to record all the money received out by the organisation each day. The total amount is then entered into the cash receipts book.

 Test your understanding 9

Complete the two sentences below with the correct options.

Batch processing is a method of processing financial documents [all together/individually] rather than [all together/individually].

Cheques and cash paid into the organisation can be listed on a [cheques and cash paid/cheques and cash received] listing before entering into the [cash payments book/cash receipts book].

This is an example of [batch processing/invoice processing] and means that [more/fewer] mistakes will be made.

5 Calculating opening and closing balances for cash

5.1 Calculating closing amounts of cash in hand and cash in the bank

Within this chapter you have been introduced to the cash book and how this is used to record all bank receipts and payments.

Some businesses will record their cash receipts and payments within the cash book, others may only deal with small amounts of cash and record these transactions separately in the petty cash book. The concept of calculating closing amounts of cash in hand and cash in the bank is the same.

The opening balance will show how much cash in hand or cash in the bank the business has at the beginning of a period. The total receipts are added as these show monies received; the total payments are deducted as these represent monies paid out; the balance shows the amount of cash in hand or cash in the bank at the end of the period.

5.2 Differences between cash in hand and cash in the bank

The main difference between calculating the closing balance of cash in hand and the closing balance of cash in the bank is that the bank account can sometimes be overdrawn.

A bank overdraft is classed as a short-term loan from the bank. The limit to which a bank account can be overdrawn is agreed with the bank and they will charge interest on any overdrawn balances. Overdrawn balances are shown as a minus figure to indicate a negative balance, thus showing that money is owed back to the bank.

Cash in hand cannot be overdrawn. Once a cash balance reaches £0, there is no cash left to spend therefore the closing balance cannot be a minus figure.

Example

How Two Ltd have the following information relating to cash in the bank for May.

Date	Description	Amount £
1st May	Opening balance	2,367.71
2nd May	Motor expenses	268.75
5th May	Supplier payments	1,642.11
10th May	Customer receipts	520.49
15th May	Wages	1,770.90
21st May	Customer receipts	911.34
29th May	Supplier payments	364.72

To calculate the balance of cash in the bank at the end of May, the following calculation would be performed:

Opening balance as at 1st May   £2,367.71

Total Receipts   £1,431.83

Total Payments   (£4,046.48)

Closing amount at the end of May   (£246.94)

The total of the opening balance and the bank receipts when added together are less than the total monies paid out, therefore the bank balance is negative which means it is overdrawn.

Test your understanding 10

Farley AV Supplies has the following information relating to cash in hand for May.

Date	Description	Amount £
1st May	Opening balance	542.25
12th May	Motor expenses	82.40
20th May	Cleaners Wages	92.00
23rd May	Cash Sales	121.84
27th May	Stationery	64.32
31st May	Postage	97.26

Use the table below to calculate the balance of cash in hand at the end of May. Use brackets or a minus sign to indicate negative values:

	Amount £
Opening balance as at 1st May	542.25
Total Receipts	121.84
Total Payments	(335.98)
Closing balance as at 31st May	328.11

8 Summary and further questions

In this chapter you learnt about how the cash book is completed and used to record payments and receipts, as well as looking at the nature of those payments, in preparation for the next chapter which looks at bank statements.

We have also looked at how petty cash is managed and shown how batch control can help accounting professionals to process information efficiently and effectively and how to calculate opening and closing balances for suppliers and customers, both for cash in hand and cash in the bank.

Let us now return to the How Two Ltd case study to apply this knowledge in context.

 Case study activity 24

Jessica has been asked to set up the following payments. For each one indicate the best method of payment from the pick list provided.

Payment	Payment method
The telephone bill for calls and line rental for the Manchester office, for which the statement is paid in full on 15th of each month.	*Direct Debit*
A fixed monthly fee of £3,750, paid on 1st of each month, to Platinum Property Management for rent of the Liverpool offices.	*Standing Order*
An urgent payment for £75 to a local contractor who is performing decorating and maintenance work in Reading, but will not work until paid.	*Faster payment bank transfer*
A refund to a small business who placed an order in error and do not have account terms with How Two Ltd. They have written to request the refund.	*Cheque*

Pick list

Cheque

Faster payment bank transfer

Direct debit

Standing order

Case study activity 25

Jessica has received the following three cheques in the week ended 20 November 20X7. Today is 20 November 20X7.

Are the cheques valid? Jessica needs to explain to her manager why easy is either suitable or unsuitable to take to the bank.

more than six month

Cheque A

ABC Bank PLC	Date: 20th November, 2016
Payee: *How Two Ltd*	no
	320.00
Three hundred and twenty pounds only	M Salinger
	M Salinger
CHEQUE NO SORT CODE ACCOUNT NO	
00073 27-60-85 5921434	

Cheque B

Plunketts Bank, Wiston no	Date: 18th November, 2017
Payee: *How Two Ltd*	89
	60.99
Sixty pounds & eighty-nine pence only	V Rogers, VCR Ltd
ninety	*Vic Rogers*
CHEQUE NO SORT CODE ACCOUNT NO	
02312 56-22-99 7421232	

Cheque C

Royston Bank Ltd NO	Date: 16th November, 2017
How TWO LTD.	
Payee: *NB Solutions Ltd*	
	406.00
Four hundred and six pounds only	on behalf of N B Solutions Ltd
	O Smart
CHEQUE NO SORT CODE ACCOUNT NO	
621001 40-08-09 6174931	

Case study activity 26

Jessica has been asked to record the following receipts and payments into the cash book:

Receipts:

Cash sale 2nd November £100.

Cash sale 3rd November £80.

Cheque from IT Geeks on the 3rd November £550.

Cheque from NB Solutions on the 4th November £225.

Payments:

Cash purchase on the 2nd November £50.

Cheque paid to MMC Ltd. on the 3rd November £450.

Cheque paid to RBC Plc. On the 4th November £340.

Cash purchase on the 5th November £65.

	DEBIT	**Cash Book**		CREDIT	
Date	**Details**	**Amount**	**Date**	**Details**	**Amount**
2/11	CASH SALES	100	2/11	Cash PURCHASE	50
3/11	CASH SALES	80	3/11	MMC Ltd.	450
3/11	IT GEEKS	550	4/11	RBC Plc.	340
4/11	NB Solutions	225	5/11	CASH PURCHASE	65

 Case study activity 27

Jessica has been asked to send a cheque to a supplier (MMC Direct) for the payment of recent orders.

Which daybook should the amount be listed in?   Cash book

Cash payment book.

KAPLAN PUBLISHING

Case study activity 28

Jessica has been asked to record the following transactions into the petty cash book and balance it off:

1/11 Opening Balance £50

Receipts:

1/11 Top up from the bank £150

Payments:

2/11 Rail fare £15

3/11 Taxi fare £25

4/11 Postage £25

Petty Cash Book					
Date	Details	Amount	Date	Details	Amount
1/11	OPENING BALANCE	50	2/11	RAIL FARE	15
1/11	BANK	150	3/11	TAXI	25
			4/11	POSTAGE	25
			30/11	BALANCE C/D	135
30/11	TOTAL	200	4/11	TOTAL	200
1/12	BALANCE B/D	135			

Case study activity 29

How Two Ltd. have provided Jessica with the following information relating to the cash in the bank for May.

She has been asked to use this information to calculate the closing balance as at 31st May.

Date	Description	Amount £
6th May	Opening balance	3,489.73
11th May	Supplier payments	1,459.26
19th May	Rent	800.00
24th May	Customer receipts	926.84
28th May	Debit card purchases	342.10
31st May	Heat & light	268.02

Use the table below to calculate the balance of cash in the bank as at 31st May. Use brackets or a minus sign to indicate negative values:

	Amount £
OPENING BALANCE AS AT 31st May	3,489.73
TOTAL RECEIPTS	926.84
TOTAL PAYMENTS	(3,869.38)
CLOSING BALANCE AT 31st May	1,547.19

Jessica has been asked whether the following statement is true or false.

Tick the correct option below.

Statement	True	False
The closing balance as at 31st May shows an overdrawn bank balance.		✓

KAPLAN PUBLISHING

Answers to chapter activities

Test your understanding 1

Date:	ABC Bank plc	£50 notes	
19/11/17	Manchester	£20 notes	60.00
		£10 notes	150.00
	Account	£5 notes	100.00
	How Two Ltd	£2 coin	
		£1 coin	25.00
No of cheques:	Paid in by	Other coin	6.00
	J Howard	Total cash	341.00
2	Sort Code Account No	Cheques	2250.00
	25-22-78 30087251	Total £	2591.00

Test your understanding 2

The paying-in slip must be dated and signed so that the bank cashier can contact the person who paid in the money in to the bank, in case there are any queries.

Test your understanding 3

Cheque A

The amount needs to be included, in numbers – in this case 500.00.

ABC Bank PLC	Date: 29th November, 2017
Payee: *NB Solutions Ltd*	
	500.00
Five hundred pounds ONLY	on behalf of How Two Ltd
	J Howard
CHEQUE NO SORT CODE ACCOUNT NO	
04312 25-22-78 30087251	

Cheque B

The amount needs to be included in written form.

ABC Bank PLC	Date: 29th November, 2017
Payee: *Armistead & Co*	
	250.50
Two hundred and fifty pounds and 50p	on behalf of How Two Ltd
	J Howard

CHEQUE NO	SORT CODE	ACCOUNT NO
04313	25-22-78	30087251

Cheque C

The date needs to be included, to state the day, month and year.

ABC Bank PLC	Date: **29th November, 2017**
Payee: *Mr P Sagan*	
	25.20
Twenty five pounds and 20p only	on behalf of How Two Ltd
	J Howard

CHEQUE NO	SORT CODE	ACCOUNT NO
04314	25-22-78	30087251

 Test your understanding 4

The statement is false.

Cheques can only be signed by authorised signatories.

Test your understanding 5

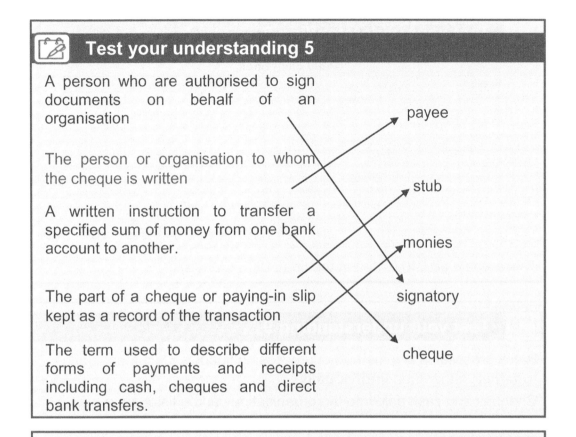

A person who are authorised to sign documents on behalf of an organisation

The person or organisation to whom the cheque is written

A written instruction to transfer a specified sum of money from one bank account to another.

The part of a cheque or paying-in slip kept as a record of the transaction

The term used to describe different forms of payments and receipts including cash, cheques and direct bank transfers.

payee

stub

monies

signatory

cheque

Test your understanding 6

	Left / right
Money received	Left
Money paid out	Right
Credit	Right
Debit	Left
£220 cash to pay for catering at NB Solutions event	Right
Bank transfer from a one-off customer for £150	Left
Cheque from Miss B Craven for £232	Left
Cheque payable to How Two Ltd for £459	Right

Test your understanding 7

The **Cash receipts book** is used to record monies received from customers.

The **Cash payments book** is used to record monies paid to suppliers.

Test your understanding 8

Petty cash book											
Receipts			Payments								
Date	Narrative	Total	Date	Narrative	Voucher no	Total	Postage	Travel	Tea & coffee	Sundry	VAT
20X1		£	20X1			£	£	£	£	£	£
03/04	Cash	100.00	03/04	Tea/coffee	0001	4.73			4.73		
			03/04	Train fare	0002	14.90		14.90			
			04/04	Stationery	0003	4.80				4.00	0.80
			05/04	Postage	0004	16.35	16.35				
			07/04	Train fare	0005	15.30		15.30			
			08/04	Milk/biscuits	0006	3.85			3.85		
						59.93	16.35	30.20	8.58	4.00	0.80

There would be £40.07 left in the tin (£100 - £59.93).

 Test your understanding 9

Batch processing is a method of processing financial documents [**all together**] rather than [**individually**].

Cheques and cash paid into the organisation can be listed on a [**cheques and cash received listing**] before entering into the [**cash receipts book**].

This is an example of [**batch processing**] and means that [**fewer**] mistakes will be made.

 Test your understanding 10

	Amount £
Opening balance as at 1st May	542.25
Total Receipts	121.84
Total Payments	(335.98)
Closing balance as at 31st May	328.11

Case study activity 24

Payment	Payment method
The telephone bill for calls and line rental for the Manchester office, for which the statement is paid in full on 15th of each month.	Direct debit
A fixed monthly fee of £3,750, paid on 1st of each month, to Platinum Property Management for rent of the Liverpool offices.	Standing order
An urgent payment for £75 to a local contractor who is performing decorating and maintenance work in Reading, but will not work until paid.	Faster payment bank transfer
A refund to a small business who placed an order in error and do not have account terms with How Two Ltd. They have written to request the refund.	Cheque

 Case study activity 25

Cheque A – the date is incorrect (2016 not 2017), making the cheque invalid

Cheque B – the written value is £60.89 whereas the numerical value of the cheque is £60.99 – these amounts do not match so the cheque is invalid

Cheque C – the cheque is actually made payable to the payer (NB Solutions) rather than the payee. Therefore as the payee is not How Two Ltd, the cheque is not valid.

 Case study activity 26

Cash Book					
Date	Details	Amount	Date	Details	Amount
2/11	Cash sale	100	2/11	Cash purchase	50
3/11	Cash sale	80	3/11	MMC Ltd.	450
3/11	IT Geeks	550	4/11	RBC Plc.	340
4/11	NB Solutions	225	5/11	Cash purchase	65

Case study activity 27

This is a payment from How Two Ltd and should therefore be listed in the **cash payments book.**

 Case study activity 28

Petty Cash Book					
Date	Details	Amount	Date	Details	Amount
1/11	Opening Balance	50	2/11	Rail fare	15
1/11	Bank	150	3/11	Taxi fare	25
			4/11	Postage	25
			30/11	Bal c/d	135
	Total	**200**		**Total**	**200**
1/12	Bal b/d	135			

Case study activity 29

	Amount £
Opening balance as at 1st May	3,489.73
Total Receipts	926.84
Total Payments	(2,869.38)
Closing balance as at 31st May	1,547.19

Statement	True	False
The closing balance as at 31st May shows an overdrawn bank balance.		✓

The cash book and bank reconciliations

Introduction

Whilst the Level 1 assessment does not require the completion of the bank reconciliation statement, you will be asked to recognise balances on the bank statement, items in the cash book which are missing from the statement and items on the bank statement which are not in the cash book.

Therefore, this chapter will explore the concept of the bank reconciliation, providing you with the background knowledge of how to correctly prepare the cash book, compare the entries in the cash book to details on the bank statement and then finally on how to prepare a bank reconciliation statement correctly.

KNOWLEDGE
Process receipts and payments
4.1 Enter receipts and payments into a cash book
4.2 Use the cash book to calculate closing amounts of cash in hand and cash in the bank
4.3 Check the closing amount of cash in the bank against the closing balance on the bank statement

CONTENTS

1 Writing up the cash book
2 Preparing the bank reconciliation statement
3 Summary and further questions

1 Writing up the cash book

1.1 Case study: an introduction

 Case study

Jessica is now ready to undertake the biggest challenge to date in her career. Her manager wants her to get an insight into the bank reconciliation - this will form part of her role in the near future.

However, for data protection and confidentiality reasons, it would be inappropriate to allow Jessica access to genuine company records until she is qualified and experienced enough to take on this role. It would also be inappropriate to allow a trainee to work with genuine records due to the scope for errors occurring. This could cause complications for the accounting department as the tracing of errors can be extremely time consuming and can have a knock on effect on other work deadlines. Therefore, Jessica will be working with scenarios and figures that have been fictitiously created for training purposes.

On completion of the tasks set, Jessica will be able to show that she can prepare the cash book correctly. She will need to compare the entries in the cash book to the details on the bank statement.

Attention to detail and accuracy when comparing the records is paramount as Jessica will then need to prepare a bank reconciliation statement. All tasks that Jessica completes will be reviewed by her manager who will provide feedback on her performance.

1.2 Balancing the cash book

Most businesses will have a separate cash receipts book and a cash payments book which form part of the double entry system. If this form of record is used, the cash balance must be calculated from the opening balance at the beginning of the period, plus the receipts shown in the cash receipts book for the period and minus the payments shown in the cash payments book for the period.

The following brief calculation will enable us to find the balance on the cash book when separate receipts and payments book are maintained.

	£
Opening balance per the cash book	X
Add: Receipts in the period	X
Less: Payments in the period	(X)
Closing balance per the cash book	X

📖 Case study

Jessica is being introduced to the process of completing a bank reconciliation for How Two Ltd. She is receiving some training from one of her colleagues who presents her with the following scenario:

Suppose that the opening balance on the cash book is £358.72 on 1 June. During June the cash payments book shows that there were total payments made of £7,326.04 during the month of June and the cash receipts book shows receipts for the month of £8,132.76.

She asks Jessica: What is the closing balance on the cash book at the end of June?

Solution

			£
Opening balance at 1 June	*1 January*		358.72
Add:	Receipts for June *January*		8,132.76
Less:	Payments for June *January*		(7,326.04)
Balance at 30 June			1,165.44

673.42
6,488.20
(6,419.37)
742.25

📝 Test your understanding 1

To check that Jessica has understood what she has just been told, she has been presented with the following scenario and asked to calculate the closing balance of the cash book:

The opening balance at 1 January in a business cash book was £673.42. During January payments totalled £6,419.37 and receipts totalled £6,488.20. *The closing balance wf 742.25*

What is the closing balance on the cash book? *cash surplus.*

Test your understanding 2

Within her training pack, Jessica is given the following:

Below is a cash book that needs updating with the receipts provided:

	£
10 May BACS	6,200
25 May Bank interest	40
31 May BACS	460

She needs to enter the amounts into the cash book

Date	Details	£	Date	Chq	Details	£
1 May	Balance b/d	526	1 May			
6 May	Shaws	630	3 May	0041	Bills Farm	2,000
6 May	Andrew Ltd	880	3 May	0042	Cows Head	3,240
10 MAY	BACS	6,200	5 May	0043	Adam Ant	840
25 MAY	BANK INTEREST	40	30 May	0044	Miles to Go	700
31 MAY	BACS	460			BALANCE	1,956
			31 MAY		BALANCE C/D	1,956
		8,736				8,736
2 JUNE	BALANCE B/D	1,956				

2 Preparing the bank reconciliation statement

2.1 Introduction

At regular intervals (normally at least once a month) the cashier must check that the cash book is correct by comparing the cash book with the bank statement.

2.2 Differences between the cash book and bank statement

At any date the balance shown on the bank statement is unlikely to agree with the balance in the cash book for two main reasons.

(a) **Items in the cash book not on the bank statement**

Certain items will have been entered in the cash book but will not appear on the bank statement at the time of the reconciliation. Examples are:

- Cheques received by the business and paid into the bank which have not yet appeared on the bank statement, due to the time lag of the clearing system. These are known as **outstanding lodgements** (can also be referred to as "uncleared lodgements").

- Cheques written by the business but which have not yet appeared on the bank statement, because the recipients have not yet paid them in, or the cheques are in the clearing system. These are known as **unpresented cheques**.

- Errors in the cash book (e.g. transposition of numbers, addition errors).

(b) **Items on the bank statement not in the cash book**

At the time of the bank reconciliation certain items will appear on the bank statement that have not yet been entered into the cash book. These can occur due to the cashier not being aware of the existence of these items until receiving the bank statements.

Examples are:

- Direct debit or standing order payments that are in the bank statement but have not yet been entered in the cash payments book.

outstanding lodgements = uncleared lodgements

- BACS or other receipts paid directly into the bank account by a customer that have not yet been entered in the cash received book.

- Bank charges or bank interest that are unknown until the bank statement has been received and therefore will not be in the cash book.

- Errors in the cash book that may only come to light when the cash book entries are compared to the bank statement.

- Returned cheques i.e. cheques paid in from a customer who does not have sufficient funds in his bank to 'honour' the cheque (see later in this chapter).

2.3 Procedure for balancing the cash book

An organisation needs to know how much it has spent, and on what. In order to gain that information a balance of the cash book needs to be calculated:

This is done as follows:

Step 1 Total both the debit and the credit side of the cash book and make a note of each total.

Step 2 Insert the higher of the two totals as the total on both sides of the ledger account leaving a line beneath the final entry on each side of the cash book.

Step 3 On the side with the smaller total insert the figure needed to make this column add up to the total. Call this figure the balance carried down (or 'Bal c/d' as an abbreviation).

Step 4 On the opposite side of the ledger account, below the total insert this same figure and call it the balance brought down (or 'Bal b/d' as an abbreviation).

An example of the method is shown on the following page, returning back to the case study.

Case study

Within the training session, Jessica's colleague works through the following example with Jessica to demonstrate the process to be followed when balancing off the cash book.

The cash book of a business has the following entries:

Cash Book			
	Debit		Credit
	£		£
Capital	1,000	Purchases	200
Sales	300	Drawings	100
Sales	400	Rent	400
Capital	500	Stationery	300
Sales	800	Purchases	400

Calculate the balance on the account and bring the balance down as a single amount.

Step 1 Total both sides of the account and make a note of the totals. (Note that these totals that are asterisked below would not normally be written into the ledger account itself.)

Cash Book			
	Debit		Credit
	£		£
Capital	1,000	Purchases	200
Sales	300	Drawings	100
Sales	400	Rent	400
Capital	500	Stationery	300
Sales	800	Purchases	400
	———		———
Sub-total debits*	3,000	Sub-total credits*	1,400

Step 2   Insert the higher total as the total of both sides.

Cash Book			
	£		£
	Debit		Credit
Capital	1,000	Purchases	200
Sales	300	Drawings	100
Sales	400	Rent	400
Capital	500	Stationery	300
Sales	800	Purchases	400
	———		———
Sub-total debits*	**3,000**	**Sub-total credits***	**1,400**
	———		———
Total	**3,000**	**Total**	**3,000**
	———		———

Step 3   Insert a balancing figure on the side of the account with the lower sub-total. This is referred to as the 'balance carried down' or 'bal c/d' for short.

Cash Book			
	Debit		Credit
	£		£
Capital	1,000	Purchases	200
Sales	300	Drawings	100
Sales	400	Rent	400
Capital	500	Stationery	300
Sales	800	Purchases	400
	———		———
Sub-total debits*	**3,000**	**Sub-total credits***	**1,400**
		Bal c/d	**1,600**
	———		———
Total	**3,000**	**Total**	**3,000**
	———		———

Step 4   Insert the balance carried down figure beneath the total on the other side of the account. This is referred to as 'bal b/d' for short.

Cash Book				
	Debit			Credit
	£			£
Capital	1,000	Purchases		200
Sales	300	Drawings		100
Sales	400	Rent		400
Capital	500	Stationery		300
Sales	800	Purchases		400
	———			———
Sub-total debits*	3,000	Sub-total credits*		1,400
		Bal c/d		1,600
	———			———
Total	3,000	Total		3,000
	———			———
Bal b/d	1,600			

The closing balance carried down at the end of the period is also the opening balance brought down at the start of the next period. This opening balance remains in the account as the starting position and any further transactions are then added into the account. In this case the balance brought down is a debit balance as there is money in the bank account making it an asset.

Test your understanding 3

Jessica has now been given another scenario to work through to demonstrate her ability to accurately balance off a cash book.

She is given the cash book for the month of March below and is required to "balance off" the cash book.

Cash Book					
Date		£	Date		£
1 Mar	Capital	12,000	3 Mar	Purchases	3,000
7 Mar	Sales	5,000	15 Mar	Computer	2,400
19 Mar	Sales	2,000	20 Mar	Purchases	5,300
22 Mar	Sales	3,000	24 Mar	Rent	1,000
			28 Mar	Drawings	2,000
		———			———
		22,000			22,000
		———			———
1 april	Bal d/d	8,300			

2.4 The bank reconciliation

 Definition

A **bank reconciliation** is simply a statement that explains the differences between the balance in the cash book and the balance on the bank statement at a particular date.

A bank reconciliation is produced by following a standard set of steps.

Step 1: Compare the cash book and the bank statement for the relevant period and identify any differences between them.

You should begin with agreeing the opening balances on the bank statement and cash book so that you are aware of any prior period reconciling items that exist.

This is usually done by ticking in the cash book and bank statement items that appear in both the cash book and the bank statement. Any items left unticked therefore only appear in one place, either the cash book or the bank statement. We saw in section 2.2 above the reasons why this might occur.

Step 2: Update the cash book for any items that appear on the bank statement that have not yet been entered into the cash book.

Tick these items in both the cash book and the bank statement once they are entered in the cash book.

At this stage there will be no unticked items on the bank statement.

(You clearly cannot enter on the bank statement items in the cash book that do not appear on the bank statement – the bank prepares the bank statement, not you. These items will either be unpresented cheques, outstanding lodgements or errors in the cash book – see 2.2 above.)

Step 3: You then need to balance the cash book to calculate the updated figure which is more realistic as the cash book now contains information on automated receipts/payments that hadn't been recorded but that have actually been received or paid.

Step 4: Prepare the bank reconciliation statement.

This will typically have the following layout:

Bank reconciliation as at 31.0X.200X

	£
Balance as per bank statement	X
Less unpresented cheques	(X)
Add outstanding lodgements	X
	———
Balance as per cash book	X
	———

Think for a moment to ensure you understand this layout.

We deduct the unpresented cheques (cheques already entered in the cash book but not yet on the bank statement), these will be obvious as they will be the payments left in the cash book unticked. We do this because when the recipient pays them into their bank, our bank balance will be reduced.

We add outstanding lodgements (cash received and already entered in the cash book), these again will be obvious because they will be receipts left in the cash book unticked. We do this because when they clear in our bank, they will increase the bank balance.

2.5 Debits and credits in bank statements

When comparing the cash book to the bank statement it is easy to get confused with debits and credits.

- When we pay money into the bank, we debit our cash book but the bank credits our account.

- This is because a debit in our cash book represents the increase in our asset 'cash'. For the bank, the situation is different: they will credit our account because they now owe us more money; in the bank's eyes we are a payable.

- When our account is overdrawn, we owe the bank money and consequently our cash book will show a credit balance. For the bank an overdraft is a debit balance because we owe them money and therefore from their perspective we are a receivable.

On the bank statement a credit is an amount of money paid into the account and a debit represents a payment. A bank statement shows the transactions from the bank's point of view rather than the business' point of view.

Note: For the purpose of your assessment you are not required to complete the bank reconciliation statement. You are required to compare the items on the bank statement with those in the cash book and identify which one's are missing from each. You will also need to be able to calculate the closing amount of the cash in the bank.

The bank reconciliation statement has been included within this chapter so that you get a good understanding of the whole process and so that you can see the reasoning behind the missing items. Bank reconciliation statements will be covered in depth in the AAT Foundation Certificate.

Example

On 30 April Tomasso's received the following bank statement as at 28 April.

Today's date is 30 April.

	QC Bank			
	QC Street, London			
To: Tomasso's	Account No 92836152		30 April 20x7	
Date	**Details**	**Payments**	**Receipts**	**Balance**
20x7		£	£	£
2 April	Bal b/f			100
3 April	Cheque 101	55		45
4 April	Cheque 103	76		(31)
6 April	Bank Giro Credit		1,000	969
9 April	Cheque 105	43		926
10 April	Cheque 106	12		914
11 April	Cheque 107	98		816
21 April	Direct Debit RBC	100		716
22 April	Direct Debit OPO	150		566
23 April	Interest received		30	596
24 April	Bank charges	10		586
28 April	Bank Giro Credit DJA		250	836

The cash book at 28 April is shown below.

Date 20x7	Details	Bank £	Date 20x7	Cheque number	Details	Bank £
	Balance b/f	100	01 April	101	Alan & Co	55
06 April	Prance Dance Co.	1,000	02 April	102	Amber's	99
23 April	Interest received	30	02 April	103	Kiki & Company	76
23 April	Graham Interiors	2,000	05 April	104	Marta	140
25 April	Italia Design	900	06 April	105	Nina Ltd	43
			07 April	106	Willy Wink	12
			08 April	107	Xylophones	98

Firstly, we see that the opening balance is £100 per both the bank statement and the cash book. Secondly, we must tick off the items in the bank statement to the cash book.

The effect of this on the bank statement can be seen below.

Date	Details	Payments £	Receipts £	Balance £
2 April	Bal b/f			100 ✓
3 April	Cheque 101	✓55		45
4 April	Cheque 103	✓76		(31)
6 April	Bank Giro Credit		✓1,000	969
9 April	Cheque 105	✓43		926
10 April	Cheque 106	✓12		914
11 April	Cheque 107	✓98		816
21 April	Direct Debit RBC	100		716
22 April	Direct Debit OPO	150		566
23 April	Interest received		✓30	596
24 April	Bank charges	10		586
28 April	Bank Giro Credit DJA		250	836

This leaves 4 items unticked on the bank statement. These transactions need to be added to the cash book and the cash book can then be balanced off.

The cash book is updated for these on the following page.

Date 20x7	Details	Bank £	Date 20x7	Cheque number	Details	Bank £
	Balance b/d	100	01 April	101	Alan & Co	✓55
06 April	Prance Dance Co.	✓1,000	02 April	102	Amber's	99
23 April	Interest received	✓30	02 April	103	Kiki & Company	✓76
23 April	Graham Interiors	2,000	05 April	104	Marta	140
25 April	Italia Design	900	06 April	105	Nina Ltd	✓43
28 April	DJA	250	07 April	106	Willy Wink	✓12
			08 April	107	Xylophones	✓98
			21 April	–	DD – RBC	100
			22 April	–	DD – OPO	150
			24 April	–	Bank charges	10
			28 April	–	Balance c/d	3,497
		4,280				4,280
29 April	Balance b/d	3,497				

Once the cash book has been updated, there are 4 items unticked on the cash book.

These are the items that will go onto the bank reconciliation, as shown below.

Bank reconciliation statement as at 28 April	£
Balance per bank statement	836
Add:	
Name: Graham's Interior	2,000
Name: Italia Design	900
Total to add	2,900
Less:	
Name: Amber's	99
Name: Marta	140
Total to subtract	239
Balance as per cash book	3,497

The bank reconciliation statement proves that the difference between the balance on the bank statement and the balance on the cash book is due to outstanding lodgements and unpresented cheques.

Test your understanding 4

FELICITY HOWE BOUTIQUE

Below is the cash book (bank columns only) of Felicity Howe Boutique for the month of April 20x7 together with her bank statement for the same period.

CASH BOOK

20x7	DETAILS	£	20X7	DETAILS	£
1 Apr	Balance b/d	1,470	2 Apr	Cheque 101129	930
9 Apr	Sales	606	4 Apr	Cheque 101130	506
12 Apr	Sales	1,048	9 Apr	Cheque 101131	834
30 Apr	Sales	550	29 Apr	Cheque 101132	410
			30 Apr	Balance c/d	994
		3,674			3,674
1 May	Balance b/d	994			

BANK STATEMENT

NORBURY BANK PLC
Southborough Branch
In account with: Felicity Howe   Account no 34578900

20X7		Payments	Receipts	Balance
01-Apr	balance b/f.			1,470
02-Apr	Cheque No. 129	930		540
05-Apr	Cheque No. 130	506		34
09-Apr	Counter Credit		606	640
12-Apr	Cheque No. 131	834		-194
12-Apr	Counter Credit		1,048	854
16-Apr	STO Hamble Comms.	75		779
17-Apr	BACS - Honey Bee		948	1,727
18-Apr	BACS - Goldfish CC	534		1,193
25-Apr	Overdraft fee	125		1,068
29-Apr	BGC S. May		610	1,678

Required:

a. Bring up to date the Cash Book making any adjustments necessary

b. Update the Cash Book and bring the balance down

c. Prepare a bank reconciliation statement as at 30 April 20x7

3 Summary and further questions

In this chapter you have learnt how to compare items in the cash book with those on the bank statement. You have also been able to identify items that are on the bank statement that have not been entered into the cash. From here you have gone on to update the accounting records accordingly.

Within this chapter you have learnt how to carry out a bank reconciliation and have presented this in the form of a bank reconciliation statement. As mentioned earlier in the chapter, in your exam you **will not** be tested on the bank reconciliation statement however you will need to demonstrate the ability to carry out all other activities set out in this chapter.

Let us return to the How Two Ltd case study for further activities to test your understanding of the topics covered in the chapter.

 Case study activity 30

Having gained considerable experience in the bookkeeping team at How Two Ltd, Jessica has been promoted and is preparing to complete her first bank reconciliations.

Before she does so, her manager wants to check that she fully understands the process. Jessica is given a list of statements and needs to decide whether each is true or false. Tick the correct box for each

Statement	True	False
An outstanding lodgement is a cheque that has been received by the business, paid into the bank, and has appeared on the bank statement		✓
An outstanding lodgement is a cheque that has been received by the business, paid into the bank, but has not yet appeared on the bank statement	✓	
An unpresented cheque is one that has been written by the business but which has not yet appeared on the bank statement	✓	
Direct debits that only show on the bank statement should be ignored		✓
Direct debits and standing orders that only show on the bank statement should be written into the cash book	✓	
Bank charges are receipts to be entered into the cash book on the debit side		✓
Errors in the cash book may only come to light when the cash book entries are compared to the bank statement	✓	

Case study activity 31

It is November 20X8. Having convinced her manager she is ready, Jessica has been promoted and is now responsible for How Two Ltd's bank reconciliations.

The cash book shows a debit balance of £204 on 30 November 20X8.

A comparison with the bank statements revealed the following:

		£
1	Cheques drawn but not presented	3,168
2	Amounts paid into the bank but not credited	723
3	Entries in the bank statements not recorded in the cash account	
	(i) Standing orders	35
	(ii) Interest on bank deposit account	18
	(iii) Bank charges	14
4	Balance on the bank statement at 30 November	2,618

Jessica needs to:

a)   Show the appropriate adjustments required in the cash book of bringing down the correct balance at 30 November 20X8.

b)   Prepare a bank reconciliation statement at that date.

Case study activity 32

Jessica is working on the accounts of How Two Ltd. Below is an extract from the bank statement for the month of July.

Date	Details	Paid Out £	Paid In £	Balance £
1st July	Balance			6,954.20
6th July	Counter credit		525.00	7,479.20
12th July	DD Utilities	216.28		7,262.92
15th July	Standing Order – Rent	800.00		6,462.92
19th July	Faster payment		255.00	6,717.92
23rd July	Bank Transfer – N Ahmed		310.00	7,027.92
24th July	Heat & light	187.52		6,840.40
26th July	Cash withdrawal	(150.00)		6,690.40
28th July	Counter credit		220.00	6,910.40
31st July	Bank Charges	14.40		6,896.00

Jessica has been asked to clarify what the closing balance was on the 23rd of July and whether this represented a positive bank balance or an overdrawn balance.

State the closing bank balance as at 23rd July and whether this was a positive balance or an overdrawn balance.

Bank Balance as at 23rd July	Positive	Overdrawn
£ 7,027.92	✓	

Jessica has been given an extract of the cash book for How Two Ltd for the month of July.

	Receipts			Payments	
Date	Details	Bank £	Date	Details	Bank £
6th July	Receivables	525.00	12th July	DD Utilities	216.28
19th July	Receivables	255.00	15th July	Rent	800.00
21st July	Cash sale	(110.00)	24th July	Heat & Light	187.52
23rd July	N Ahmed	310.00	31st July	Bank Charges	14.40
28th July	Receivables	220.00			

Jessica has been asked to provide her manager with information on any items that are missing from the bank statement or the cash book.

Compare the items from the extract of the bank statement with the items in the cash book and complete the following sentences:

The item missing from the bank statement is a _cash sale_

for an amount of £ _110.00_ .

The item missing from the cash book is a _cash withdrawal_

for an amount of £ _150.00_ .

This should be included in the _right / credit_ side of the cash book.

Answers to chapter activities

 Test your understanding 1

	£
Opening balance	673.42
Payments	(6,419.37)
Receipts	6,488.20
Closing balance	742.25

The closing balance is £742.25 cash surplus.

 Test your understanding 2

Updated cash book:

Date	Details	£	Date	Chq	Details	£
1 May	Balance b/d	526				
6 May	Shaws	630	3 May	0041	Bills Farm	2,000
6 May	Andrew Ltd	880	3 May	0042	Cows Head	3,240
10 May	BACS	6,200	5 May	0043	Adam Ant	840
25 May	Bank Interest	40	30 May	0044	Miles to Go	700
31 May	BACS	460				
			31 May		Balance c/d	1,956
		8,736				8,736
1 June	Balance b/d	1,956				

Test your understanding 3

Cash Book

Date		£	Date		£
1 Mar	Capital	12,000	3 Mar	Purchases	3,000
7 Mar	Sales	5,000	15 Mar	Non-current asset	2,400
19 Mar	Sales	2,000	20 Mar	Purchases	5,300
22 Mar	Sales	3,000	24 Mar	Rent	1,000
			28 Mar	Drawings	2,000
			31 Mar	Balance c/d	8,300
		———			———
		22,000			22,000
		———			———
1 Apr	Balance b/d	8,300			

Test your understanding 4

a. Bring up to date the Cash Book making any adjustments necessary

CASH BOOK

20x7		£	20x7		£
1 Apr	Balance b/d	1,470✓	2 Apr	Cheque 101129	930✓
9 Apr	Sales	606✓	4 Apr	Cheque 101130	506✓
12 Apr	Sales	1,048✓	9 Apr	Cheque 101131	834✓
30 Apr	Sales	550	29 Apr	Cheque 101132	410
			30 Apr	Balance c/d	994
		3,674			3,674
1 May	Balance b/d	994✓			

BANK STATEMENT

20x7		Payments	Receipts	Balance
01 Apr	Balance b/f			1,470✓
02 Apr	Cheque 101129	930✓		540
05 Apr	Cheque 101130	506✓		34
09 Apr	Counter credit		606✓	640
12 Apr	Cheque 101131	834✓		(194)
12 Apr	Counter credit		1,048✓	854
16 Apr	STO Hamble Comms	75✓		779
17 Apr	BACS – Honey Bee		948✓	1,727
18 Apr	BACS – Goldfish CC	534✓		1,193
25 Apr	Overdraft fee	125✓		1,068
29 Apr	BGC S May		610✓	1,678

b. Update the Cash Book and bring the balance down

FELICITY HOWE BOUTIQUE

CASH BOOK

20x7				20x7		
30 April	Balance b/d.	994.00✓				
	Honey Bee	948.00✓		16 April	Hamble Comms.	75.00✓
	S. May	610.00✓		18 April	Goldfish CC	534.00✓
				25 April	Bank charges	125.00✓
					Balance c/d.	1,818.00
		£	2,552.00		£	2,552.00
1 May	Balance b/d.	1,818.00				

c. Prepare a bank reconciliation statement as at 30 April 20x7

Felicity Howe Boutique Bank reconciliation statement as at 30 April	£
Balance per bank statement	1,678
Add:	
Name: Sales	550
Total to add	550
Less:	
Name: 101132	410
Total to subtract	410
Balance as per cash book	1,818

Case study activity 30

Statement	True	False
An outstanding lodgement is a cheque that has been received by the business, paid into the bank, and has appeared on the bank statement		✔
An outstanding lodgement is a cheque that has been received by the business, paid into the bank, but has not yet appeared on the bank statement	✔	
An unpresented cheque is one that has been written by the business but which has not yet appeared on the bank statement	✔	
Direct debits that only show on the bank statement should be ignored		✔
Direct debits and standing orders that only show on the bank statement should be written into the cash book	✔	
Bank charges are receipts to be entered into the cash book on the debit side		✔
Errors in the cash book may only come to light when the cash book entries are compared to the bank statement	✔	

Case study activity 31

a)

Cash book			
	£		£
Balance b/d	204	Sundry accounts	
Interest on deposit account	18	Standing orders	35
		Bank charges	14
		Balance c/d	173
	222		222
Balance b/d	173		

b)

BANK RECONCILIATION STATEMENT AT 30 NOVEMBER 20X8

	£
Balance per bank statement	2,618
Add Outstanding lodgements	723
	3,341
Less Unpresented cheques	(3,168)
Balance per cash account	173

 Case study activity 32

Bank Balance as at 23rd July	Positive	Overdrawn
£7,027.92	✓	

Complete the sentences:

The item missing from the bank statement is a **cash sale**
for an amount of **£110.**

The item missing from the cash book is a **cash withdrawal**
for an amount of **£150.**

This should be included in the **credit** side of the cash book.

Using accounting software to complete bookkeeping tasks

Introduction

This chapter will give you an insight into the features and benefits of different types of accounting software. It will also look at the advantages of using computerised accounting in comparison to manual bookkeeping.

When choosing which software package would be most suitable for an organisation, the advantages and disadvantages of each should be carefully assessed.

This chapter will look at each of these in turn to allow you to make your own assessment in different situations.

Having looked the different type of software options available, it is worth reconsidering some of the data security measures which were established in Chapter 1.

KNOWLEDGE
Understand the role of a bookkeeper
1.2 The importance of timely and accurate information
Understand the benefits and risks of using accounting software to complete bookkeeping tasks
5.1 Features and benefits of accounting software compared to manual bookkeeping
5.2 Advantages and disadvantages to users of different types of accounting software
5.3 Accounting software security

CONTENTS

1. Computerised accounting systems
2. Different types of accounting software
3. Summary and further questions

1 Computerised accounting systems

1.1 Case study: an introduction

 Case study

As part of her apprenticeship, Jessica has been asked to consider the accounting systems used by different organisations and perform such research, not only for her use in her own career, but to feed back to her manager at How Two Ltd.

The focus of Jessica's initial research is her uncle's business. Mr Howard is a sole trader, specialising in electrical services. He informs Jessica that although he currently uses a manual bookkeeping system, he is keen to move to a computerised accounting package, but doesn't know much about them.

Jessica has agreed to research the different features of accounting software and compare it to manual bookkeeping methods to identify whether transferring to a computerised accounting software package would be advantageous for his business.

She will then look into the different types of accounting software and to outline the advantages and disadvantages of each. She has been asked to present her findings to her manager and provide a recommendation for the future for How Two Ltd, as well as for Mr Howard's business.

1.2 The use of computerised accounting systems

Manual accounting requires the bookkeeper or accountant to post all transactions manually either into journal ledgers or into spreadsheets via a computer program such as Excel. The reason that this is considered manual is because each transaction has to be entered individually into the accounting records which can be very time-consuming.

For very small organisations, a simple spreadsheet to record monies in and out of the business may be sufficient. However, once a business becomes larger or more complex, it can be more effective and less time-consuming to use a computerised bookkeeping system.

There are many proprietary versions on the market, each of which works in a similar way. However, they will each offer different approaches to data entry, presentation of reports and so on, as well as additional 'extras' such as stock management modules, budgeting and tax planning.

Some systems also allow a company to integrate a computerised payroll function.

It very much depends on the needs of a business as to which system they would use. Assessing what a business requires a system to do for them is really important when deciding on the best package to use.

1.3 The benefits of computerised accounting systems

The main benefits of using a computerised bookkeeping system in comparison to a manual system are:

- **It enables quicker, more efficient processing of data** – financial transactions can be entered into the accounting system in batches which speeds up the process of data entry. It will perform calculations such as VAT, additions and subtractions automatically which not only improves efficiency but reduces the risk of human error. Batch processing also helps to improve speed and efficiency, further information on batch control is provided later in this chapter.

- **Cost** – hardware and software prices have fallen dramatically over the last thirty years, making a computerised system affordable to all organisations. In addition, the automation of various accounting processes enables individuals to focus their time on other tasks which contributes to the successful operation of an organisation.

- **There is no need for manual processing of data** – computerised bookkeeping systems complete all the double entry automatically. This reduces the risk of errors within the accounting records and helps to ensure that the financial reports produced are more accurate.

- **Fewer mathematical errors** – because the system completes all the double entry and other mathematical functions (e.g. calculation of percentages) there is reduced opportunity for human error.

- **Accounting documents (e.g. invoices, statements etc.) can be generated automatically** – within a computerised accounting system, accounting documents can be tailored to meet the needs of the company. They can also incorporate company details, logos etc. and are produced easily with the click of a button. This again helps with efficiency as it allows a company to automate what would be a lengthy process if completed manually.

- **The reporting process** – the range of information that can be easily produced in reports is wide and varied, meaning businesses can report to various internal and external groups (e.g. management, directors, shareholders, banks etc) in an appropriate format. As the calculations within these reports are performed automatically, it means that the information contained within is usually more accurate and reliable.

- **Data can be imported or exported to and from other programs** – computerised accounting systems allow data to be easily transferred into and out of other programs – e.g. a spreadsheet or word processing package. This allows you to work more flexibly and prevents the risk of duplication within accounting processes.

1.4 The features of computerised accounting systems

Integrated accounting software interlinks multiple functions within the accounting process.

For example, sales, purchases, the bank, the subsidiary ledgers and the general ledger all work with one another to ensure efficiency and accuracy within the accounting records. Double-entry is completed automatically - essentially, a transaction is entered into the system and all affected accounts and ledgers are automatically updated within the program, reducing the risk of error.

 Case study

How Two Ltd have sold a suite of computer accessories to a national IT company.

As soon as the sale is made and entered onto the system, the inventory levels will automatically decrease. The sale will be recorded in the relevant accounts and the bank account balance will increase to reflect the income received.

If this was completed manually, it would be a long drawn out process and the risk of human error would be quite high as the transaction is being recorded in numerous places.

Tools and wizards can be used for every accounting process, from setting up new customer/supplier records, creating price lists, showing opening balances, maintaining bank accounts, updating the nominal ledger and running an audit trail. You can also generate sales orders and control stock, print invoices, credit notes and statements, produce history and financial reports. The list of information available is endless, and these wizards have been integrated to make accounting easier on a day-to-day basis. However it is important that the initial entry is made accurately, otherwise this can cause issues with the financial data.

The tools and wizards speed up the accounting process and assures accuracy so long as the correct information is inputted to the system for it to work with. They also leave less room for errors as only one accounting entry is needed for each transaction rather than two (or three) for a manual system. By processing financial information in this way, it promotes client confidence in the accounting company as their records are updated in a timely manner. It also saves the business money as there is a lot less time spent inputting manual transactions.

All accounting systems have help menus available to users if they are unsure of how to process a transaction or perform a certain function. On the toolbar at the top of the screen, you can click 'Help' which will bring up a menu. From here you can either search for key words i.e. 'process a supplier invoice' and this will bring up a list of help sheets which contain guidance on how to complete this task. Alternatively, you can click  through the different topics within the help menu which again will provide necessary information relating to different functions within the program and their use.

The help menus are a really useful tool for those who are new to using accounting software. Some people even use these to produce their own 'process notes' to form part of the training schedule for new staff members. They also help a business by reducing the amount of training needed by individuals in the organisation and as a result this will increase productivity within the department.

1.5 Processing sales and purchase transactions

Accounting software can provide multiple benefits to processing customer and supplier transactions. Pro formas can be created quickly and easily for documents such as purchase orders, and invoices and a company house style can be adopted so they represent the branding of the organisation. When a business provides a quotation to a customer, the system can automatically perform calculations and the information can be stored within the software, making it easy to retrieve when required.

If the customer accepts the quotation, the software can easily convert the information within the quotation into an invoice format and the customer account will then automatically update to show an amount owed to the business. The double entry surrounding the invoice is also performed automatically, meaning the accounting records are always kept up to date. If an invoice requires an update for example an item had been missed or there was an error inputting the original value, the amendment only needs to be made in one place and all other records will update automatically. Alternatively, if a customer queries an invoice or has misplaced it for some reason, duplicate invoices can easily be generated from the software. This is beneficial to the customer as queries can be dealt with quickly and efficiently, portraying a positive image of you and the organisation.

1.6 Automating the sales and purchase process

If a customer or supplier invoice recurs on a regular basis, the system can be set up to process these transactions automatically. For example, if a business rents out office space to a client on a monthly basis, they can set up a recurring invoice within the system for a particular amount which can be sent at a set time in the month. Furthermore, email templates allow advanced automation of communications such as invoices, payment reminders etc. These can be scheduled to be sent automatically and the customer/supplier record will be updated with a note to show what has been sent/received. The only issue with this is if the frequency or amount changes. The bookkeeper needs to be made aware of any changes so that the information can be updated within the system and accurate records are communicated/kept.

Accounting software allows multiple invoices to be scanned into the system at one time. It will then automatically scan and check the information within the invoices to make sure they are accurate and free from error. Any issues will be highlighted by the system and can then be checked by the bookkeeper, who will investigate appropriately following the organisation's processes. The system will also allocate codes to the invoices which are then checked by the bookkeeper for accuracy. This is another major benefit to the organisation as it reduces vast amounts of time when processing customer/supplier invoices.

Once the customer/supplier invoices have been agreed within the system, it will then automatically match amounts received into/paid out of the bank to those invoices. For example, if an invoice was sent to a customer on the 1st July and payment was due on the 31st July, the system will recognise the amount due/customer reference from the automatic bank feed and will allocate the receipt to the relevant invoice. The customer account within the accounting software is automatically updated, along with the cash book. If the amount received was different to the amount expected, the system will recognise this and identify the issue so it can be reviewed and rectified as appropriate.

When a business buys goods from the same supplier regularly, the system will recognise this and automatically match transactions based on previous transactions. The only issue with this is if purchases from one supplier need to be coded to multiple accounts, therefore it is essential that the bookkeeper reviews any automatic matches before agreeing them in the system. This helps to keep the information accurate within the financial records.

1.7 Impact on business relationships

Accounting software helps maintain positive business relationships with credit suppliers. When a credit account is opened with a supplier, terms are agreed for when payment for goods/services should be made. The bookkeeper will set the supplier record up within the system and will input the payment terms agreed i.e. 10, 14, 30 days etc. If an amount is due to a supplier, a reminder will be generated to indicate that you need to pay. If the bank account is linked, automated payments can be set up so that they are generated automatically. Automated remittances can also be set up so that when a payment is made, the systems sends a remittance advice to the supplier to tell them how much has been paid and what invoices/credit notes have been taken into account. This creates efficient communication with the supplier and gives them confidence in the organisation's ability to pay amounts due on time.

Test your understanding 1

Identify whether the following statements are true or false.

Tick the correct option for each.

Statement	True	False
Individual transactions are always entered into accounting software manually		✓
Accounting software reduces the risk of human error	✓	
Recurring entries will always remain the same when they have been set up in the system		✓
Quotations are automatically converted to sales invoices in accounting software	✓	
Accounting software can suggest automatic matching of invoices based on previous transactions	✓	
Accounting software does not automatically allocate the amount received to the cash book or customer account		✓
Automated payments to suppliers can be set within the accounting software	✓	

1.8 Reporting

Computerised accounting packages automatically pull all relevant ledger entries for the period reports. Manual accounting takes much longer therefore computerised accounting enables reports to be completed much quicker.

Historically, when manual accounts were produced, reporting could take days (sometimes weeks) as all calculations would have to be performed manually and depending on the amount of data required within the report meant that this could be a lengthy process. Nowadays most reports can be produced at the click of a button and the information contained within them is up to date at the point in which the report was produced. This means that information viewed is a lot more reliable and business decisions can be made much more quickly based on the information given.

Reports can be produced which will help the management to instantly monitor and control the business.

 Case study

When discussing accounting software systems with her manager, Jessica asks her manager for an example of how computerised reports have had a real impact in the past. Her manages explains that an issue was identified with unpaid invoices.

In this instance, the aged debtor's/receivables analysis showed which customer accounts were overdue, how much they owed and how old the debt was. This helped the credit control department to see which debts needed chasing immediately. As a result, this report helps with a very important process in accounting, as the business needs income to operate and if the customers are not paying their debts on time, this could lead to cash flow problems.

If the business has cash flow problems, it could not have enough money to pay its suppliers, which could lead to delays in getting products for resale to customers. In this instance, it would not take long for any business to fail.

Similar to the example given above, aged creditors/payables reports are useful to determine when payment is due to suppliers. A business does not want to pay amounts due too early as again, this may lead to cash flow issues. It is important that these reports are generated regularly and monitored closely to ensure financial stability for the organisation.

Example

The Aged Debtors (also called the Aged Receivables) Analysis shows details of any monies outstanding from credit customers. It also breaks the debts down into timescales of 30, 60, 90 and 90+ days so that you can see how old any particular debt is which helps with knowing which are a priority to chase for payment.

Time: 22:31:29

Aged Debtors Analysis (Detailed)

Date From:	01/01/1980	Customer From:
Date To:	31/08/2020	Customer To: ZZZZZZZZ

Include future transactions: No
Exclude later payments: No

 ** NOTE: All report values are shown in Base Currency, unless otherwise indicated **

A/C: CAM004　Name: Campbell & Dunn　　　Contact: Julian Dunn　　　Tel: 01346 231412

No	Type	Date	Ref	Details	Balance	Future	Current	Period 1	Period 2	Period 3	Older
29	SI	31/08/2020	4895	8 x Televisions	4,003.20	0.00	4,003.20	0.00	0.00	0.00	0.00
				Totals:	4,003.20	0.00	4,003.20	0.00	0.00	0.00	0.00

Turnover: 3,336.00
Credit Limit £ 0.00

A/C: HAS004　Name: W Haslam　　　Contact: William Haslam　　　Tel: 01346 859234

No	Type	Date	Ref	Details	Balance	Future	Current	Period 1	Period 2	Period 3	Older
30	SI	31/08/2020	4896	Paper & Ink	105.84	0.00	105.84	0.00	0.00	0.00	0.00
				Totals:	105.84	0.00	105.84	0.00	0.00	0.00	0.00

Turnover: 713.20
Credit Limit £ 0.00

A/C: PAR006　Name: Miss S Pargenter　　　Contact: Sarah Pargenter　　　Tel: 01346 554776

No	Type	Date	Ref	Details	Balance	Future	Current	Period 1	Period 2	Period 3	Older
27	SI	31/08/2020	4893	TV Installation	180.00	0.00	180.00	0.00	0.00	0.00	0.00
				Totals:	180.00	0.00	180.00	0.00	0.00	0.00	0.00

Turnover: 150.00
Credit Limit £ 0.00

A/C: POP002　Name: Mrs H Poppy　　　Contact: Harriett Poppy　　　Tel: 01346 855777

No	Type	Date	Ref	Details	Balance	Future	Current	Period 1	Period 2	Period 3	Older
25	SI	31/08/2020	4891	Laptop	270.00	0.00	270.00	0.00	0.00	0.00	0.00
31	SC	31/08/2020	25	Faulty Laptop	-270.00	0.00	-270.00	0.00	0.00	0.00	0.00
				Totals:	0.00	0.00	0.00	0.00	0.00	0.00	0.00

Turnover: 0.00
Credit Limit £ 0.00

		Grand Totals:	4,289.04	0.00	4,289.04	0.00	0.00	0.00	0.00

Example

The Aged Creditor's (sometimes called the Aged Payables) analysis shows details of any monies owed to credit suppliers. It breaks the outstanding amounts down into timescales of 30, 60, 90 and 90+ days so that you can see how old any particular debt is and who to make a priority for payment.

An example is shown on the next page.

```
Time:  22:42:23                      Aged Creditors Analysis (Detailed)

Date From:               01/01/1980                              Supplier From:
Date To:                 31/08/2020                              Supplier To:     ZZZZZZZZ

Include future transactions:  No
Exclude later payments:       No

               ** NOTE: All report values are shown in Base Currency, unless otherwise indicated **

A/C:   MP002    Name:   Mills Paper Products        Contact:   Shaun Squire          Tel:    01726 378918

No:   Type  Date        Ref     Details      Balance    Future   Current   Period 1   Period 2   Period 3    Older
36    PI    31/08/2020  10092   Paper and Ink  195.02     0.00    195.02      0.00       0.00       0.00      0.00

                                Totals:        195.02     0.00    195.02      0.00       0.00       0.00      0.00

Turnover:                       162.52
Credit Limit £                    0.00

A/C:   OI001    Name:   Octopus Inks Ltd          Contact:   Sheila Cribbley        Tel:    0191 252 4132

No:   Type  Date        Ref     Details      Balance    Future   Current   Period 1   Period 2   Period 3    Older
35    PI    31/08/2020  2203    Laptops and   371.11     0.00    371.11      0.00       0.00       0.00      0.00

                                Totals:        371.11     0.00    371.11      0.00       0.00       0.00      0.00

Turnover:                       309.26
Credit Limit £                    0.00

                                Grand Totals:  566.13     0.00    566.13      0.00       0.00       0.00      0.00
```

It is common for customer/supplier queries to be raised. Using accounting software helps to locate information quickly and easily and allows for individual customer/supplier reports to be generated immediately.

This is helpful as individual records can be used as evidence to solve a customer/supplier query. Amendments to these records can be made easily and all other records will be automatically updated to reflect any changes. A full supplier report follows on the next page.

Example

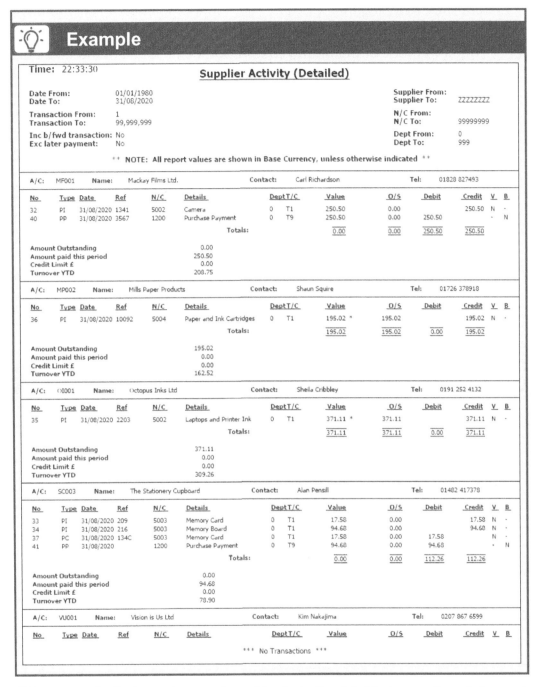

Time: 22:33:30

Supplier Activity (Detailed)

Date From:	01/01/1980
Date To:	31/08/2020
Transaction From:	1
Transaction To:	99,999,999
Inc b/fwd transaction:	No
Exc later payment:	No

Supplier From:	
Supplier To:	ZZZZZZZZ
N/C From:	
N/C To:	99999999
Dept From:	0
Dept To:	999

** NOTE: All report values are shown in Base Currency, unless otherwise indicated **

A/C: MF001   Name: Mackay Films Ltd.   Contact: Carl Richardson   Tel: 01828 827493

No	Type	Date	Ref	N/C	Details	Dept	T/C	Value	O/S	Debit	Credit	V	B
32	PI	31/08/2020	1341	5002	Camera	0	T1	250.50	0.00		250.50	N	-
40	PP	31/08/2020	3567	1200	Purchase Payment	0	T9	250.50	0.00	250.50		-	N
					Totals:			0.00	0.00	250.50	250.50		

Amount Outstanding	0.00
Amount paid this period	250.50
Credit Limit £	0.00
Turnover YTD	208.75

A/C: MP002   Name: Mills Paper Products   Contact: Shaun Squire   Tel: 01726 378918

No	Type	Date	Ref	N/C	Details	Dept	T/C	Value	O/S	Debit	Credit	V	B
36	PI	31/08/2020	10092	5004	Paper and Ink Cartridges	0	T1	195.02 *	195.02		195.02	N	-
					Totals:			195.02	195.02	0.00	195.02		

Amount Outstanding	195.02
Amount paid this period	0.00
Credit Limit £	0.00
Turnover YTD	162.52

A/C: OI001   Name: Octopus Inks Ltd   Contact: Sheila Cribbley   Tel: 0191 252 4132

No	Type	Date	Ref	N/C	Details	Dept	T/C	Value	O/S	Debit	Credit	V	B
35	PI	31/08/2020	2203	5002	Laptops and Printer Ink	0	T1	371.11 *	371.11		371.11	N	-
					Totals:			371.11	371.11	0.00	371.11		

Amount Outstanding	371.11
Amount paid this period	0.00
Credit Limit £	0.00
Turnover YTD	309.26

A/C: SC003   Name: The Stationery Cupboard   Contact: Alan Pensill   Tel: 01482 417378

No	Type	Date	Ref	N/C	Details	Dept	T/C	Value	O/S	Debit	Credit	V	B
33	PI	31/08/2020	209	5003	Memory Card	0	T1	17.58	0.00		17.58	N	-
34	PI	31/08/2020	216	5003	Memory Board	0	T1	94.68	0.00		94.68	N	-
37	PC	31/08/2020	134C	5003	Memory Card	0	T1	17.58	0.00	17.58		N	-
41	PP	31/08/2020		1200	Purchase Payment	0	T9	94.68	0.00	94.68		-	N
					Totals:			0.00	0.00	112.26	112.26		

Amount Outstanding	0.00
Amount paid this period	94.68
Credit Limit £	0.00
Turnover YTD	78.90

A/C: VU001   Name: Vision is Us Ltd   Contact: Kim Nakajima   Tel: 0207 867 6599

No	Type	Date	Ref	N/C	Details	Dept	T/C	Value	O/S	Debit	Credit	V	B

*** No Transactions ***

Other reports that can be produced include the trial balance, the statement of profit and loss and the statement of financial position to show real-time information about the business.

- **The trial balance** is essentially a list of all accounts within the system and their balances at any one point in time.

  With computerised accounting, a user simply selects the 'trial balance' from the reports section and prints it off. All of the debits and credits are automatically created and the accounts automatically balanced off. The information contained within the trial balance is in real time, meaning that it is up to date to the point at which you have run the report and much more accurate that doing this manually.

- **The statement of profit and loss** report contains all of the accounts that relate to the income and expenses of the business, but it does it does not include any information on the company's assets or liabilities. Again, using the accounting software system, it would be produced in real-time at the point at which the report was produced.

  This report is one of the required financial statements at the end of an accounting year and is useful for making business decisions.

  Managers would typically review the information within the profit and loss account to see whether the figures appear to be correct. If something does not look quite right, the accounting system allows users to drill into the figures and produce more detailed analysis on the income and expenses by running the analysis reports for the required accounts. This means that the reporting process not only increases productivity but it also reduces the stress levels of staff and enables them to work more efficiently.

⍾ Example

The Profit and Loss report includes information on all of the income and expenses of a business.

Time: 22:57:28   **Profit and Loss**

From: Month 1, September 2019
To: Month 12, August 2020

Chart of Accounts: Default Layout of Accounts

	Period		Year to Date	
Sales				
Product Sales	17,718.28		17,718.28	
		17,718.28		17,718.28
Purchases				
Purchases	8,735.43		8,735.43	
		8,735.43		8,735.43
Direct Expenses				
Sales Promotion	208.33		208.33	
		208.33		208.33
Gross Profit/(Loss):		8,774.52		8,774.52
Overheads				
Gross Wages	255.50		255.50	
Rent and Rates	666.67		666.67	
Travelling and Entertainment	6.67		6.67	
Printing and Stationery	106.51		106.51	
Maintenance	4.00		4.00	
General Expenses	5.65		5.65	
		1,045.00		1,045.00
Net Profit/(Loss):		7,729.52		7,729.52

- The **Statement of Financial Position** (Balance Sheet) is another important report both for accounting and business planning.

  The Balance Sheet report includes information on all of the assets and liabilities of a business, but it does not include any information on the company's income or expenses. This report is also one of the required financial statements at the end of an accounting year.

 Example

The financial position (balance sheet) report includes information on all of the assets and liabilities of a business.

Time: 22:58:38

Balance Sheet

From: Month 1, September 2019
To: Month 12, August 2020

Chart of Accounts: Default Layout of Accounts

	Period		Year to Date	
Fixed Assets				
Motor Vehicles	5,500.00		5,500.00	
		5,500.00		5,500.00
Current Assets				
Debtors	4,289.04		4,289.04	
Deposits and Cash	602.36		602.36	
Bank Account	5,904.88		5,904.88	
		10,796.28		10,796.28
Current Liabilities				
Creditors : Short Term	566.13		566.13	
VAT Liability	1,000.63		1,000.63	
		1,566.76		1,566.76
Current Assets less Current Liabilities:		9,229.52		9,229.52
Total Assets less Current Liabilities:		14,729.52		14,729.52
Long Term Liabilities				
		0.00		0.00
Total Assets less Total Liabilities:		14,729.52		14,729.52
Capital & Reserves				
Share Capital	7,000.00		7,000.00	
P & L Account	7,729.52		7,729.52	
		14,729.52		14,729.52

There are also reports relating to bank payments and receipts over a specified period.

The **Bank Payments Analysis** report will show an analysis of all payments that have gone through the Bank Current Account.

Example

The Bank Payments Analysis report includes all payments out of the bank.

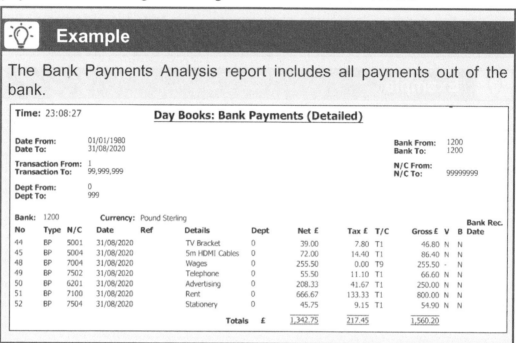

The **Bank Receipts Analysis** is similar but shows receipts rather than payments.

Example

The Bank Receipts Analysis report includes all payments into the bank.

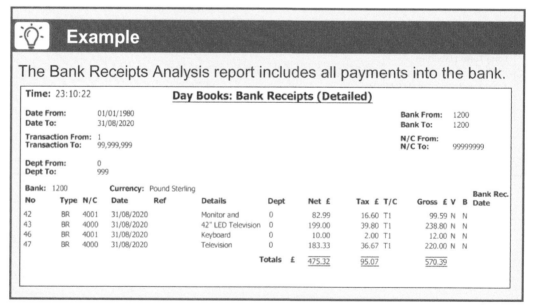

You can also run a **Bank Payments and Receipts Analysis** report which shows both payments and receipts.

Likewise, the **Cash Payments Analysis** and **Cash Receipts Analysis** show all cash payments received and made.

KAPLAN PUBLISHING

This is just a small selection of the reports that are available to view within most accounting software systems.

It really depends on the needs of the business as to which report is the most suitable for each particular task. Reports can be customised to include as much or as little information as required, making them adaptable to all types of business.

Templates for financial reports are available to meet the needs of individual organisations where logos and business-related information can be included. All businesses have many clients and users of financial reporting, it would therefore not be cost-effective or possible to design individual report layouts for every client/user of the software.

Whilst there are many reports available with different options for layouts and the information contained within, it would be impossible to be able to meet the needs of every individual user.

Test your understanding 2

Identify whether the following statements are true or false.

Tick the correct option for each.

Statement	True	False
An individual customer account report will show amounts due from all credit customers		✓
An aged payables report details the age of and amounts due to credit suppliers	✓	
Bank receipt and payments reports can be generated for specified periods of time	✓	
Amendments to customer/supplier records will not reflect on the reports unless specified		✓

Test your understanding 3

Consider the following statement:

An advantage of producing reports using accounting software is that it shows real-time financial information

Put a tick in the correct box to show if the statement is true or false.

Options	✓
True	✓
False	

1.9   Importing and exporting data

 Definitions

Importing data means taking information such as a file from one location on a computer to another location on a computer so that you can work with or use that file/information in a different format.

Exporting data is the same in reverse – sending data from one location in your computer to another location, either internally or externally.

Information that can be imported or exported can come in many formats which include files produced by other programs such as spreadsheets, word processors or other accounting packages.

In accounting, this is a really useful tool as not all organisations will use accounting software for their day-to-day operations.

 Example

A company may use a database to store all customer/supplier information. This information can be imported into the accounting software package to save inputting it twice. This information includes:

- customer information
- supplier information
- stock information
- asset data.

Financial transactions computed in one type of software cannot be imported into another type of software. Accounting transactions need to be produced at source within the accounting software.

The most common tool used in accounting is exporting data from the accounting software into spreadsheet format using a program such as Excel.

Reports produced within the accounting software can be exported to spreadsheet format and then the data can be manipulated to suit the needs of the business.

For example, a company might produce an aged debtor's/receivables report and export this into Excel. From here they can then add or remove information as required and then produce charts and graphs to make the information easier to see at a glance. They may do this month on month so that they can spot any trends in the data which will enable them to take appropriate action within the credit control department.

KAPLAN PUBLISHING

Many organisations will use the import/export function in their day-to-day operations as sometimes the accounting package that they are using is limited in terms of the information that can be produced and how it can be manipulated. Importing and exporting data not only saves time processing large volumes of information, but it allows an organisation to work more flexibly with the information given.

It also reduces the risk of human error as the same information isn't being manually inputted to a number of different places which helps to prevent duplicating entries within the accounting records. It enables businesses to work more sustainably as it reduces the need to work from paper-based documentation which in turn improves efficiency and productivity, as multiple users can view information at the same time from the system.

 Example

Historically, bank statements were provided in paper format and manually reconciled in the accounting software. The bookkeeper would have to identify any discrepancies between the bank statement and the accounting records and manually enter the information into the software.

Advances in technology allow for bank statements to be downloaded from online banking systems into a comma-separated value (CSV) file. A CSV file is a plain text file that contains a list of data, which in this case would be the list of transactions within the bank statement. This file can be imported into the accounting software to remove the need to manually enter every transaction. Not only does this save time, but it reduces the risk of human error.

As mentioned in an earlier chapter, bank accounts can also be directly linked to the accounting software via a live bank feed. This allows finance professionals to view information in real-time and provides wider accessibility to those who are authorised to see this information.

Bank payments/receipts analysis reports can be generated quickly and reviewed by senior management to help prepare budgets/monitor spending etc. These reports can be generated for specified periods of time i.e. a particular month, to help identify trends in company income/expenditure.

CSV – comma-separated value.

Test your understanding 4

Identify whether the following statement is true or false.

Tick the correct option.

Statement	True	False
A CSV file is used to import/export data to/from third party software/apps.	✓	

Test your understanding 5

What are the benefits of being able to import and export data to and from other programs?

Tick all that apply.

Options	✓
It saves time	✓
It reduces the risk of human error	✓
To be able to communicate information in different formats	✓
It ensures all data is backed up	
It enables all accounting transactions to be modified	
To be able to work with data more flexibly	✓

Test your understanding 6

If you are unsure how to complete a task, what do you click on?

Put a tick in the correct box.

Options	✓
Help menu	✓
Tools menu	
File menu	
Task menu	

KAPLAN PUBLISHING

2 Different types of accounting software

2.1 'Off the shelf' accounting software

Many accounting software packages can be bought 'off the shelf', from retail outlets or suppliers. They typically come in a box with a CD to load the software onto a computer and a user manual to help with set up and instructions of how to process financial transactions.

You may have come across some of these in your day-to-day work but examples include: Sage (there are many versions of this), Quickbooks and CCH. You will find that these are available to purchase from retail outlets specialising in computer or office goods or online via their websites. 'Off the shelf' accounting packages are easy to install and usually have a step by step wizard to help you set up your accounting platform.

The main advantage of 'off the shelf' accounting software is the cost. It works out cheaper than some other software types as effectively you purchase a license for a certain number of users at a fixed fee. This cost is then spread out across multiple users and once purchased, there are no further costs unless you wish to upgrade the software to a later version.

For a small business, they may decide that the current version of the software is sufficient for their day-to-day operations and therefore they may decide not to upgrade. If they do upgrade, they will only pay for the upgrade and, again, this is a fixed, one-off amount. With 'off the shelf' software, there are external training courses and webinars available which takes the ownership away from the employer. Many suppliers of 'off the shelf' software also have helpdesks that users of the system can contact if they are experiencing problems; members of their specialist teams will assist, rather than problems having to be dealt with internally.

'Off the shelf' software can be complicated to use (especially for small businesses) and may contain sections that are not needed. It tries to offer something for every kind of company and therefore is not specific to one particular industry. This may mean a shortfall for specialist businesses, which could be a disadvantage. If this is the case, companies may have to alter the way they operate to fit in with the software's limitations, possibly resulting in further training for staff and new processes. It can also take some time for new users to learn how to use the software properly which could slow down the production of financial information in the early stages of use. However, in comparison to manual accounting, an 'off the shelf' accounting package will dramatically increase speed and productivity within an accounts department and reduce the risk of human error.

2.2   Bespoke accounting software

Bespoke accounting software is designed and written to meet the individual needs of an organisation. When choosing this option for accounting, a business will look at all aspects of their day-to-day operations and decide what it is that they want the system to do for them, and what information they would like the system to produce.

Software developers will then be brought in to design and implement the system; this could be done in house (for larger organisations) or by an external company who specialise in doing this. If taking the latter option, it is important that the company has access to the source code for the software. If they do not have the source code for the software, there is a danger that the business can be exposed.

The main disadvantage of using bespoke accounting software is that it takes time to develop, implement and test the software before it can be used. If it does not work how the company desire, it will take additional time to go back and amend it. All of this comes at a cost and it can become expensive in relation to 'off the shelf' software packages.

Another disadvantage is that all staff will need specialised training on how to use the software. This will have to be done internally which again comes at a cost. Overall, using bespoke software proves a very expensive although sophisticated option, especially for large specialist businesses.

There are many advantages of bespoke accounting software. As it is made to work how the company likes to work and to fit their business needs, it means that if a company changes the way it works, the software can be changed to meet this demand.

The software is continuously developed and updated, so it should never become outdated which can prove to be a massive benefit to the company. As the software is generated internally, this means that there are no licensing costs or annual fees in comparison to 'off the shelf' accounting software. If users of the system are experiencing problems, these can be solved in house rather than having to contact an external help desk which means less supervision should be needed.

Bespoke software could also potentially offer a company a competitive advantage because you can design specialist features that may not be used/available to your competitors.

2.3   Cloud-based accounting software

> ### 🔍 Definition
>
> **Cloud computing** refers to the delivery of various computing services online via web-based applications, using a network of servers connected to the internet rather than a direct connection to local servers or in-house networks.
>
> Cloud computing allows files to be stored and managed remotely, meaning that data can be downloaded from any location.

Cloud-based accounting software is a relatively new way of accounting, which enables all accountancy tasks to be completed online and for the data to then be safely stored remotely, off the premises and 'in the cloud', meaning that all data is protected from natural disasters such as floods and fires.

Storing information in the cloud increases the safety of stored information where the chances of unauthorised access from external sources are virtually nil.

Most common applications have evolved and are now offering this service such as SageOne, Xero, Quickbooks, Kashflow and Clearbooks. Many companies that have moved towards a cloud-based version of accounting feel that it has revolutionised the way in which they work.

The software is available to authorised users anywhere, on any device that has an internet connection. This means that the user does not necessarily have to be in the office in order to access the software and complete their duties. Users can even download applications onto their smart phones and complete their day-to-day accounting transactions whilst on the move. Consequently, accounting is more flexible and urgent tasks can easily be completed on an ad hoc basis. → for specific purpose.

LATIN = TO THIS.

SOFTWARES
OFF THE SHELF ACCOUNTING
CLOUD — BASED ACCOUNTING
BESPOKE ACCOUNTING

device device device device device device

> **Example**
>
> A customer was chasing a credit note which was due three weeks ago.
>
> If the company is using a desktop version of accounting software, the credit note would need to done in the office. If no one is available to create it, the credit note would still not be raised.
>
> Using cloud accounting enables the user to view the customer account via the internet or via their smartphone app, they can then gather the required information, create the credit note and send it straight away. Not only does this increase productivity, but it presents a good impression of the company and creates solid relationships with customers.

From a management perspective this is also a more productive new way of working. Managers may not necessarily be available in the office all of the time. Cloud-based accounting means that they are not restricted to viewing activity and productivity on the company premises. This enables a smooth flow of work and action to be taken much more quickly if productivity slows or work is not being completed in the correct manner.

Cloud-based accounting is a cost-effective way of working because the company computer costs are reduced. Companies pay a monthly subscription for access to the software for a specific number of users. This means that there is no limit to the number of users who are able to access the program and different levels of access can be set which helps to protect company data.

Another advantage of cloud-based accounting is that all software maintenance, version upgrades, system administration costs and server failures are managed by the cloud accounting service provider. In terms of cash flow for a company, this is excellent as the management know exactly how much they are paying and with this being paid monthly, there are no unexpected costs or additional upgrade fees. However, it may not be cost effective for a small company to keep paying subscription fees compared to purchasing 'off the shelf' software. A small company may only have a handful of users so having to pay a monthly subscription to be able to use the software may work out more expensive than if they purchased an 'off the shelf' package.

Another disadvantage to cloud based accounting is that companies have no direct control over their information. The server which is supplied and controlled by the software provider could be anywhere outside the UK. Different countries have different rules and this could mean that a government in another country could be looking at your remotely stored files.

+ shifts according provider

In addition to this, updates may be a problem. The software provider will decide what additional features they are going to add to the program and when this will happen. This means that users can only have what the accounting provider offers and can only update processes when the general software update occurs. Ultimately this does not allow much flexibility in terms of being able to easily change the way companies work to reflect the ever changing demands of their business.

There can be problems when backing up data, as most cloud accounting software providers do not have the ability for a company to take a backup of its data and export it or save it to their own computer system; they are simply able to print out selected reports. This means that changing to another package or just keeping a long-term record without having to keep paying the monthly subscription can then become a problem.

2.4 Choosing the correct software: 'off the shelf' vs bespoke

When comparing 'off the shelf' software with bespoke software, the following should be considered before choosing which is the right option for an organisation:

Cost

* 'Off the shelf' software involves the purchase price of the product. There is then usually an annual license fee to pay; companies have to pay a fee per user of the software.

* Bespoke software is extremely expensive at the outset. It is impossible to give a price as it is dependent on the size and complexity of the software build that the company needs. It will always cost many thousands of pounds however as you own the software, there are no license fees.

Levels of support for users

* 'Off the shelf' software has so many users that there is a wealth of online community support. Many software programs provide online 'web chat', e-mail and telephone support facilities. Some software providers charge for maintenance and support functions.

* In relation to bespoke software, there are no means of direct self-help support or online communities, however, as there is direct access to the developer who will provide support, this means that this is not necessary.

Timeframe for development

- 'Off the shelf' software has already been developed and therefore once you have purchased the package, the software is loaded onto a computer and is instantly available to start using. The only problem that some users may encounter at this point is whether or not they know how to use the software.

- Bespoke software takes months to develop and the more complex software builds can take as long as a year, dependent on how many developers are working on it. Once developed, the software then needs to be tested and any problems detected and amended before any data can be transferred into it. The added problem of transferring old data from another program into the new one will probably follow, although some of the information may be exported from an old program depending on how the new bespoke version has been designed. This means that the initial setup could take some time and all of the information from the old system must be checked for accuracy to ensure the integrity of the data.

Range of functions used by the business

- 'Off the shelf' software has so many functions available that most companies will not need all of them and therefore there will be some functions that they will never use at all. The software is designed under a 'one size fits all' basis in an attempt to suit all business needs, so what functions one company uses another may not.

- Bespoke software only has functions that an individual company has specified that they need. These should be designed and implemented to fit in with the company's processes to ensure smooth automation and increased productivity where possible.

Frequency and ease of updates

- Updates are available with 'off the shelf' software, it depends on the software provider used as to whether there is a fee for this service. The software updates will be decided upon by the software provider and will not necessarily match the demands of an individual business. In addition to this, updates are installed as and when the software provider decide, not necessarily in a timeframe to suit a particular business' needs.

- Updates are free with bespoke software and will be agreed with the program designers. If a particular function within the program needs to be added or amended due to company expansion for example, then this will be done in a timeframe that suits the business needs. The program developers if working with an external company will charge for this service.

Level of training required to use the software

- When introduced, 'off the shelf' software usually comes with training needs for an organisation's staff. Employees need to learn how to navigate the software to meet the needs of the organisation. Each user will have different tasks to complete using the program. This means that depending on the user, there may be quite a lot of new ways of working to learn. This can increase cost and slow down productivity. The software provider will provide external training courses as well as webinars/online videos for them to use to help them get to grips with how the system works.

- Bespoke software needs very little training, as it is built to function in the same way as the company works. If a whole new system is built and all users are new to it, staff could get involved in the testing phase to get them used to using it. All training would be conducted in house with the developers or senior staff members who have been involved in the changeover.

Type of subscription

- 'Off the shelf' subscriptions vary by software provider and can include some or all of the following charges: upgrades, software support, monthly or annual licensing fees, per user fee, per-website or installation licenses.

- There are no subscription fees with bespoke software because the company owns the software.

Test your understanding 7

Match the following features to the relevant software by ticking the correct one.

	Bespoke Software	'Off the Shelf' Software
Already developed		✓
Tailored to company specification	✓	
Instant installation		✓
Takes time to develop and install	✓	
Requires a subscription		✓
No subscription needed	✓	

2.5   Choosing the correct software: traditional vs cloud

Cost

- Traditional accounting software can be costly, as well as set up costs there are costs involved in system upgrades. In addition to this, customer support can be expensive.

- With cloud software there are no upfront fees for hardware packages such as servers - instead smaller fixed monthly fees are paid. The only downside to this is that it does involve committing to a contract. With there being no way of backing up data to the organisation's computer hardware, it also makes transferring from a cloud-based version back to traditional software more difficult.

Levels of support for users

- With traditional accounting software, support is usually made available via telephone during office hours. This can end up being quite costly, time consuming and is not always convenient for those who work longer hours or whose working hours are outside of the traditional 9 – 5 Monday to Friday.

- Cloud-based software users usually feel much more supported because support is available online 24/7. This is much more flexible for those who work unsociable hours, or for those who might want to complete their business' bookkeeping duties in the evening.

Range of functions used by the business

- Often traditional accounting software will only work across one platform. The functions available using traditional software are also restricted to whatever is built in to the program they are using.

- All accounting functions can be accessed via the cloud. A range of functions are available and these are regularly reviewed and updated free of charge by the software provider. Different levels of access to different functions can be set for the varying levels of job roles within the organisation.

Frequency and ease of updates

- Traditional accounting updates can be expensive and the user has to remember to do them. In order to run the updates, there must be sufficient space on the server and this can sometimes take considerable time to complete. The updates with traditional software are not always as up to date as other types of software and are not always easy to accomplish.

- Cloud-based accounting updates are automatically processed by the server. Notifications of updates are communicated to the user by the software provider so that the company can utilise the software properly as the technology evolves. The cost of upgrades is included in the monthly subscription and therefore no additional costs are incurred.

Upgrade capacity

- With traditional accounting, upgrades are not always possible due to the storage capacity of the computer system. This then involves the costly task of having to expand the system memory in order to install the upgrade.

- With cloud-based accounting, there is no danger of running out of space to upgrade as this is managed by the service provider. The cost of your monthly fee however, is dependent on the size of your storage package.

Level of training required to use the software

- There are many different training options available with both traditional software and cloud-based accounting, these include:

  - external training by the software provider
  - courses run by an accredited training company
  - online webinars and training videos
  - user manuals.

Access from multiple devices

- Traditional accounting is restricted to working on one computer, if the user wanted to take information away from the office to work with elsewhere it would mean saving their work to a device such as a USB stick. This poses a security risk as sensitive information could be lost in transportation.

- With cloud-based accounting, users can access and work with their software on multiple devices from anywhere with an internet connection - for example, on laptops, ipads/tablets and mobile telephones.

Type of subscription

- Traditional accounting subscriptions can include a one-off fee with the potential for additional costs for upgrades etc. If licenses are put in place, they are done so on a per user basis.

- Cloud-based accounting requires a contract commitment with the service provider and a monthly subscription fee.

Access to the internet

- Traditional accounting does not require an internet connection.
- An authorised user can access cloud-based software anywhere in the world where there is an internet connection.

Test your understanding 8

You have received an e-mail to say that you may have overlooked something within the company accounts but you are on holiday abroad. It cannot wait until you return home.

Which software would allow you to access the information?

Put a tick in the correct box.

Options	✔
'Off the shelf'	
Bespoke	
Cloud-based	✓

Test your understanding 9

Different types of software have different advantages.

Match the relevant software to its statement.

	Cloud	Bespoke	'Off the Shelf'
You can access it anywhere in the world with an internet connection	✓		
Is developed to meet the individual company needs		✓	
Can be changed to meet the changing demands of a company		✓	
Can be used on any device (laptop, tablet, smartphone)	✓		
Loads instantly onto a computer			✓
Has a widespread self-help community forum			✓
Has online support 24/7	✓		

3 Summary and further questions

In this chapter we have considered why organisations use computerised accounting systems and the different types of software available, including 'off the shelf' packages, bespoke products and cloud-based applications. You should have a good understanding of the advantages and disadvantages of all of these types of software and which are most appropriate for different organisations.

We have also looked in depth at security software and the risks and threats presented by computerised accounting.

Let us return to our case study to see how Jessica applies this knowledge.

 Case study activity 33

Jessica is now required to feed back to her manager after her research. She is asked to state the benefits of using accounting software compared to the existing manual accounting system.

Which of the following are advantages of using accounting software? Tick all correct answers.

Options	✓
Money can be saved as no accounting staff are required	
All accounting software packages offer online chat support	
Data can be processed more efficiently and accurately	✓
Invoices and statements can be generated automatically	✓
It removes the threat of viruses	
It reduces the likelihood of mathematical errors	✓
Data can easily be exported to other programs	✓
GDPR is no longer a consideration	

Case study activity 34

Having decided that an accounting software system is required, Jessica's uncle asks her whether to buy an 'off the shelf' product or a cloud-based accounting solution.

He asks for her advice on the matter. Which TWO of the following statements would be correct advice for her to offer?

	✓
With cloud-based accounting software, it is not necessary to be in the office as applications can be accessed anywhere on any device, as long as there is an internet connection. This means greater flexibility and easier access to data.	✓
Updates are not as easy and are more expensive with cloud-based accounting systems. Furthermore, the user needs to remember to run the updates, unlike 'off the shelf' packages where updates are automatic and quicker.	
'Off the shelf' accounting software often comes with much better support – this is available 24 hours a day, 7 days a week, via online chat communities and therefore is better suited for those working long hours.	
Traditional accounting software can prove more expensive, as there are both set up costs and the additional upgrade costs. Cloud-based software is usually paid for by a monthly subscription, so although there is a contract, the fee is fixed.	✓
All accounting functions can be accessed via the cloud and therefore it is easier for everyone to access the data, including customers and individuals with no connection to the company. Everyone has the same level of access, which is fairer.	

Case study activity 35

Jessica has been asked to help her colleague find some sales information. Which **two** of the following reports would show How Two Ltd's sales figures?

Report	✔
Trial Balance	✓
Aged creditors (payables) report	
Aged debtors (receivables) report	
Balance sheet report	
Profit and loss report	✓
Bank receipts analysis report	

Answers to chapter activities

Test your understanding 1

Statement	True	False
Individual transactions are always entered into accounting software manually		✓
Accounting software reduces the risk of human error	✓	
Recurring entries will always remain the same when they have been set up in the system		✓
Quotations are automatically converted to sales invoices in accounting software	✓	
Accounting software can suggest automatic matching of invoices based on previous transactions	✓	
Accounting software does not automatically allocate the amount received to the cash book or customer account		✓
Automated payments to suppliers can be set within the accounting software	✓	

Test your understanding 2

Statement	True	False
An individual customer account report will show amounts due from all credit customers		✓
An aged payables report details the age of and amounts due to credit suppliers	✓	
Bank receipt and payments reports can be generated for specified periods of time	✓	
Amendments to customer/supplier records will not reflect on the reports unless specified		✓

Test your understanding 3

An advantage of producing reports using accounting software is that it shows real-time financial information

Options	✓
True	✓
False	

Test your understanding 4

Statement	True	False
A CSV file is used to import/export data to/from third party software/apps.	✓	

Test your understanding 5

Options	✓
It saves time	✓
It reduces the risk of human error	✓
To be able to communicate information in different formats	✓
It ensures all data is backed up	
It enables all accounting transactions to be modified	
To be able to work with data more flexibly	✓

Test your understanding 6

Options	✔
Help menu	✔
Tools menu	
File menu	
Task menu	

Test your understanding 7

	Bespoke Software	'Off the Shelf' Software
Already developed		✔
Tailored to company specification	✔	
Instant installation		✔
Takes time to develop and install	✔	
Requires a subscription		✔
No subscription needed	✔	

Test your understanding 8

Options	✔
'Off the shelf'	
Bespoke	
Cloud-based	✔

Test your understanding 9

	Cloud	Bespoke	'Off the Shelf'
You can access it anywhere in the world with an internet connection	✓		
Is developed to meet the individual company needs		✓	
Can be changed to meet the changing demands of a company		✓	
Can be used on any device (laptop, tablet, smartphone)	✓		
Loads instantly onto a computer			✓
Has a widespread self-help community forum			✓
Has online support 24/7	✓		

Case study activity 33

Statement	✓
Money can be saved as no accounting staff are required	
All accounting software packages offer online chat support	
Data can be processed more efficiently and accurately	✓
Invoices and statements can be generated automatically	✓
It removes the threat of viruses	
It reduces the likelihood of mathematical errors	✓
Data can easily be exported to other programs	✓
GDPR is no longer a consideration	

Case study activity 34

Options	✓
With cloud-based accounting software, it is not necessary to be in the office as applications can be accessed anywhere on any device, as long as there is an internet connection. This means greater flexibility and easier access to data.	✓
Updates are not as easy and are more expensive with cloud-based accounting systems. Furthermore, the user needs to remember to run the updates, unlike 'off the shelf' packages where updates are automatic and quicker.	
'Off the shelf' accounting software often comes with much better support – this is available 24 hours a day, 7 days a week, via online chat communities and therefore is better suited for those working long hours.	
Traditional accounting software can prove more expensive, as there are both set up costs and the additional upgrade costs. Cloud-based software is usually paid for by a monthly subscription, so although there is a contract, the fee is fixed.	✓
All accounting functions can be accessed via the cloud and therefore it is easier for everyone to access the data, including customers and individuals with no connection to the company. Everyone has the same level of access, which is fairer.	

Case study activity 35

Report	✓
Trial Balance	✓
Aged creditors (payables) report	
Aged debtors (receivables) report	
Balance sheet report	
Profit and loss report	✓
Bank receipts analysis report	

Mock Assessment 1 – Bookkeeping Fundamentals

Introduction

The following is a Mock Assessment to be attempted in exam conditions.

You should attempt and aim to complete EVERY task.

Read every task carefully to make sure you understand what is required.

Where the date is relevant, it is given in the task.

Both minus signs and brackets can be used to indicate negative numbers UNLESS task instructions say otherwise.

You must use a full stop to indicate a decimal point.

You may use a comma to indicate a number in the thousands, but you don't have to.

The assessment includes 9 tasks.

The total number of marks available for this assessment is 100.

Time allowed: 90 minutes.

1 Mock Assessment Questions

Task 1 (10 marks)

a) State whether the following are the responsibility of a bookkeeper within an organisation by putting a tick in the correct box. **(3 marks)**

	Yes	No
Entering sales invoices and credit notes onto the system	✓	
Maintaining the cash book	✓	
Approving salary increases for sales staff		✓

b) State whether the following statements are true or false by putting a tick in the relevant box. **(2 marks)**

Statement	True	False
Making an underpayment to a supplier is good for business as it will increase the profit figure.		✓
Spending time tracing and correcting errors in the bookkeeping system is good for business as it is a cost-effective way of ensuring information is accurate	✓	✓

c) Your supervisor tells you that there are some issues with customer accounts this month. Identify whether the following situations would impact on the outstanding amounts due from credit customers.

Tick the relevant box next to each option. **(3 marks)**

Statement	Could impact the amounts due	Could not impact the amounts due
An underpayment from a credit customer	✓	
A cash sale overstated in the accounting records	✓	✓
An invoice to a credit customer has been duplicated in the accounting records	✓	✓

d) Your supervisor is completing the quarterly VAT return, but cannot finalise this without all of the invoices being inputted onto the system by the end of the day. She has asked you to complete this task, but you know the volume of invoices is too much to do in the timeframe given. What should you do?

Tick the correct option from the actions below. **(1 mark)**

Options	✓
Enter the invoices as quickly as possible	
Ask your colleague to help you, they only started with the business on Monday therefore they have no set tasks to complete today	
Speak with your supervisor and explain there is too much work to do in the time given	✓

e) You have completed an internal report for your manager to show the actual purchases compared with budgeted purchases for the month of July. After sending the report over, you recognise there were some errors within the calculations. What could be a possible consequence of this?

Tick the correct option from the below options. **(1 mark)**

Options	✓
Incorrect tax payments could be made to HMRC	
Incorrect business decisions could be made in relation to future budgets	✓
There would be no consequences as the system should have highlighted any errors	

Task 2 (10 marks)

a)   Insert an item from the following list into the right hand column of the table below to identify the term described.

You will not need to use all of the items. **(2 marks)**

Description	Term described
A transaction when an organisation buys goods or services and pays its supplier immediately	*cash purchase*
An organisation that is owed money for goods or services supplied.	*a receivable/debtor*

a payable/creditor

Pick list

A cash sale   A cash purchase   A credit sale

A credit purchase   A receivable/debtor   A payable/creditor

b)   Place a tick in the appropriate column of the table below to show whether each of the items listed is an example of an asset, a liability, income or expenditure.

You should not place more than one tick against each item.
(3 marks)

Item	Asset	Liability	Income	Expenditure
Cash sales			✓	
Rent				✓
Office computers	✓			

c)   Refer to the following transactions and complete the table to show the dual effect of each transaction. Use the picklist below, you can use each option more than once if required. **(4 marks)**

Description	Effect 1	Effect 2
A business took out a bank loan which was paid into the business bank account today. The loan will be paid back over 4 years.		
A business purchased a new van, paying for it immediately by bank transfer		

Pick list

Increase Liabilities   Increase Assets   Decrease Capital

Increase Capital   Decrease liabilities   Decrease Assets

d) Identify whether the following statement is true or false by ticking the correct option below. **(1 mark)**

Statement	True	False
The accounting equation will always balance.		

Task 3 (14 marks)

a) Organisations issue and receive different documents when buying and selling goods.

Complete the sentences below by inserting the most appropriate option from the following pick list: **(4 marks)**

- a purchase order
- a receipt
- an invoice
- a statement of account
- a remittance advice
- a credit note
- a goods returned note

i) An organisation sends _____ listing the items returned to the customer and showing the amount refunded.

ii) An organisation sends _____ to a supplier listing the items it wishes to purchase.

iii) An organisation sends _____ to a customer detailing all the transactions that took place between them and the customer in a given period of time.

iv) An organisation sends _____ to a supplier along with items returned that are not fit for purpose.

b) You are the bookkeeper for Sunnyside Ltd. You are preparing a sales invoice for the following items: 12 x Hanging Baskets and 18 x Ceramic Plant Pots from Happydays PLC.

The list price of the Hanging Baskets is £17.90 and the list price of the Ceramic Plant Pots is £15.50. The purchase order has been checked and the number used was PO1090.

Sunnyside Ltd. have agreed 14 day payment terms with Happydays PLC. VAT is charged at the standard rate of 20% and today's date is 28th November 202X.

Complete the following purchase order with the following information:

- Customer name
- Supplier name
- Date
- PO number
- Product pricing
- Net
- VAT
- Total

(10 marks)

Sales Invoice

Sunnyside Ltd.

476 Laneside Road

Oxford

OX10 5WD

VAT Reg No. 397 8682 00

Telephone No: 01346 572354

To: Happydays PLC.   Date:

Wayside Business Park

Taunton   P.O. Number:

TN5 6NQ

Quantity	Description	Unit Price	Price
12	Hanging Baskets		
15	Ceramic Plant Pots		
		Net	
		VAT	
		Total	
	Payment terms agreed:		

Task 4 (8 marks)

A supply of paper has been delivered to Alpha Ltd by Pixie Paper. The purchase order sent from Alpha Ltd, and the invoice from Pixie Paper, are shown below.

Alpha Ltd.
121 Baker St
Newcastle
NE1 7DJ

Purchase Order No. PO1792

To: Pixie Paper
Date: 5 Aug 202X

Please supply 50 boxes of A4 paper product code 16257
Purchase price: £10 per box, plus VAT
Discount: less 10% trade discount, as agreed.

Pixie Paper
24 Eden Terrace
Durham
DH9 7TE

VAT Registration No. 464 392 401

Invoice No. 1679

Alpha Ltd
121 Baker St
Newcastle
NE1 7DJ

9 Aug 202X

50 boxes of A4 paper, product code 16257 @ £11 each

Net	£550
VAT	£100
Total	£600

Terms: 30 days net

Check the invoice against the purchase order and answer the following questions.

a) Consider the following statements relating to the invoice provided by Pixie Paper when checked against the purchase order.

Tick to indicate whether they are true or false. **(3 marks)**

Statement	True	False
The correct product has been supplied		
The correct quantity of goods has been supplied		
The correct net price has been calculated		

b) What is the main reason for any errors on this invoice? **(1 mark)**

_____

c) What would be the net amount charged if the invoice was correct? **(1 mark)**

£

d) What would be the VAT amount charged if the invoice was correct? **(1 mark)**

£

e) What would be the total amount charged if the invoice was correct? **(1 mark)**

£

f) Based on the information provided, what action should be taken? Tick the most appropriate answer. **(1 mark)**

Action	✓
The invoice should be filed but not paid	
The invoice should be referred back to a supervisor	
The invoice should be paid	

Task 5 (14 marks)

Three sales credit notes have been partially entered into the relevant day book below:

GGD Ltd	
117 Vinefield Place	
Warminster	
Kent WA1 1BB	
Credit Note 552	**Date: 1 Dec 202X**
	£
250 products GUP @ £2.00	500.00
VAT @ 20%	100.00
Gross amount refunded	600.00
Terms: Net monthly account	

Day Associates	
2 London Road	
Becksley	
Kent BE7 9MN	
Credit Note 35	**Date: 10 Dec 202X**
	£
24 products Y12 @ £5.75	138.00
VAT @ 20%	27.60
Gross amount refunded	165.60
Terms: Net monthly account	

Cohen PLC	
25 Main Road	
Rexsome	
Herefordshire HR2 6PS	
Credit Note 1168	**Date:23 Dec 202X**
	£
80 products Y12 @ £7.10	568.00
VAT @ 20%	113.60
Gross amount refunded	681.60
Terms: Net monthly account	

a)   Given this information:

i)   Enter the correct name of the day book in the space provided.

ii)   Complete the entries in the day book by inserting the missing figures for each of the credit notes.

iii)   Total the day book. **(8 marks)**

| | day book

Date 202X	Details	Credit note number	Total £	VAT £	Net £
1 Dec	GGD Ltd	552		100.00	
10 Dec	Day Associates	138	165.60	27.60	
23 Dec	Cohen PLC	1168	681.60		568.00
	Totals				

b)   You recently started trading with a new supplier. Below is a list of transactions between you and the supplier for December 202X.

Document Type	Total Amount (£)
Opening balance	422.11
Invoice	450.00
Credit Note	125.00
Invoice	324.50
Invoice	675.35
Remittance	325.00
Credit Note	121.00

Complete the following table to calculate how much you owe to the supplier at the end of December. You do not need to enter minus signs or brackets in your answer. **(5 marks)**

	£
Opening balance	
Total of invoices	
Total of credit notes	
Remittance advice	
Amount owed at the end of December	

c) Identify which of the following would be a useful source of information when identifying amounts due from a credit customer using accounting software.

Tick the most appropriate answer from the options below: **(1 mark)**

Options	✓
Aged payables analysis	
Profit & loss report	
Aged receivables analysis	
Cash sales listing	

Task 6 (18 marks)

a) You are working on the payments side of the cash book. There are four bank payments to record.

Cash Purchases Listing

Date	Paid to	Details	Net (£)	VAT (£)	Total (£)
2/12/2X	J Carroll	Cleaning	80.00	16.00	96.00
12/12/2X	Rymann	Stationery	42.50	8.50	51.00

Payments to trade payables

Date	Supplier	£
8/12/2X	ABS Ltd.	455.00
20/12/2X	PnP Express	525.60

Complete the payments side of the cash book shown below.

Enter details into the relevant columns, and enter figures to complete each column. Total each column and check your work by cross casting your figures. **(10 marks)**

Cash book extract – payments side

Date	Details	Bank (£)	VAT (£)	Trade payables (£)	Cleaning (£)	Stationery (£)
2/12/2X	J Carroll	96.00				
8/12/2X	ABS Ltd.	455.00				
12/12/2X	Rymann	51.00				
20/12/2X	PnP Express	525.60				
Totals		1127.60				

b) Identify whether each of the following transactions would be included in the payments side of the cash book, the receipts side of the cash book, or whether it would not appear in the cash book.

Tick the relevant box to indicate your answer. **(5 marks)**

Transaction	Payments side	Receipts side	Would not appear in cash book
Cash sales			
A credit note received from a credit supplier			
Capital transferred to the business by its' owner			
Motor vehicle expenses			
A sales invoice			

c) Identify whether the following would be input as a cash payments or cash receipts. Tick the relevant box to indicate your answer. **(3 marks)**

Description	Cash Receipts	Cash Payments
Counter credits		
Cash withdrawals		
Bank charges		

Task 7 (10 marks)

You have the following information about cash in hand.

Date	Details	Amount (£)
30/11/2X	Amount counted at the end of the day	125.00
2/12/2X	Cash sales	225.00
4/12/2X	Paid for postage	25.00
6/12/2X	Paid a train fare	80.00
10/12/2X	Cash sales	154.00
15/12/2X	Cash sales	201.50
19/12/2X	Paid a taxi fare	18.50
21/12/2X	Paid the cleaner	50.00

a)   Complete the table to calculate the closing amount of cash in hand on the 21st December. You do not need to use minus signs or brackets in your answer. **(4 marks)**

Cash in hand	£
Opening amount on 1st December 202X	
Total receipts	
Total payments	
Closing amount on 21st December 202X	

b) You have the following extract from the business bank statement.

Bank statement

Date 20XX	Details	Paid out £	Paid in £	Balance £
01 Dec	Balance b/d			4,550
03 Dec	Counter credit – S Callaghan		75	4,625
9 Dec	Counter credit – B Wadhurst		800	5,425
13 Dec	Faster Payment – Waterloo plc	120		5,305
14 Dec	Cheque – P Umpkin	951		4,354
19 Dec	Counter credit – S Top		115	4,469
20 Dec	Cheque – Simply Stationery		70	4,539
21 Dec	Cheque - Geordie Gas	180		4,359
26 Dec	BACS Receipt – H.I. Light		720	5,079
27 Dec	BACS Receipt – R Winder		99	5,178

What is the closing balance on the bank statement on 14th December? **(1 mark)**

c) You also have an extract from the cash book for December covering the same period of time.

Cash book

Details	Reference	Bank	Details	Reference	Bank
Balance b/d		4,550	P Umpkin	Cheque	951
S Callaghan	Counter credit	75	Waterloo plc	Faster Payment	120
B Wadhurst	Counter credit	800	Geordie Gas	Cheque	180
S Top	Counter credit	115	R Williams	Faster Payment	240
Simply Stationery	Cheque	70			
R Winder	BACS Receipt	99			

Compare the extracts from the bank statement and the cash book, and complete the following sentences: **(5 marks)**

		✔		
The item that is missing from the bank statement is….	a cheque			
	A counter credit			
	A faster payment		for an amount of	£
	A BACS payment			
	A BACS receipt			

		✔		
The item that is missing from the cash book is….	a cheque			
	a counter credit			
	a faster payment		for an amount of	£
	a BACS payment			
	a BACS receipt			

		✔	
The missing item will need to go on the….	receipts		side of the cash book.
	payments		

Task 8 (8 marks)

a) Match the features in the picklist below to the relevant heading within the table. **(4 marks)**

Off the shelf software	Bespoke software

Picklist:

Updates are made regularly and with ease

Reporting is tailored specifically for the needs of your business

Costs are fixed and can be easily budgeted for

The system can be adapted in line with the organisation's processes

b) Identify which of the following is an advantage of cloud based accounting software. **(1 mark)**

Cloud based accounting software…..	✓
…..produces financial reports in real-time	
…..requires memory on the server to store financial information	
…..can produce reports that are specifically tailored to your business	
…..can be backed up at any time to your computer	

c) Which of the following would be an indicator of a manual bookkeeping system? Tick the most appropriate option. **(1 mark)**

Options	✓
It is a cheap way of accounting for a small business	
It is quicker	
It is more accurate	
Reports can be produced easily	

d) Which **two** of the following reports would show a sale made in cash? **(2 marks)**

Report	✓
Cash payments analysis	
Aged creditors report	
Cash receipts analysis	
Balance sheet report	
Sales analysis	

KAPLAN PUBLISHING

Task 9 (8 marks)

a) Professional accountants are required to undertake continuing professional development (CPD). State which one of the five fundamental principles is safeguarded by CPD.

Tick the correct ethical principle from the options below. **(1 mark)**

Options	✓
Objectivity	
Integrity	
Professional competence & due care	
Professional behaviour	
Confidentiality	

b) A professional accountant who complies with the law, brings no disrepute on the profession and is perceived as being ethical by other people has complied with the fundamental principle of:

_____.

Tick the correct ethical principle from the options below. **(1 mark)**

Options	✓
Objectivity	
Integrity	
Professional competence & due care	
Professional behaviour	
Confidentiality	

c) As a bookkeeper it is important to observe confidentiality.

Show whether the following statement is true or false. **(1 mark)**

Statement	True	False
If a manager asks to see confidential information, you should let them see it.		

d) Place the correct threats to data security from the picklist below next to each of the following definitions. **(3 marks)**

Definition	Threat
Unauthorised access or control to a computer network with a motive of altering information or stealing information for personal gain.	
Being contacted by someone via email who is posing as HMRC and asking for you to provide your bank details to receive a refund.	
A computer program which attaches itself to files and then duplicates itself to cause harm to your computer.	

Picklist:

A Virus

Hacking

Phishing

e) Which **two** of the following can protect accounting software against threats? **(2 marks)**

Options	✓
Only have one log in so that you know exactly who has access to the system	
Have unlimited access for all registered users of the accounting system	
Encrypt files so that they are only readable by authorised users	
Ensure that passwords are changed regularly	
Always work remotely rather than in an office	

Mock Assessment 2 – Bookkeeping Fundamentals

Introduction

The following is a Mock Assessment to be attempted in exam conditions.

You should attempt and aim to complete EVERY task.

Read every task carefully to make sure you understand what is required.

Where the date is relevant, it is given in the task.

Both minus signs and brackets can be used to indicate negative numbers UNLESS task instructions say otherwise.

You must use a full stop to indicate a decimal point.

You may use a comma to indicate a number in the thousands, but you don't have to.

The assessment includes 9 tasks.

The total number of marks available for this assessment is 100.

Time allowed: 90 minutes.

1 Mock Assessment Questions

Task 1 (10 marks)

a) Show whether the following statements are true or false. **(2 marks)**

Statement	True	False
A bookkeeper is able to authorise all financial transactions.		
A bookkeeper is responsible for preparing and checking financial documentation.		

b) Identify whether the following statements are true or false.

Tick the correct box from the options below. **(3 marks)**

Statement	True	False
If a client is suspected of money laundering, the bookkeeper should speak to them about it .		✓
A bookkeeper is required to follow the ethical principles of the profession.	✓	
A bookkeeper is responsible for making business decisions based on the financial information.	⩗	✓

c) Identify **TWO** potential effects of untimely information by selecting the appropriate options from the list below. **(2 marks)**

Statement	✓
It helps build a good rapport with suppliers as they can delay payments.	
It is better to take time when processing entries regardless of timescales.	
It can delay the receipt of goods from suppliers.	
It can lead to management making good business decisions.	
Compliance deadlines may be missed, leading to penalties being imposed.	

d) Complete the following sentence. **(1 mark)**

		✓
A bookkeeping error can result in…	authorisation of the purchase of an asset	
	duplicated payments to suppliers	

e) A bookkeeper issued a sales invoice to a customer. The total was overstated by £250.

What effects might this overstatement have on the business? Tick the box to complete the sentence. **(1 mark)**

		✓
This could result in the customer making an…	underpayment	
	overpayment	✓

f) Complete the following sentence. **(1 mark)**

		✓	
The overstatement…	could	✓	…affect the recorded profit of the business
	could not		

Task 2 (10 marks)

a) Insert an item from the following pick list into the right hand column of the table below to categorise the item described.

You will not need to use all of the items. **(3 marks)**

Description	Category
A bank loan obtained by an organisation to fund expansion plans	*liability*
Amounts due from credit customers	*asset*
An injection of cash into the business by its owner	*capital*

Pick list

Asset   Liability   Income

Expenditure   Capital

b) When a business makes a profit, how does this affect the capital figure?

Tick the correct option from the list below. **(1 mark)**

Options	✓
The capital will remain the same	
The capital will increase	✓
The capital will decrease	

c) When a business has more expenses than income, it results in a:

Select the correct option below. **(1 mark)**

Options	✓
Profit	
Loss	✓

d) Which TWO of the following, accurately represent the accounting equation?

Select two options from the list below. **(2 marks)**

Equation	✓
Capital = Assets + Liabilities	
Assets = Capital + Liabilities	✓
Assets – Capital = Liabilities	✓
Assets = Capital - Liabilities	

e) A business receives a cheque from one of its credit customers.

Complete the following sentences to show the effects of this transaction. **(2 marks)**

	Select one	
It will....	increase	the amount recorded in the business bank account
	decrease	
It will	increase	the amount the business records as outstanding from their receivables
	decrease	

e) Identify which of the one of the following statements is true.

Tick the correct option from the list of statement provided. **(1 mark)**

Statement	✓
Every transaction will affect the bank account in the bookkeeping system.	
Every bookkeeping transaction will affect at least two records.	
Every transaction within the bookkeeping system will increase assets and decrease liabilities.	

Task 3 (14 marks)

a) Organisations issue and receive different documents when buying and selling goods.

Complete the sentences by inserting the most appropriate option from the following pick list: **(2 marks)**

- a purchase order
- a receipt
- an invoice
- a statement of account
- a remittance advice
- a credit note

i) An organisation sends _____ to a customer with details of items purchased, the amount owing and the terms of payment.

ii) An organisation sends _____ to a creditor accompanying a payment, listing items included in that payment.

b) Insert an item from the following pick list into the right hand column of the table below to identify the term described.

You will not need to use all of the items. **(2 marks)**

Description	Term described
A person or organisation who is owed money due to sales made on credit.	
A transaction to sell goods when the payment is made one month later.	

Pick list

A cash sale	A cash purchase	A credit sale
A credit purchase	A debtor/receivable	A creditor/payable

c) You are the bookkeeper for Pens & Paper Ltd, a supplier of print and stationery products.

One of your customers is I Do Designs, are a supplier of specialist wedding stationery including invitations and table plans. They have returned some goods to you. The goods returned note is shown below and has already been checked against the products returned.

**I Do Designs
84 Hornsea Way
Colchester
CO21 4XU**

GOODS RETURNED NOTE

Pens and Paper Ltd.
Unit 4a Dialstone Business Park
Sheffield
S23 4LE

30 Nov 202X

Reference: GRN2214

Product Code	Description	Reason for return	Unit Price (£)	Quantity
A4GLX	1 Box of A4 Silver Gloss Card	Damaged	28.80	2
TON4G	LG Printer Toner	The wrong size	32.50	1

The following information is available:

- The last two credit notes issued within the system were CN2241 and CN2242

- Today's date is 27th November 202X

- The amounts stated on the goods returned note are VAT exclusive

Complete the sales credit note on the following page. **(10 marks)**

Credit note

Unit 4a Dialstone Business Park
Sheffield
S23 4LE

VAT Reg No. 7423546338

To: [   ]

84 Hornsea Way
Colchester
CO21 4XU

Date: [   ]

Credit Note
Number: [   ]

Product Code	Description	Quantity	Unit Price	Price
A4GLX	1 Box of A4 Silver Gloss Card	[ ]	28.80	
TON4G	LG Printer Toner	1	32.50	
			Net	
			VAT	
			Total	

Task 4 (8 marks)

a) You work for ABC Ltd. You have a goods returned note and a purchases credit note. Check that the information entered on the credit note is correct.

Mark all highlighted boxes with a tick or cross to show if they have been input accurately. **(7 marks)**

ABC Ltd.
123 High Street
Manchester
M23 1RD

Goods Returned Note

XYZ Ltd.
Sunnyside
Beach Business Park
LN1 5NQ

30 Nov 202X

Description	Reason for return	Unit Price (£)	Quantity
S123	Damaged	10.99	2
RC557	The wrong size	12.50	1

XYZ Ltd.
Sunnyside
Beach Business Park
LN1 5NQ

Credit Note

ABC Ltd.
123 High Street
Manchester
M23 1RD

2 Dec 202X

Description	Quantity	✓ / x	Unit Price (£)	✓ / x	Total	✓ / x
S123	1		19.09		19.09	
RC557	1		12.50		12.50	
				Net	31.59	
				VAT	6.28	
				Total	37.90	

b) Complete the following sentence based on the above. **(1 mark)**

		✓
Based on the information I have, I will.....	accept the credit note and input it onto the system	
	process the credit note but raise it with my supervisor as an issue	
	refer the credit note to my supervisor	

Task 5 (14 marks)

a) Three purchase invoices have been partially entered into the purchase day book.

GGD Ltd 117 Vinefield Place Warminster Kent WA1 1BB	
Invoice 3575	**Date:21 October 202X**
	£
70 units of SPLAT @ 12.75	892.50
VAT @ 20%	178.50
Total	1,071.00
Terms: Net monthly account	

Day Associates 2 London Road Becksley Kent BE7 9MN	
Invoice 35	**Date:22 October 202X**
	£
2400 units of AA12 @ £0.55	1,320.00
VAT @ 20%	264.00
Total	1,584.00
Terms: Net monthly account	

Cohen PLC

25 Main Road

Rexsome

Herefordshire HR2 6PS

Invoice 1164	Date:23 October 202X

	£
40 units of Y12 @ £14.20	568.00
VAT @ 20%	113.60
Total	681.60

Terms: Net monthly account

Using this information to:

i)   Enter the correct name of the day book in the space provided.

ii)   Complete the entries in the day book by inserting the missing figures for each of the invoices.

iii) Total the day book.   **(8 marks)**

[_____] **day book**

Date 202X	Details	Invoice	Total £	VAT £	Net £
21 Oct	GGD Ltd	3575		178.50	892.50
22 Oct	Day Associates	35	1,584.00		1,320.00
23 Oct	Cohen PLC	1164	681.60	113.60	
	Totals				

b) You recently started trading with a new credit customer who you owed £325.00 to at the beginning of the month. Below is a list of transactions between you and the customer for November 202X.

Document Type	Total Amount (£)
Remittance	325.00
Invoice	221.00
Credit Note	54.00
Invoice	556.96
Remittance	167.00
Credit Note	54.26
Invoice	339.50

Complete the following table to calculate how much is owed by the customer at the end of November. Enter minus signs or brackets to indicate negative figures in your answer. **(5 marks)**

	£
Opening balance	
Total of invoices	
Total of credit notes	
Remittance advice	
Amount owed at the end of November	

c) Should the business record the amount owing from the customer at the end of November as an asset or a liability? **(1 mark)**

Task 6 (18 marks)

a)   You are working on the receipts side of the cash book. For this task you may ignore VAT.

The following cash sales were counted and put into the safe.

Date	Details	Total (£)
20/12/2X	Cash Sales	42.00

The following amounts were received from credit customers.

Date	Customer	Payment Type	Total (£)
15/12/2X	Mayor & Sons	Faster Payment	655.90
22/12/2X	C Whelan	Cheque	224.60

Complete the receipts side of the cash book shown below.

Enter details into the relevant columns, and enter figures to complete each column.

Total each column and check your answer by cross casting your figures.
(8 marks)

Cash book extract – receipts side

Details	Bank (£)	Cash (£)	Trade Receivables (£)	Cash Sales (£)
Mayor & Sons	655.90		655.90	
Cash Sales				
C Whelan				
Totals				

b) You are working on the payments side of the cash book. There is a cash payment that needs to be entered into the payments side of the cash book.

The supplier is Locksmiths Ltd. The cash payment is for a repair on 10/12/2X at £25 exclusive of VAT. VAT is charged at 20%.

Enter the payment into the payments side of the cash book.
(4 marks)

Cash book extract – payments side

Date	Details	Bank (£)	VAT (£)	Trade payables (£)	Repairs (£)	Stationery (£)
10/12/2X						

c) Identify whether the following statements are true or false by ticking the appropriate option from the list below. **(6 marks)**

Statement	True	False
Interest received will be entered into the payments side of the cash book		
VAT will appear in both the cash receipts book and the cash payments book		
Debit card payments will show in the cash payments book		
Remittance advice notes will be entered into the cash payments book		
Items that have been entered into the cash book will automatically appear on the bank statement		
Cheque book stubs are used to record receipts from credit customers		

Task 7 (10 marks)

You have the following information about cash in hand.

Date	Details	Amount (£)
30/11/2X	Amount counted at the end of the day	180.00
4/12/2X	Cash sales	120.00
5/12/2X	Cash sales	75.00
10/12/2X	Paid for lunch for a meeting	30.00
19/12/2X	Paid for refreshments for the office	15.00
21/12/2X	Cash sales	143.00
23/12/2X	Paid a taxi fare	21.50
24/12/2X	Cash sales	70.00

a) Complete the table to calculate the closing amount of cash in hand on the 21st December. Use minus signs or brackets to indicate negative amounts in your answer. **(4 marks)**

Cash in hand	£
Opening amount on 1st December 202X	
Total receipts	
Total payments	
Closing amount on 24th December 202X	

b) You have the following extract from the business bank statement.

Bank statement

Date 202X	Details	Paid out £	Paid in £	Balance £
01 Dec	Balance b/d			5,168
03 Dec	BACS receipt – R Brown		250	5,418
9 Dec	Counter credit – A Bate		425	5,843
13 Dec	Cheque – Trafalgar plc	120		5,723
14 Dec	Faster payment – P Tuller	138		5,585
19 Dec	Faster payment – R Brown		300	5,885
20 Dec	Cheque – Printer Palace	400		5,485
21 Dec	BACS payment - English Electrics	180		5,305
26 Dec	Counter credit – C Beamer		175	5,480
27 Dec	Faster payment – M Boulden		180	5,660

What is the closing balance on the bank statement on 19th December?
(1 mark)

c) You also have an extract from the cash book for December covering the same period of time.

Cash book

Details	Reference	Bank	Details	Reference	Bank
Balance b/d		5,168	Trafalgar plc	Cheque	120
R Brown	BACS receipt	250	P Tuller	Faster payment	138
A Bate	Counter credit	425	Printer Palace	Cheque	400
R Brown	Faster payment	300			
M Boulden	Faster payment	180			
C Beamer	Counter credit	175			
A Parker	Counter credit	195			

Compare the extracts from the bank statement and the cash book, and complete the following sentences. **(5 marks)**

		✓		
The item that is missing from the bank statement is....	a cheque			
	A counter credit			
	A faster payment		for an amount of	£
	A BACS payment			
	A BACS receipt			

		✓		
The item that is missing from the cash book is....	a cheque			
	a counter credit			
	a faster payment		for an amount of	£
	a BACS payment			
	a BACS receipt			

		✓	
The missing item will need to go on the....	receipts		side of the cash book.
	payments		

Task 8 (8 marks)

a) Match the features in the picklist below to the relevant heading within the table. **(4 marks)**

Traditional Accounting Software	Cloud Software

Picklist:

No need for an internet connection
Can be paid in monthly instalments with no upfront fees for hardware
All financial information is securely stored on the server
Can be synced with your phone or tablet so that you can work on the move

b) Identify which **one** of the following is an advantage of bespoke software in comparison to 'of the shelf' software. **(1 mark)**

Bespoke accounting software…..	✔
…..can evolve over time to match your changing requirements	
…..is available immediately and therefore is more efficient	
…..requires less in house training	
…..is cheaper in comparison to 'off the shelf' software	

c) Which **one** of the following would be an indicator of cloud based software? **(1 mark)**

Options	✓
Development and installation will only take about two weeks	
Updates are run automatically and are included in the price	
Developed and built to meet your specific needs; it is flexible	
Can be easily modified to match your specific requirements	

d) Identify whether the following statements are true or false by ticking the correct option from the list below. **(2 marks)**

Statement	True	False
Accounting software allows customer statements to be produced in real time.		
Accounting software allows data to be imported from third party software and apps.		

Task 9 (8 marks)

a) Place the correct threats to data security from the picklist below next to each of the following statements. **(3 marks)**

Definition	Threat
One of the clerks has been processing transactions all day and then clicks on the wrong processing option, to delete them all in error.	
You have been working on a project for nearly a month. When you come to work on it again and try to open it, an error message comes up to say that there's something wrong with the document.	
You have been processing month end adjustments all morning and then your screen freezes and the software shuts down automatically.	

Picklist

Corrupt file

Software crashes

Accidental deletion

b) Which **two** of the following can protect accounting software against threats? **(2 marks)**

Options	✓
Give all users of the system a specific way of setting their password so that you can access it on their behalf even if they leave suddenly	
Implement firewalls on all hardware and software	
Enlist different levels of access rights depending on the user	
Ensure that a backup is taken once a week in case of a fire or flood	

KAPLAN PUBLISHING

c) Identify whether the following statements are true or false by ticking the correct option. **(3 marks)**

Statement	True	False
Money laundering is a criminal offence but you cannot be imprisoned as a result of it.		
The ethical principle of objectivity is about being straightforward and honest in all professional and business relationships.		
CPD activities contribute to the ethical principle of professional competence.		

Mock Assessment Answers – Bookkeeping Fundamentals

1 Mock Assessment One : Answers

Task 1 (10 marks)

a) State whether the following are the responsibility of a bookkeeper within an organisation by putting a tick in the correct box. **(3 marks)**

	Yes	No
Entering sales invoices and credit notes onto the system	✓	
Maintaining the cash book	✓	
Approving salary increases for sales staff		✓

b) State whether the following statements are true or false by putting a tick in the relevant box. **(2 marks)**

Statement	True	False
Making an underpayment to a supplier is good for business as it will increase the profit figure.		✓
Spending time tracing and correcting errors in the bookkeeping system is good for business as it is a cost-effective way of ensuring information is accurate		✓

c) Your supervisor tells you that there are some issues with customer accounts this month. Identify whether the following situations would impact on the outstanding amounts due from credit customers. **(3 marks)**

Statement	Could impact the amounts due	Could not impact the amounts due
An underpayment from a credit customer	✓	
A cash sale overstated in the accounting records		✓
An invoice to a credit customer has been duplicated in the accounting records	✓	

KAPLAN PUBLISHING

d) Your supervisor is completing the quarterly VAT return, but cannot finalise this without all of the invoices being inputted onto the system by the end of the day. She has asked you to complete this task, but you know the volume of invoices is too much to do in the timeframe given. What should you do? **(1 mark)**

Options	✓
Enter the invoices as quickly as possible	
Ask your colleague to help you, they only started with the business on Monday therefore they have no set tasks to complete today	
Speak with your supervisor and explain there is too much work to do in the time given	✓

e) You have completed an internal report for your manager to show the actual purchases compared with budgeted purchases for the month of July. After sending the report over, you recognise there were some errors within the calculations. What could be a possible consequence of this? **(1 mark)**

Options	✓
Incorrect tax payments could be made to HMRC	
Incorrect business decisions could be made in relation to future budgets	✓
There would be no consequences as the system should have highlighted any errors	

Task 2 (10 marks)

a) Insert an item from the following list into the right hand column of the table below to identify the term described. **(2 marks)**

Description	Term described
A transaction when an organisation buys goods or services and pays its supplier immediately	A cash purchase
An organisation that is owed money for goods or services supplied.	A payable/ creditor

b) Place a tick in the appropriate column of the table below to show whether each of the items listed is an example of an asset, a liability, income or expenditure. **(3 marks)**

Item	Asset	Liability	Income	Expenditure
Cash sales			✓	
Rent				✓
Office computers	✓			

c) Refer to the following transactions and complete the table to show the dual effect of each transaction. Use the picklist below, you can use each option more than once if required. **(4 marks)**

Description	Effect 1	Effect 2
A business took out a bank loan which was paid into the business bank account today. The loan will be paid back over 4 years.	Increase Assets	Increase Liabilities
A business purchased a new van, paying for it immediately by bank transfer	Increase Assets	Decrease Assets

d) Identify whether the following statement is true or false by ticking the correct option below. **(1 mark)**

Statement	True	False
The accounting equation will always balance.	✓	

Task 3 (14 marks)

a) Complete the sentences below by inserting the most appropriate option from the following pick list: **(4 marks)**

  i) An organisation sends **a credit note** listing the items returned to the customer and showing the amount refunded.

  ii) An organisation sends **a purchase order** to a supplier listing the items it wishes to purchase.

  iii) An organisation sends **a statement of account** to a customer detailing all the transactions that took place between them and the customer in a given period of time.

  iv) An organisation sends **a goods returned note** to a supplier along with items returned that are not fit for purpose.

b) You are the bookkeeper for Sunnyside Ltd. You are preparing a sales invoice for the following items: 12 x Hanging Baskets and 18 x Ceramic Plant Pots from Happydays PLC.

The list price of the Hanging Baskets is £17.90 and the list price of the Ceramic Plant Pots is £15.50. The purchase order has been checked and the number used was PO1090.

Sunnyside Ltd. have agreed 14 day payment terms with Happydays PLC. VAT is charged at the standard rate of 20% and today's date is 28th November 202X. **(10 marks)**

Sales Invoice

Sunnyside Ltd.

476 Laneside Road

Oxford

OX10 5WD

VAT Reg No. 397 8682 00

Telephone No: 01346 572354

To: Happydays PLC.

Wayside Business Park

Taunton

TN5 6NQ

Date: **28/11/202X**

P.O. Number: **PO1090**

Quantity	Description	Unit Price	Price
12	Hanging Baskets	17.90	214.80
15	Ceramic Plant Pots	15.50	232.50
		Net	447.30
		VAT	89.46
		Total	536.76

Payment terms agreed:	14 days

Task 4 (8 marks)

a) Consider the following statements relating to the invoice provided by Pixie Paper when checked against the purchase order. **(3 marks)**

Statement	True	False
The correct product has been supplied	✓	
The correct quantity of goods has been supplied	✓	
The correct net price has been calculated		✓

b) What is the main reason for any errors on this invoice? **(1 mark)**

The 10% trade discount has not been applied.

c) What would be the net amount charged if the invoice was correct? **(1 mark)**

£450.00

d) What would be the VAT amount charged if the invoice was correct? **(1 mark)**

£90.00

e) What would be the total amount charged if the invoice was correct? **(1 mark)**

£540.00

f) Based on the information provided, what action should be taken? **(1 mark)**

Action	✓
The invoice should be filed but not paid	
The invoice should be referred back to a supervisor	✓
The invoice should be paid	

Task 5 (14 marks)

a) **Sales returns** day book

Date 202X	Details	Credit note number	Total £	VAT £	Net £
1 Dec	GGD Ltd	552	**600.00**	100.00	**500.00**
10 Dec	Day Associates	138	165.60	27.60	**138.00**
23 Dec	Cohen PLC	1168	681.60	**113.60**	568.00
	Totals		**1,447.20**	**241.20**	**1,206.00**

(8 marks)

b) Complete the following table to calculate how much you owe to the supplier at the end of December. **(5 marks)**

	£
Opening balance	422.11
Total of invoices	1,449.85
Total of credit notes	(246.00)
Remittance advice	(325.00)
Amount owed at the end of December	1,300.96

c) Identify which of the following would be a useful source of information when identifying amounts due from a credit customer using accounting software. **(1 mark)**

Options	✓
Aged payables analysis	
Profit & loss report	
Aged receivables analysis	✓
Cash sales listing	

Task 6 (18 marks)

a) **Cash book extract – payments side** (10 marks)

Date	Details	Bank (£)	VAT (£)	Trade payables (£)	Cleaning (£)	Stationery (£)
2/12/2X	J Carroll	96.00	**16.00**		80.00	
8/12/2X	ABS Ltd.	455.00		**455.00**		
12/12/2X	Rymann	51.00	**8.50**			42.50
20/12/2X	PnP Express	525.60		**525.60**		
Totals		1127.60	**24.50**	980.60	80.00	42.50

b) Identify whether each of the following transactions would be included in the payments side of the cash book, the receipts side of the cash book, or whether it would not appear in the cash book. **(5 marks)**

Transaction	Payments side	Receipts side	Would not appear in cash book
Cash sales		✔	
A credit note received from a credit supplier			✔
Capital transferred to the business by its' owner		✔	
Motor vehicle expenses	✔		
A sales invoice			✔

c) Identify whether the following would be input as a cash payments or cash receipts. **(3 marks)**

Description	Cash Receipts	Cash Payments
Counter credits	✔	
Cash withdrawals		✔
Bank charges		✔

Task 7 (10 marks)

a) Complete the table to calculate the closing amount of cash in hand on the 21st December. **(4 marks)**

Cash in hand	£
Opening amount on 1st December 202X	125.00
Total receipts	580.50
Total payments	(173.50)
Closing amount on 21st December 202X	532.00

b) What is the closing balance on the bank statement on 14th December? **(1 mark)**

£4,354

c) **(5 marks)**

The item that is missing from the bank statement is….	a cheque		for an amount of	£240
	A counter credit			
	A faster payment	✓		
	A BACS payment			
	A BACS receipt			

The item that is missing from the cash book is….	a cheque		for an amount of	£720
	a counter credit			
	a faster payment			
	a BACS payment			
	a BACS receipt	✓		

The missing item will need to go on the….	receipts	✓	side of the cash book.
	payments		

Task 8 (8 marks)

a) Match the features in the picklist below to the relevant heading within the table. **(4 marks)**

Off the shelf software	Bespoke software
Updates are made regularly and with ease	Reporting is tailored specifically for the needs of your business
Costs are fixed and can be easily budgeted for	The system can be adapted in line with the organisation's processes

b) Identify which **one** of the following are advantages of cloud based accounting software. **(1 marks)**

Cloud based accounting software.....	✔
.....produces financial reports in real-time	✔
.....requires memory on the server to store financial information	
.....can produce reports that are specifically tailored to your business	
.....can be backed up at any time to your computer	

c) Which of the following would be an indicator of a manual bookkeeping system? Tick the most appropriate option. **(1 mark)**

Options	✔
It is a cheap way of accounting for a small business	✔
It is quicker	
It is more accurate	
Reports can be produced easily	

d) Which **two** of the following reports would show a sale made in cash? **(2 marks)**

Report	✓
Cash payments analysis	
Aged creditors report	
Cash receipts analysis	✓
Balance sheet report	
Sales analysis	✓

Task 9 (8 marks)

a) Professional accountants are required to undertake continuing professional development (CPD). State which one of the five fundamental principles is safeguarded by CPD. **(1 mark)**

Options	✓
Objectivity	
Integrity	
Professional competence & due care	✓
Professional behaviour	
Confidentiality	

b) A professional accountant who complies with the law, brings no disrepute on the profession and is perceived as being ethical by other people has complied with the fundamental principle of: **(1 mark)**

Options	✓
Objectivity	
Integrity	
Professional competence & due care	
Professional behaviour	✓
Confidentiality	

c) As a bookkeeper it is important to observe confidentiality.

Show whether the following statement is true or false. **(1 mark)**

Statement	True	False
If a manager asks to see confidential information, you should let them see it.		✓

d) Place the correct threats to data security from the picklist below next to each of the following definitions. **(3 marks)**

Definition	Threat
Unauthorised access or control to a computer network with a motive of altering information or stealing information for personal gain.	**Hacking**
Being contacted by someone via email who is posing as HMRC and asking for you to provide your bank details to receive a refund.	**Phishing**
A computer program which attaches itself to files and then duplicates itself to cause harm to your computer.	**A Virus**

e) Which **two** of the following can protect accounting software against threats? **(2 marks)**

Options	✓
Only have one log in so that you know exactly who has access to the system	
Have unlimited access for all registered users of the accounting system	
Encrypt files so that they are only readable by authorised users	✓
Ensure that passwords are changed regularly	✓
Always work remotely rather than in an office	

2 Mock Assessment Two: Answers

Task 1 (10 marks)

a) Show whether the following statements are true or false. **(2 marks)**

Statement	True	False
A bookkeeper is able to authorise all financial transactions.		✓
A bookkeeper is responsible for preparing and checking financial documentation.	✓	

b) Identify whether the following statements are true or false. **(3 marks)**

Statement	True	False
If a client is suspected of money laundering, the bookkeeper should speak to them about it .		✓
A bookkeeper is required to follow the ethical principles of the profession.	✓	
A bookkeeper is responsible for making business decisions based on the financial information.		✓

c) Identify **TWO** potential effects of untimely information by selecting the appropriate options from the list below. **(2 marks)**

Statement	✓
It helps build a good rapport with suppliers as they can delay payments.	
It is better to take time when processing entries regardless of timescales.	
It can delay the receipt of goods from suppliers.	✓
It can lead to management making good business decisions.	
Compliance deadlines may be missed, leading to penalties being imposed.	✓

d)   Complete the following sentence. **(1 mark)**

A bookkeeping error can result in...	authorisation of the purchase of an asset	
	duplicated payments to suppliers	✓

e)   A bookkeeper issued a sales invoice to a customer. The total was overstated by £250.

What effects might this overstatement have on the business? **(1 mark)**

This could result in the customer making an...	underpayment	
	overpayment	✓

f)   Complete the following sentence. **(1 mark)**

The overstatement...	could	✓	...affect the recorded profit of the business
	could not		

Task 2 (10 marks)

a)   Insert an item from the following pick list into the right hand column of the table below to categorise the item described. **(3 marks)**

Description	Category
A bank loan obtained by an organisation to fund expansion plans	Liability
Amounts due from credit customers	Asset
An injection of cash into the business by its owner	Capital

b)   When a business makes a profit, how does this affect the capital figure? **(1 mark)**

Options	✓
The capital will remain the same	
The capital will increase	✓
The capital will decrease	

KAPLAN PUBLISHING

c) When a business has more expenses than income, it results in a: **(1 mark)**

Options	✓
Profit	
Loss	✓

d) Which TWO of the following, accurately represent the accounting equation? **(2 marks)**

Equation	✓
Capital = Assets + Liabilities	
Assets = Capital + Liabilities	✓
Assets – Capital = Liabilities	✓
Assets = Capital - Liabilities	

e) A business receives a cheque from one of its credit customers.

Complete the following sentences to show the effects of this transaction. **(2 marks)**

It will….	**increase**	the amount recorded in the business bank account
It will	**decrease**	the amount the business records as outstanding from their receivables

e) Identify which of the one of the following statements is true. **(1 mark)**

Statement	✓
Every transaction will affect the bank account in the bookkeeping system.	
Every bookkeeping transaction will affect at least two records.	
Every transaction within the bookkeeping system will increase assets and decrease liabilities.	

Task 3 (14 marks)

a) Complete the sentences by inserting the most appropriate option from the following pick list: **(2 marks)**

i) An organisation sends **an invoice** to a customer with details of items purchased, the amount owing and the terms of payment.

ii) An organisation sends **a remittance advice** to a creditor accompanying a payment, listing items included in that payment.

b) Insert an item from the following pick list into the right hand column of the table below to identify the term described. **(2 marks)**

Description	Term described
A person or organisation who is owed money due to sales made on credit.	A debtor/ receivable
A transaction to sell goods when the payment is made one month later.	A credit sale

c)

Credit note

Pens & Paper Ltd

Unit 4a Dialstone Business Park
Sheffield
S23 4LE

VAT Reg No. 7423546338

To: **I Do Designs**

84 Hornsea Way
Colchester
CO21 4XU

Date: **27/11/202X**

Credit Note Number: **CN2243**

Product Code	Description	Quantity	Unit Price	Price
A4GLX	1 Box of A4 Silver Gloss Card	2	28.80	57.60
TON4G	LG Printer Toner	1	32.50	32.50
			Net	90.10
			VAT	18.02
			Total	108.12

(10 marks)

Task 4 (8 marks)

a)

	XYZ Ltd. Sunnyside Beach Business Park LN1 5NQ					
	Credit Note					

ABC Ltd.
123 High Street
Manchester
M23 1RD

2 Dec 202X

Description	Quantity	✓ / x	Unit Price (£)	✓ / x	Total	✓ / x
S123	1	x	19.09	x	19.09	x
RC557	1	✓	12.50	✓	12.50	✓
				Net	31.59	
				VAT	6.28	x
				Total	37.90	

(7 marks)

b) Complete the following sentence based on the above. **(1 mark)**

Based on the information I have, I will…..	accept the credit note and input it onto the system	
	process the credit note but raise it with my supervisor as an issue	
	refer the credit note to my supervisor	✓

Task 5 (14 marks)

a) **Purchases** day book

Date 202X	Details	Invoice	Total £	VAT £	Net £
21 Oct	GGD Ltd	3575	**1,071.00**	178.50	892.50
22 Oct	Day Associates	35	1,584.00	**264.00**	1,320.00
23 Oct	Cohen PLC	1164	681.60	113.60	**568.00**
	Totals		**3,336.60**	**556.10**	**2,780.50**

(8 marks)

b) Complete the following table to calculate how much is owed by the customer at the end of November. Enter minus signs or brackets to indicate negative figures in your answer. **(5 marks)**

	£
Opening balance	325.00
Total of invoices	1,117.46
Total of credit notes	(108.26)
Remittance advice	(492.00)
Amount owed at the end of November	842.20

c) Should the business record the amount owing from the customer at the end of November as an asset or a liability? **(1 mark)**

An asset

Task 6 (18 marks)

a) **Cash book extract – receipts side (8 marks)**

Details	Bank (£)	Cash (£)	Trade Receivables (£)	Cash Sales (£)
Mayor & Sons	655.90		655.90	
Cash Sales		42.00		42.00
C Whelan	224.60		224.60	
Totals	880.50	42.00	880.50	42.00

b) **Cash book extract – payments side (4 marks)**

Date	Details	Bank (£)	VAT (£)	Trade payables (£)	Repairs (£)	Stationery (£)
10/12/2X	Locksmiths Ltd	30.00	5.00		25.00	

c) Identify whether the following statements are true or false by ticking the appropriate option from the list below. **(6 marks)**

Statement	True	False
Interest received will be entered into the payments side of the cash book		✔
VAT will appear in both the cash receipts book and the cash payments book	✔	
Debit card payments will show in the cash payments book	✔	
Remittance advice notes will be entered into the cash payments book	✔	
Items that have been entered into the cash book will automatically appear on the bank statement		✔
Cheque book stubs are used to record receipts from credit customers		✔

Task 7 (10 marks)

a) Complete the table to calculate the closing amount of cash in hand on the 21st December. Use minus signs or brackets to indicate negative amounts in your answer. **(4 marks)**

Cash in hand	£
Opening amount on 1st December 202X	**180.00**
Total receipts	**408.00**
Total payments	**(66.50)**
Closing amount on 24th December 202X	**521.50**

b) What is the closing balance on the bank statement on 19th December? **(1 mark)**

£5,885

c) Compare the extracts from the bank statement and the cash book, and complete the following sentences. **(5 marks)**

The item that is missing from the bank statement is….	a cheque		for an amount of	£195
	A counter credit	✓		
	A faster payment			
	A BACS payment			
	A BACS receipt			

The item that is missing from the cash book is….	a cheque		for an amount of	£180
	a counter credit			
	a faster payment			
	a BACS payment	✓		
	a BACS receipt			

The missing item will need to go on the….	receipts		side of the cash book.
	payments	✓	

Task 8 (8 marks)

a) Match the features in the picklist below to the relevant heading within the table. **(4 marks)**

Traditional Accounting Software	Cloud Software
No need for an internet connection	Can be paid in monthly instalments with no upfront fees for hardware
All financial information is securely stored on the server	Can be synced with your phone or tablet so that you can work on the move

b) Identify which **one** of the following is an advantage of bespoke software in comparison to 'of the shelf' software. **(1 mark)**

Bespoke accounting software…..	✓
…..can evolve over time to match your changing requirements	✓
…..is available immediately and therefore is more efficient	
…..requires less in house training	
…..is cheaper in comparison to 'off the shelf' software	

c) Which **one** of the following would be an indicator of cloud based software? **(1 mark)**

Options	✓
Development and installation will only take about two weeks	
Updates are run automatically and are included in the price	✓
Developed and built to meet your specific needs; it is flexible	
Can be easily modified to match your specific requirements	

KAPLAN PUBLISHING

d) Identify whether the following statements are true or false by ticking the correct option from the list below. **(2 marks)**

Statement	True	False
Accounting software allows customer statements to be produced in real time.	✓	
Accounting software allows data to be imported from third party software and apps.	✓	

Task 9 (8 marks)

a) Place the correct threats to data security from the picklist below next to each of the following statements. **(3 marks)**

Definition	Threat
One of the clerks has been processing transactions all day and then clicks on the wrong processing option, to delete them all in error.	Accidental deletion
You have been working on a project for nearly a month. When you come to work on it again and try to open it, an error message comes up to say that there's something wrong with the document.	Corrupt file
You have been processing month end adjustments all morning and then your screen freezes and the software shuts down automatically.	Software crashes

b) Which **two** of the following can protect accounting software against threats? **(2 marks)**

Options	✓
Give all users of the system a specific way of setting their password so that you can access it on their behalf even if they leave suddenly	
Implement firewalls on all hardware and software	✓
Enlist different levels of access rights depending on the user	✓
Ensure that a backup is taken once a week in case of a fire or flood	

c) Identify whether the following statements are true or false by ticking the correct option. **(3 marks)**

Statement	True	False
Money laundering is a criminal offence but you cannot be imprisoned as a result of it.		✓
The ethical principle of objectivity is about being straightforward and honest in all professional and business relationships.		✓
CPD activities contribute to the ethical principle of professional competence	✓	

KAPLAN PUBLISHING

INDEX

KAPLAN PUBLISHING